TEMPLES
of the GRAIL

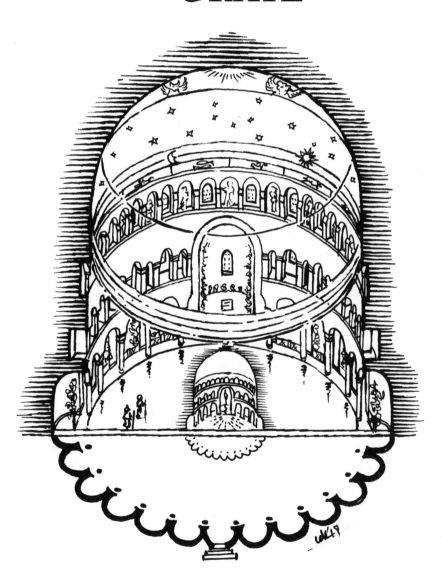

About the Authors

John Matthews (Oxford, UK) is a *New York Times* bestselling author who has written more than one hundred books on myth, faery, the Arthurian legends, and Grail studies. John has appeared on the History Channel and Discovery Channel, and he was an advisor and contributor on Jerry Bruckheimer's film *King Arthur*.

Gareth Knight (Essex, UK) has spent four decades actively investigating and writing about the Western Magical Tradition and the Qabalistic symbolism. He is one of the world's foremost authorities on magic and the active use of symbolism. In 1976 he was awarded an honorary doctorate for his work in the field, and he has acted as a consultant for Jungian analysis and for television producers in the area of archetypal symbolism.

To Write to the Authors

If you wish to contact the authors or would like more information about this book, please write to the authors in care of Llewellyn Worldwide Ltd. and we will forward your request. Both the authors and publisher appreciate hearing from you and learning of your enjoyment of this book and how it has helped you. Llewellyn Worldwide Ltd. cannot guarantee that every letter written to the authors can be answered, but all will be forwarded. Please write to:

John Matthews
Gareth Knight
℅ Llewellyn Worldwide
2143 Wooddale Drive
Woodbury, MN 55125-2989
Please enclose a self-addressed stamped envelope for reply,
or $1.00 to cover costs. If outside the U.S.A., enclose
an international postal reply coupon.

Many of Llewellyn's authors have websites with additional information and resources. For more information, please visit our website at http://www.llewellyn.com.

TEMPLES
of the GRAIL
The Search for the World's Greatest Relic

JOHN MATTHEWS
GARETH KNIGHT

Llewellyn Publications
WOODBURY, MINNESOTA

FIRST EDITION
First Printing, 2019

Book design by Rebecca Zins
Cover design by Shannon McKuhen
Cover image: *The Temple of the Holy Grail* by Eduard von Steinle/Superstock/DeAgostini
Illustrations © Wil Kinghan

Llewellyn is a registered trademark of Llewellyn Worldwide Ltd.

Library of Congress Cataloging-in-Publication Data
Names: Matthews, John, author. | Knight, Gareth author. | Albrecht, von
    Scharfenberg, active 13th century. Jüngere Titurel. English.
Title: Temples of the Grail : the search for the world's greatest relic /
    John Matthews, Gareth Knight.
Other titles: Sone de Nansay (Roman d'aventures). English.
Description: First edition. | Woodbury, Minnesota : Llewellyn Publications,
    2019. | Includes bibliographical references and index.
Identifiers: LCCN 2019004310 (print) | LCCN 2019007073 (ebook) | ISBN
    9780738757797 () | ISBN 9780738757759 (alk. paper)
Subjects: LCSH: Grail—Legends—History and criticism. | Sone de Nansay
    (Roman d'aventures) | Albrecht, von Scharfenberg, active 13th century.
    Jüngere Titurel. | Literature, Medieval—History and criticism. |
    Arthurian romances—History and criticism.
Classification: LCC PN686.G7 (ebook) | LCC PN686.G7 M2865 2019 (print) | DDC
    398.26—dc23
LC record available at https://lccn.loc.gov/2019004310

Llewellyn Publications
A Division of Llewellyn Worldwide Ltd.
2143 Wooddale Drive
Woodbury MN 55125-2989
www.llewellyn.com

Printed in the United States of America

I have made the temple worthy of Christians,
so that they may learn by studying its shape and design.

◆ ◆ ◆

The Later Titurel, 516.2

CONTENTS

CONTENTS

♦ ♦ ♦

SONE DE NANSAY
translated by Gareth Knight 27

♦ ♦ ♦

CONTENTS

✦✦✦

CONTENTS

✦ ✦ ✦

ACKNOWLEDGMENTS

We would like to thank the various people consulted in the writing of this book, especially Dr. Simon Wilson for his expert analysis of *Der Jüngere Titurel* and the Church of Ettal; to David Elkington for his careful reading of various drafts of the manuscript and his comments thereon, and for first pointing us to the East; to Janet Piedelato for venturing into the depths of the New York Public Library to examine and comment on the papers of Arthur Upham Pope and Phyllis Ackerman. A very big thank you to Melanie Kinghan for her translation of the essay by Sulpiz Boisserée, carried out with exemplary care in the midst of a busy life. Special thanks, as always, to Caitlín Matthews for all her support, for taking time out of her busy schedule to point out avenues of research we might otherwise have missed, and for translating passages from Latin and French.

Needless to say, we are solely responsible for any errors of fact that escaped our notice. Despite working with the first scholarly edition of *Sone de Nansay* by Goldschmidt, we could not have ventured far down the path without access to the edition prepared by Dr. Claude Lachet, whose commentary and modern French translation were also immensely useful.

Thanks also to our editor at Llewellyn, Bill Krause, and the rest of the production team for making the process flow smoothly. Grateful thanks to Wil Kinghan for drawing the diagrams included in this book.

Note: For a full range of illustrations, including of the
Takht-e Taqdis and other sacred sites, go to Hallowquest.org.uk
and click on "Grail Temples."

✦ ✦ ✦

INTRODUCTION

THE JOURNEY TO THE GRAIL

For nearly a thousand Years the peoples of
Europe were intensely absorbed and emotionally
agitated by a series of strange legends about a sacred
object of magical power called the Holy Grail.

♦ ♦ ♦

A. U. Pope, *Persia and the Holy Grail*

The story of the Grail has long revolved around two essential questions: Does it—or did it—exist, and if so, where is it? A third question—What is its purpose?—though often asked, has always been perceived as a personal thing. If you look for the Grail, you may never find it…but then again, perhaps you will. It is a slippery thing, this wondrous relic, and all questions concerning it are suspended in time.

The first question may be addressed by asking another: What is it? If we are looking for a physical object, the choices are multitudinous, the most popular being a cup or chalice, a shallow dish, a book, a stone, or a bloodline. There are almost as many claimants around the world for the actual Grail as any would-be seeker could wish for: the Valencia Chalice in Spain, the Nanteos Cup in Wales, the Antioch Chalice in New York. All are well attested and have their own followers. All are, in some sense, Grails. Not *the* Grail, perhaps—if such a thing really exists—but sacred objects made holy by the beliefs of countless pilgrims.

Yet, whilst all of these are the Grail—none of them are *the* Grail. We might, perhaps, call them "impressions"—shadows or extensions that each, in its own way, embody the mystical aspects of the object that has been called by this name for at least two thousand years. The very idea of the Grail is the foundation for an outpouring of texts in both verse and prose that

♦ ♦ ♦

dominated the literature of the Western world from the twelfth to fifteenth centuries—the period referenced in the quotation heading this introduction.

So much for the first question; what about the second: Where is it? Again, this has been the subject of a multitude of studies, books, films, and theories, some utterly mad and unlikely, others plausible, and still more persuasive. Again, to generalize, it could be said that the Grail is everywhere and nowhere, and that to seek a physical home for it is as unnecessary as it is to seek an actual cup, stone, book, or bloodline.

However, the medieval storytellers who first recorded the continuing journey of the Grail (its origins remained as mysterious to them as it is to us) believed in the *physical* existence of both the relic and its hiding place. For most of them, it was the cup from which Jesus drank when he celebrated the Last Supper with his disciples and which later caught some of his holy blood, but because it was seen as a physical thing, it required a physical home.

Where else, then, should one put a relic as sacred as this but in a chapel, or even a temple, probably contained within the sheltering walls of a castle? Such a place must be extraordinary, beautiful, and as grand as it possibly could be. Maybe it was not even made by human hands, but with the assistance of angelic powers. Whatever form it was to take, it must be splendid, mysterious, and—most important of all—hard to find, because it was widely known that any and all spiritual and transformative experiences must involve a search, a journey, and a set of challenging circumstances: a statement that perfectly describes the quest for the Grail.

When Sir Lancelot, in Thomas Malory's fifteenth-century novel *Le Morte d'Arthur*, comes after many adventures to the Chapel of the Grail, an unearthly voice warns him not to enter. Hesitating outside the door, he nontheless looks within and sees

> a table of silver, and the Holy Vessel, covered with red samite, and many angels about it … and before the Holy Vessel … a good man clothed as a priest. And it seemed he was at the sacring of the mass.[1]

Watching the events that follow, Lancelot sees the celebrant holding aloft the image of a wounded man, as though he would make with it an offering at the altar. And, when it seems as though the priest would fall from the effort, Lancelot enters the chamber, motivated purely by a desire to help. But he is struck down by a breath of angelic fire and blinded by the light of the Grail.

This demonstrates that the way is a hard one, for it consists of entering the temple of the Grail, which is designed to serve as a test for all who wish to share in the mysteries. Lancelot's

---

1. Malory, *Le Morte d'Arthur*, 2000.

◆ ◆ ◆

experience is echoed by many who set out unprepared and who end up being blinded by what they cannot understand. However, the way towards the home of the Grail can offer a means of knowing, of understanding the light. Many temples have fallen in ruins, but it is said that the true temple can never be destroyed. We would do well to keep this in mind as we examine some of the images assumed by that imperishable temple throughout its long history, hoping that we may thus learn something of our own part in the continuing mysteries of the Grail.

In a recent book, the writer John Michael Greer suggested that the mystery of the Grail could be seen as a simple metaphor for the churches raised in such proliferation during the Middle Ages. Citing the presence of a mystical spear and chalice, the glorious light which surrounds them, and the often fatal consequences of approaching the sacred vessel without first repenting one's sins, he says:

> The tall central steeple rising from the body of the church west of the sanctuary is the spear standing upright before the chalice of the Mass; stained glass windows and myriads of lamps make it a container glowing with light; the Masses celebrated in it are forbidden to those who are guilty of mortal sins but provide the virtuous with spiritual food; the nave of the church … gets its name from the typological metaphor of a ship …[2]

Greer is correct in the importance of the symbolic references to be found within the buildings. To go further, however, the descriptions of the sacred edifices designed to hold the Grail require a deeper analysis, taking into account the detailed symbolism at every point, both of the buildings and the rituals that took place there. As we shall see later in this book, these buildings, which have been called "stone books," could indeed be read by those with the knowledge to do so, and the answers thus produced will be seen to throw a new and crucial light on the history of the Grail.

The Grail story is immensely complex, each aspect leading to others, like side roads, and they in turn to still more. Here we are concentrating on a particular aspect as it relates to the whole. The story of the Grail Temples and their guardians anchors the myth in the world while at the same time admitting the mystical and the otherworldly. Thus we pick our way, by routes seeming trackless, from one part of the forest to another, up mountains, through valleys, and into cities, castles, and temples—always remembering that the Grail is at the center, and that if we follow the signs left by earlier seekers, we shall reach our goal.

In this book we are not setting out to prove that the Grail exists or what or where it is, although inevitably these questions will be discussed in the context of our exploration. What

---

2. Greer, *The Secret of the Temple*, 98.

we shall do is look at two intimately connected themes: the place where the Grail was *believed* to lie and why this was deemed so important; and what happened to the knights and pilgrims who found their way to this mystical centre.

This last is part of the most fundamental aspect of the Grail, and it brings us to the third question: What does it do? The effect of standing before the Grail—whether in a medieval past or a magical present—was clearly powerful and lives at the heart of the mystery. An examination of the places where the Grail was believed to be hidden and the transformation it wrought upon those who found their way there opens the door to a deeper realization of what the Grail is beyond the theories and physical objects that represented it.

For some of the answers, we shall be looking at two medieval texts, neither of which have been translated into English before (except in the form of brief quotations) and which give us important new clues to the location of the Grail's possible homes and the physical building on which they were based.

These two important but neglected romances are the anonymous French thirteenth-century epic *Sone de Nansay*[3] and the German *Der Jüngere Titurel* ("The Later Titurel") attributed to Albrecht of Scharfenburg and dating from the same era.[4] Both these works give detailed accounts of the home of the Grail. A third text and its associated documents, the *Letter of Prester John*, will be seen to add yet more extraordinary details pointing to an actual location of the Grail's resting places.[5]

The figure of Prester John himself—as mysterious in his own way as the Grail itself, and whose protector he is said to be—is a semi-mythical priest and king whose kingdom was sought throughout the Middle Ages. By following clues within a letter supposedly written by Prester John himself and sent to several of the crowned heads of medieval Europe, we shall see that the Grail Temple was widely believed to exist, and that its location was known by many, though understood by almost none.

This brings into question a further important aspect of the Grail myth: its effect on the history of humankind and the way in which it has been perceived, openly and in secret, by various groups of people, from the Templars to the Mormons. One of the principal aspects of this is the existence of certain families who are deemed guardians of the sacred relic and whose connection with the Grail extends back for many generations. This is not some mysterious

3. Goldschmidt, *Sone von Nausay*, 1899; Lachet, *Sone de Nansay*, 2012, 2014.

4. Hahn, *Albrecht: Der Jüngere Titurel*, 1842.

5. Brewer, *Prester John*, 2012.

✦ ✦ ✦

bloodline but an actual historically known family and its connection with a figure known as the Swan Knight. Their importance will be explored here as a further doorway into the work of the Grail (see appendix 1).

From these conundrums, among many we shall encounter in our exploration of the temples of the Grail, we intend to offer a fresh set of clues to one of the greatest mysteries of all time and an essential part of our continued spiritual evolution.

John Matthews and Gareth Knight
Oxford and Braintree, 2018

◆ ◆ ◆

1

SACRED SPACE

Just to be in the presence of the Grail
no man could age or die…

♦ ♦ ♦

Wolfram von Eschenbach, *Parzifal*

It is hardly surprising that the idea of a home for the Grail should come to the fore in the vast body of literature and myth that grew up around the sacred vessel during the Middle Ages. The mysterious relic—which could be at one and the same time a chalice, a book, a stone, or a person—was seen as existing both on the earth and at a remove from it. In the poem *The Later Titurel*,[6] which we shall be examining later in detail, it hovers above the world, untouched by human hands and supported by angels. In the *Perceval* of Chrétien de Troyes[7] and the *Parzifal* of Wolfram von Eschenbach,[8] it is kept in a secret chamber within a great castle. In *Sone von Nausay*,[9] a neglected thirteenth-century text that we shall explore later, it is kept on a fortified island in the sea. Elsewhere it is kept in an earthly paradise ruled over by a priestly king named John.

The idea of creating buildings that acted as initiatic chambers, opening up a process that enabled those who visited them to experience vision and relegation, had already been around for a long while before the Middle Ages. The Romans—especially the emperor Augustus—created a building program that included the restoration of temples to the gods laid out in

6. Wolf, *Albrecht von Scharfenberg Jüngerer Titurel.*

7. De Troyes, *Perceval: The Story of the Grail.*

8. Wolfram von Eschenbach, *Parzival.*

9. Goldschmidt, *Sone von Nausay.*

♦ ♦ ♦

such a way as to make them stages on the initiatic journey of boy into manhood.[10] So, too, the Christian churches and cathedrals—many of them under construction during the period when the Grail romances were being written—were intended to show those who entered them how to live life according to God's wishes. And so, as we shall hope to show, the temples and castles of the Grail were designed to have the same effect, whether they were rendered in words or stone.

All of these ideas come together in the idea of a Grail Temple, a permanent home where the sacred vessel awaited those who went in search of it. Virtually every surviving text on this subject composed between the twelfth and fifteenth centuries includes a version of this, and though they vary in detail, all point towards a single idea: that the buildings described as the home of the Grail are as important as the relic itself. That they may also be based on more than one actual building is something we hope to demonstrate in this book.

To understand how the nature of the Grail Temple evolved, we need to look first at a poem by Chrétien de Troyes (1130–1191), left unfinished at the time of his death and added to by no less than four "continuators," who extended the original 9,000 lines of the poem to 54,000.

Argument still rages as to sources on which Chrétien drew, with some insisting that he was the first writer to connect the enigmatic Grail with the Arthurian world, while others maintain that he drew upon much older sources, in all likelihood of Jewish origin, which can be traced back to within a hundred years of Christ's ministry (see chapter 6). Whatever the truth, it is Chrétien's undoubted genius that gave us the first recognizable Grail story, one which contains most of the elements later expanded in works such as those of his near contemporary Robert de Boron and the immense collection of texts gathered into the sequence known as the Lancelot-Grail.[11]

Chrétien's poem *Perceval, ou le Conte du Graal* (the Story of the Grail) was composed somewhere between 1188 and 1191. It literally breaks off in the middle of a sentence, supposedly with the death of its author. The story it tells can be summarized as follows:

> Perceval is brought up by his mother in the forest, in ignorance of the ways of the world. There he happily hunts game with roughly made throwing spears. Then one day he meets three knights in the wood. Thinking them angels because of the brilliance of their armour, he questions them concerning their origin. Learning

10. See Vukovic, "Initiation in the Mysteries of Augustus: The Liberalia and *Forum Augustum*."

11. *The Lancelot-Grail: The Old French Arthurian Vulgate and Post-Vulgate in Translation*, edited by Norris Lacy. [Previously known as the Vulgate cycle.]

from them of Arthur's court and the institution of knighthood, he vows to go there in search of adventure, and ignoring his mother's anguished request that he should remain with her, he rides off on an ancient mount to find his way in the world of chivalry. Before he departs his mother gives him last-minute advice, but without a context for Perceval to fully comprehend it: always to give help to any women in distress, but take no more from them by way of reward than a kiss—though if one should also wish to give him a ring, let him take that also.

Armed with this advice, the first person whom Perceval encounters is a beautiful woman in a scarlet pavilion, whose ring he takes and whom he kisses, but against her will. He then proceeds to Arthur's court, where he enters in time to witness the arrival of a red knight who spills wine in the queen's lap and carries off her golden cup. Still mindful of his mother's instructions, Perceval pursues the knight, kills him, and returns the cup to the queen.

From the court he then sets out on further adventures, meeting with a nobleman who gives him training in chivalry and counsels him not to be talkative. Perceval arrives at the castle of the mysterious Fisher King, whom he finds presiding over a hall in which a noble man lies upon a couch. The king presents Perceval with a sword, which he accepts unthinkingly. A procession then passes through the hall, led by a squire carrying a spear from which blood drips upon the ground, followed by two squires, each carrying a ten-branched candlestick. After this comes a damsel carrying a "grail" which blazes with a light so bright that it puts out the light of the candles and of the stars. Following her is another maiden carrying a *talleors* (variously translated as a dish, a bowl, a casket, or a tabernacle).

Perceval watches all this but fails to ask its meaning. He retires for the night and on waking finds the castle deserted. Thinking the company have gone hunting, he no sooner crosses the moat than the drawbridge descends. Perceval then encounters a damsel cradling the body of a knight in her arms and lamenting bitterly. She is his cousin and tells him that the Fisher King has long since received a wound in the thighs, which has never healed, though it might well have done so had Perceval asked the meaning of "the procession of the grail." She also informs him that the sword he was given at the castle will break if he is not careful, but that in such a case he can restore it by dipping it in a lake near which its maker, the smith Trebuchet, dwells.

Returning to Arthur's court, Perceval is upbraided by a hideous damsel who appears from nowhere to mock him for so foolishly failing to ask the question that would have healed the king and made his country prosperous again. Determined to right this wrong and to learn more of the mysterious Grail, Perceval sets forth again and after many adventures meets with a band of pilgrims, who reproach

◆ ◆ ◆

him for bearing arms on Good Friday. Five years have passed since he left Arthur's court, and in his eagerness to discover more about the Grail, he has forgotten God. Perceval confesses his sins to a forest hermit and learns from him that his mother died of grief after he left her. He also learns that the Fisher King is the son of an older king who served by a single host from the Grail that keeps him alive.

Perceval feels great remorse but has still not rediscovered the Castle of the Grail. Here the story changes course to deal with the adventures of Gawain, which have nothing to do with the Grail, and the poem ends before Chrétien has brought the story back to Perceval.

The First Temple

This eminently mysterious story, which almost certainly drew upon legends then circulating, perhaps orally, throughout Europe, seems at first glance somewhat removed from the later, overtly Christianised retellings. Chrétien gives the word *Grail* a lowercase g, and only towards the end of Perceval's adventures (in a section believed by some commentators to have been added later) does he call it "holy."

However, it is Chrétien's description of the castle of the Fisher King and the inner sanctum where the Grail is housed that concern us here. There is a substantial amount of evidence to suggest that it was based upon a much older structure—nothing less than the First Temple of Solomon, built according to biblical and Jewish historical sources on the Temple Mount of Jerusalem to house the Ark of the Covenant. Destroyed in circa 587 BC by King Nebuchadnezzar, the temple was subsequently rebuilt circa 832 BC and destroyed again in circa 422 BC, though these dates vary according to rabbinical or secular estimates.

Buildings following instruction dating from even more ancient texts such as the Tanakh (also known as the Hebrew Bible and upon which the Old Testament of the Christian Bible is based) existed well into the period when Chrétien lived, and descriptions provided by travellers were accessible—if not generally then almost certainly in the rabbinical school founded in Chrétien's native city of Troyes, to which he could well have had access.

According to the Tanakh, Solomon's Temple was built following a Phoenician design, though since people who were neither architects nor engineers compiled the descriptions given, it is difficult to arrive at an exact idea of what the temple looked like. However, it is the symbolic references that are of greatest interest here, in particular as these relate to the inner sanctum, or Holy of Holies, where the Ark of the Covenant was kept. The more we look at the avowed meaning of the temple, the more we can see how well it fits with the idea of the Grail.

Also known as the "Inner House" (Heb. 9:3), it measured 20 cubits in length, breadth, and height. (Another measure that describes it as 30 cubits high is believed to be an indication that the floor was raised. A cubit could be anything between 18 and 21 inches, based on the length of an arm from elbow to fist.) The floor and wainscots were clad in cederwood, and both walls and floor were overlaid with gold weighing roughly 20 tons. Two statues of cherubim, made of olive wood and 10 cubits high and with a wingspan of 10 cubits, stood side by side, their wings touching the walls. Between these stood the Ark of the Covenant, containing the tablets of Moses, inscribed with the Ten Commandments issued by the Hebrew God to his prophet.

However, the most important aspect of the Holy of Holies was that it housed the Presence of God (also known as the *Shekinah*, or Wisdom). The Solomonic temple was thus a concretization of an idea that began with the revelation of Moses, who created the first tabernacle to contain the ark and later extended it into the image of the temple itself. From within his holy house, God spoke "from above the mercy seat, from between the two cherubim that are upon the Ark of the Covenant."[12] But the tabernacle was never intended as a permanent home, and it was left to Solomon to complete the fashioning of a final resting place for the ark in Jerusalem.

Solomon himself was given the plan of the temple by God, who commanded the creation of a sanctuary on the earth modeled upon the ark itself "after the pattern of the Tabernacle."[13] So to, the creator of the Grail Temple, Titurel, received his instructions from angels and was given a ground plan on which to build.[14]

According to oral tradition, as recorded in Jewish texts, some dating from as early as the second century BC, those who carried the Ark of the Covenant were miraculously carried as if in a vehicle that seemed to float and in which they "soared … like angels."[15] The ark itself, while it was still in transit, was seen as God's throne, but when it came to rest, it became the heart of the temple. According to the Jewish Talmud,[16] the temple became a symbolic representation of "the foundation stone" upon which the earth was created; while in Kabbalistic lore Jerusalem is seen as the centre of the world, the temple the center of Jerusalem, and the ark the centre of the temple.[17]

---

12. Exodus 25:22. See plate 1 for a ground plan of Solomon's Temple showing the position of the Holy of Holies.

13. Exodus 25:8–9.

14. *The Later Titurel*. See chapter 4.

15. Schayer, "The Meaning of the Temple," 360.

16. Yoma 54b in: Polarno, *The Talmud*.

17. Schayer, "The Meaning of the Temple."

◆ ◆ ◆

This is very much how the great temple of the Grail in the thirteenth-century romance *The Later Titurel*, which we shall be examining later, is described. The walls of that temple surround an inner shrine wherein is a miniature replica of the building made to house the Grail.

Just as the mysteries of the Grail combined aspects of mind, heart, and spirit, in Jerusalem, worshippers entering the outer court of the Temple were said to have reached Eden; beyond this, in the Holy of Holies, the dwelling place of God within the Ark—or the Chapel of the Grail—are the mysteries of the heavenly world, where the concerns of mind and body are left behind. It is as though, looking out of a window, the eye was lead beyond a glimpse of the immediate world, to gaze up into the heavens, and on looking there was suddenly able to see beyond, through all the dark gulfs of space to the Throne of God itself, there to be lost in light.

Of the several non-biblical accounts of the Solomonic temple which exist, that of the Islamic historian Ibn Khaldun is one of the most interesting, for in it he states that the vaults below the temple, which have been mistakenly believed to be the stables for Solomon's horses, were built to form a vacuum between the earth and the building itself, so that malign influences might not enter it from below.[18] As we shall see, there is another site known as the Stable of Solomon, which possesses a powerful connection to the Grail mysteries and may be the origin of the much-discussed story of the Templars' search for the treasure below the Temple Mound.

By medieval times, when the original site of the Solomonic temple had become a Muslim shrine, the chamber mentioned by Ibn Khaldun had become known as a place of entrance and exit for the spirits of the dead, while of the original structure nothing now remained above ground. The Crusaders, however, continued to refer to the building as the *Templum Dominum* (Temple of God), and it became sacred to the three major religions of the time. For the Jews it was the site of Solomon's Altar of the Holocausts, while to the Muslims it was the place from which the Prophet had begun his night journey to heaven. For a time it rivaled Mecca in importance and was attributed with the property of "hovering" above the earth. Thus the geographer Idrisi referred to it in 1154 as "the stone which rose and fell" (*lapis lapsus exilians*), which recalls Wolfram von Eschenbach's description, in his thirteenth-century poem *Parzival*, of the Grail itself as *lapis exilis*, sometimes interpreted as "the stone which fell from heaven." In the poem of *The Later Titurel*, which we shall examine later, the Grail itself hovers above the earth, held by angels.

It seems that here we have a paradigm for the entire history of the Grail and of the temple built to house it. According to Wolfram, the Grail is a stone, an emerald, which fell from the

18. Ibn Khaldun, *The Muqaddimah*.

+ + +

crown of Lucifer and entered the sphere of the earth; thus it can also be said to have "fallen." Another account, which we shall explore shortly, says that Seth, the third son of Adam and Eve, brought the Grail into the world from Paradise. In the Middle Ages, according to the writings of Robert de Boron and others it has become the vessel used by Christ to perform the first Eucharist. Thus it is hallowed and the world, like the lost Eden, is redeemed, so that it too "rises," while the stones used in the building of the temple and the design for its construction are also said to "fall from heaven" in *The Later Titurel*.

The Hebrew Grail

Most of the information regarding the Solomonic temple was available to Chrétien in either Hebrew or Christian documents of the time. There is a very strong possibility, advanced by several scholars,[19] that Chrétien himself may have been a *converso*, a convert from Judaism to Christianity. His description of the Grail chapel and the hall where Perceval witnesses the procession of the Grail can be shown to derive from the description of the Holy of Holies.[20] Professor Urban Tigner Holmes summarized these parallels in his 1947 paper "A New Interpretation of Chrétien's Conte del Graal"[21] commenting on Chrétien's description:

> Then he [Perceval] saw before him in the valley
> The top of a tower which appeared.
> Had you gone as far as Beirut
> No finer could you have found.
> Square it was, of stone also,
> With smaller towers on either side.
> The hall was before the tower
> And the loges before the hall …[22]

A few lines further on, we find:

> The valet remained in the logia
> Until he escorted him to the Lord,

19. See in particular Gaster, *Studies & Texts*, vol. II, 898, 895; Weinraub, *Chrétien's Jewish Grail*; Holmes and Klenke, *Chrétien, Troyes and the Grail*; Holmes, *Chrétien de Troyes*; Adolf, *Visio Pacis, Holy City and Grail*.

20. See Elkington, *The Quest for the Face of God* (forthcoming) for a detailed analysis of this aspect. Also Adolf, *Visio Pacis, Holy City and Grail*.

21. Holmes, "A New Interpretation of Chrétien's *Conte del Graal*."

22. De Troyes, *Conte du Graal (Perceval)*, 3075–3080. Trans. Caitlín Matthews.

◆ ◆ ◆

Which two more pages soon advised
And with them he was led
Into the hall, which was square
As long as it was wide.
In the centre of the hall, lying in a bed,
A fine nobleman he saw
Who had grizzled hair…
Before him was a built-up fire
Of seasoned logs, fiercely burning
Within a hearth of four pillars.
Space enough there as for 400 men
To sit about that fire—
For each a comfortable place.
The pillars were strong enough
To support a chimney made of bronze.[23]

This is followed by the famous Grail procession, the bleeding lance, some golden candlesticks bearing ten candles each, and finally a girl carrying "a grail." The meal that follows is laid on a table of ivory.

Professor Holmes sums this up succinctly:

> The loges through which Perceval enters before he finds himself in the hall are porticoes before the front of the Temple: "*porticum vero ante frontem*" (Chronicles 3.4). Other correspondences are: the copper or brass pillars (3 Kings 7.15–16); the square-shaped hall (2 Paralip. 3.8)[24]; Chrétien's table of ivory set upon trestles of ebony which corresponds to the shewbread table with trestles of setim wood (Exodus 25.28). Concerning the Temple one Bible text says: "And he made ten candlesticks of gold according to their form and set them in the Temple, five on the right hand and five on the left" (02 Paralip. 4.7). These candelabra (*aurea decem*) surely did not mean the ten-branched candelabra in the Temple of Solomon, but a medieval reader might be pardoned for interpreting in that way.[25]

It is more than likely that Chrétien knew of the continuing traditions that associated Joseph of Arimathea with relics of the Passion of Jesus and understood by the word *grail* (in its many forms as *greal, graal, gradalis*) something specific and far from the somewhat "vague" assump-

---

23. De Troyes, *Conte du Graal (Perceval)*, 3069–3077, 3083–3090. Trans. Caitlín Matthews.

24. Paralip. = Paralipomenon, an alternate name for the two books of Chronicles, Kings and Ezra—the history-oriented books of the Old Testament.

25. Holmes, "A New Interpretation of Chrétien's *Conte del Graal*."

◆ ◆ ◆

tions usually attributed to him.[26] He would also have encountered travellers' descriptions of Jerusalem and of the remains of the Solomonic temple and had access to several popular and widely disseminated guidebooks. *The City of Jerusalem*, written circa 1187 by the great Jewish traveller Benjamin of Tudela, drew upon many of these and provided details that easily could have added to Chrétien's image of the temple.

There he could have read:

> The other building is called the Temple of Solomon; it is the palace built by Solomon, King of Israel … a very substantial structure, composed of large stones, and the like of which is not to be seen anywhere in the world.[27]

Benjamin also makes an intriguing reference to the Hebrew prophet Daniel, which may well have given Chrétien further material for his work (see chapter 6).

In *Perceval*, of course, there is no Ark of the Covenant, but this is replaced by a relic every bit as sacred to the medieval Christian world as the Ark was to the Jews: the Holy Grail. In connecting the two, Chrétien seems to have understood the importance not only of the object itself but also of the building in which it was kept.

The Tabut

The links with Solomon and his temple to the greater glory of God do not end here. Two important facts remain to be considered. The first concerns the Ark of the Covenant, which may be seen as the Grail of its age. A well-founded tradition of the Ethiopian Church maintains that the Ark was removed from Jerusalem before the destruction of the temple by Menelik, a child of Solomon and the Queen of Sheba. The supposed original Ark is still kept in the cathedral at Aksum in modern-day Ethiopia and has remained a central part of sacred practice within the Ethiopian Church. Known as the Tabut (from the Arabic *tabut 'al 'ahdi*, Ark of the Covenant), it is carried in procession at the festival of Epiphany to the accompaniment of singing, dancing, and feasting, which recalls the time when "David and all the house of Israel brought up the Ark of the Lord with shouting and with the sound of the trumpet."[28]

Replicas of the Tabut are kept in every church in Ethiopia, and where these are large enough to possess a Holy of Holies, this representation of the Ark is kept within, as it was in the

---

26. See particularly Neitze, *Perceval and the Holy Grail*, and Bruce, *The Evolution of Arthurian Romance*.

27. Signer, Adler, and Asher, *The Itinerary of Benjamin of Tudela*.

28. 2 Samuel 6:15.

◆ ◆ ◆

Temple of Solomon at Jerusalem. Every priest must posses one of these copies in order to celebrate the mysteries.

It is possible that we have here one of the contributing factors of the Grail story. It has been pointed out[29] that stories concerning a quest for a sacred object, undertaken by the fatherless son of a queen (i.e., Menelik), may well have reached the West, where they became the basis for another story of a fatherless child (Perceval) who goes upon such a quest. Add to this the nature of the Ark itself, along with the fact that apart from the *Kebra Nagast*,[30] in which this story is told in full, the only other known source is Arabic, which suggests that the frequently noted oriental influences in the twelfth-century poem of *Parzifal* by Wolfram von Eschenbach may be traced to this legend.

Wolfram speaks of the Grail being brought to earth by a troop of angels where "a Christian progeny bred to a pure life had the duty of keeping it."[31] Here we enter the world of Robert de Boron's mysterious Grail family (see chapter 6), while the *Kebra Nagast* tells how Menelik brings the Ark out of Israel to reside in a specially protected temenos in Ethiopia.

We have heard how Lancelot fared when he entered the chapel of the Grail to help the "man dressed like a priest" who was serving at the Mass. Even though his intention is good, he is not permitted to touch or look upon the mystery. So, too, in the story of the Ark's journey from Gebaa, described in the biblical book of Kings, when it had reached the threshing floor of Nachon, the oxen pulling the cart on which the Ark rode began to kick and struggle and "tilted the Ark to one side; whereupon Oza put out his hand and caught hold of it. Rash deed of his, that provoked the divine anger; the Lord smote him, and he died there beside the Ark."[32]

It is clear from this that those who care for a sacred relic must maintain a respectful distance from it—though in Robert de Boron's poem of *Joseph*, in which he tells the story of Joseph of Arimathea and his acquiring of the Grail from the hands of Jesus himself, we also find the story of Sarracynte, wife of Evelake of Sarras, whose mother had for a time shared the guardianship of the Grail in the shape of a host and kept it in a box that is specifically described as "an ark."[33] She at least was allowed to touch it without harm, though such instances are rare in the mythos. Generally the mystery is too great to be looked upon or touched by one who is

29. Adolf, "Oriental Sources for Grail Romances," 306–23.

30. Budge, *The Kebra Negast*.

31. Wolfram von Eschenbach, *Parzival*, 232.

32. 2 Kings 6–8.

33. De Boron, *Joseph d'Arimathea*.

◆ ◆ ◆

unprepared. A visit to the temple of the Grail must come first and its tests overcome before the revelation of the mystery can take place.

A New Temple

While Chrétien may well have considered the original Solomonic temple as a serious model for the hall of the Grail castle, he could also have visited a building inspired or copied from the actual Holy of Holies. This remarkable edifice was created at the command of a knight named Arnoul the Elder in circa 1117 and is described by Lambert d'Ardres in his *Historia Comitum Ghisnensium*, written between 1194–98.[34] Although this work focused primarily on the lives and deeds of Lambert's master, Count Baudouin II, Count d'Ardres, and his eldest son, Arnoul de Guines, it also references the previous Arnoul (the Elder) who commanded the building of a castle at Ardres (now part of the Pas-de-Calais Department of Northern France), which included

> steps and winding stairs from one area to another, from the house to the kitchen, from one room to another, then from the house itself to the "logium," which took its name appropriately and for the following reason: for they used to sit there in pleasure to talk, it was derived from logos; then from the logium to the oratory or chapel made in a similar way to the tabernacle of Solomon in its design of canopy and pictures.[35]

This is interesting for a number of reasons. The Greek word *logion* actually means "saying" or "word" or even "oracle."[36] Lambert is correct in noting that it derives from *logos*, but the word carried a weightier meaning: the Word of God, as it appears in the opening of St. John's Gospel.[37] The word *logion* is also used for the breastplate traditionally worn by the high priest of the Solomonic temple, suggesting that Arnoul the Elder was drawing upon earlier Hebrew traditions, as well as acknowledging the Christian Gospels.[38] As we shall see later, the appearance of the name Arnoul, in this context, is of great significance (see chapters 2 and 3).

Later, somewhere around 1169, Arnoul's ancestor, Baudouin II, created a curious circular tower at Guines (also within the Pas-de-Calais area) that included

---

34. Loomis, *Arthurian Legends in Medieval Art*; Holmes, "The Arthurian Tradition in Lambert d'Ardres"; Holmes and Klenke, *Chrétien, Troyes and the Grail*.

35. Holmes, "The Arthurian Tradition in Lambert d'Ardres," Latin translation by Kresimir Vukovic.

36. Thayer's Greek Lexicon, http://biblehub.com/greek/3051.htm.

37. John 1: 1–2.

38. We are grateful to Dr. Kresimir Vukovic for drawing our attention to this. See also http://biblehub.com/interlinear/apostolic/exodus/28.htm.

◆ ◆ ◆

rooms, dwellings and lodgings and curved paths, such as that of a labyrinth ... he built a chapel of Solomonian glory with wondrous flooring of stones and timber ... [not far from] the gates of the building. [39]

It became common practice among the Crusader knights to chip off fragments of the rock upon which the Temple of Solomon had once stood. These they would take home as talismans of their visit to the Holy Land. Arnoul the Elder is thus said to have brought back one such piece to his home at Ardres in 1177, along with a fragment of the Spear of Antioch and some of the Manna of Heaven (though how he obtained the latter is not related). According to Lambert, Arnoul then proceeded to have built a castle to house these holy relics, a castle of curious design indeed. It was here that Arnoul laid to rest the objects he had brought with him, and it is interesting to note that these objects coincide with the Hallows of the Grail. The spear had long been identified with that which had pierced the side of Christ, and as such had become one of the features of the Grail myth. Manna, the holy food of heaven, can be seen as the substance that the Grail provides, either physically or in spiritual form. The stone from Jerusalem was part of the "stone which rose and fell" and thus recalled the Grail stone described by Wolfram. So here we have, assembled in a temple or castle constructed to resemble the Solomonic temple, all the elements of the Grail Hallows originating from the Holy Land.

Troyes, home to Chrétien and a centre of Jewish learning, was close enough to Ardres for the poet to have visited there, and Chrétien's patron, Philip d'Alcase, who gave him the *métier* and *sens* of his work, was a close friend of Baudouin's. Even if Chrétien had never set foot in the curiously wrought building, he would have heard of it and almost certainly had it described by his patron. Both Philip and Baudouin would have visited the city of Jerusalem and seen the site of the original temple during the Crusades. Certainly Philip d'Alsace was in the Holy Land from 1177–8 and could very easily have brought back a description (either in writing or from personal observance), which he included in his commission of a poem from Chrétien. Philip's own father, Thierry, had himself brought back a phial of the Holy Blood, which he gifted to the church of the Holy Sepulcher in Bruges.

39. Ibid., translation by Dr. Kresimir Vukovic.

◆ ◆ ◆

The Grail Chapel of Karlstein

The castle of Guines is not the only such site to be based on the idea of the Grail and the Temple of Solomon. Karlstein, which lies twelve miles outside Prague in the Czech Republic on a wooded hill near the Beroun River,[40] was built between 1348 and 1365, soon after the first flowering of Grail literature, by the German king and Bohemian emperor Charles IV. A natural mystic, Charles seems to have possessed a profound understanding of the Grail. Karlstein was consciously built to reflect this, as the following description demonstrates:

> The adornment of the walls in the various chapels to be found in the castle, with their quantities of semi-precious stones and gold, the way in which the light is disused through these semi precious stones which—set in gilded lead—take the place of window glass, lead one to conclude that Charles IV knew about the [esoteric] powers of precious stones and gold. The small chapel of St. Catherine, for example, is a veritable gem; the entire walls, up to the ceiling, are inlaid with semi-precious stones such as amethyst, jasper, cornelian and agate, while the cross vaulting above has a blue background, adorned with roses … According to tradition it was here that Charles IV withdrew every year from Good Friday to Easter Sunday in order to meditate in undisturbed privacy …[41]

As we shall see, there are aspects of this which are very close indeed to a vastly extended description of the Grail Temple found in *The Later Titurel*, which we shall explore fully in chapter 4. Charles's choice of the Easter period to withdraw to his private Grail chapel is striking. This period, of course, is not only associated with the Passion of Christ, but also with the Grail mysteries, which were said to take place at the same time. This is reflected in the design of the castle, and throughout the building are murals that follow the narrative of the Grail.

These images guide the seeker towards the great tower of the castle that is approached across a narrow bridge, echoing the Sword Bridge of the Grail story told by Chrétien. Within the tower is the Chapel of the Holy Cross, decorated in semi-precious stones, beneath a roof representing the sun, moon, and stars, interspersed with the motif of roses. The windows are formed of pure topaz, amethyst, and almandine, through which the light enters in bands of glorious colour.

The overall symbolism of the building is clear: it shows the path of the initiate learning, forgetting, relearning, following the path of spiritual alchemy until he is able to cross the perilous

---

40. Matthews, *The Grail: Quest for Eternal Life.*
41. Allen, *A Christian Rosecreutz Anthology.*

✦ ✦ ✦

bridge and enter the chamber of the mysteries. The parallels need hardly be spelled out. This is indeed a representation of the chapel of the Grail.

The Christian Grail

If we are correct in describing Chrétien's work as of Jewish origin, it was left to another writer, his near-contemporary Robert de Boron, to connect the imagery of the temple and the mysterious Grail with the mystery of the Eucharist and the story of the Last Supper. Little is known about Robert's life, though internal evidence within his work places him in the late twelfth and early thirteenth centuries. He was the author of at least two surviving poems, all set within the world of the Arthurian legends. His *Merlin* exists only in fragments and a later prose rendition, but his greatest achievement is the *Joseph d'Arimathie*, which was probably written either at roughly the same time as Chrétien's *Conte du Graal* or shortly after. It is also possible that a third work, now known as the *Didot Perceval* after its nineteenth-century discoverer, may be a prose version of a now-lost original in which Robert told the story of Perceval from his own point of view.

Robert wrote his first poem for a lord named Gautier de Montbéliard, who is possibly indefinable with a lord of Montfaucon who left for the Holy Land in 1202 and died there in 1212. If this is a correct identification,[42] stories brought back by Gautier could be seen as a source for Robert's later work and to have enabled him access to accounts of an actual building located in the East (see chapter 7). Robert himself must have been in service to Gautier over a lengthy period of time, as he took the name "de Boron" from a village near his patron's home. In *Joseph* he calls himself *meister* (clerk); later he uses the title *messire* (knight), so that it is sometimes assumed that he was both a poet and a knight.

Whether he was following Chrétien or had an independent source remains uncertain, though his reference to his fellow author tells us that Robert certainly knew Chrétien's work. Pierre le Gentil, who made the connection between Robert and the Lord of Montfaucon, suggests that his mention of Avalon means that Robert wrote his *Joseph d'Arimathie* after 1191, when the monks at Glastonbury claimed to have discovered the coffins of King Arthur and Queen Guinevere, thus linking the site with the Arthurian and Grail legends. If this is correct, it places Robert as a follower of Chrétien rather than a contemporary.

In any case, Robert changed the direction of the Grail story forever. By making Perceval the great-nephew of Joseph of Arimathea, he ensured that we could never look at the youthful

---

42. le Gentil, "The Work of Robert de Boron and the *Didot Perceval*."

hero with the same eyes again: during the course of his adventures, he changes from a hopeless young knight into a fully fledged Grail guardian.

Through his writing, Robert joined the story of the previously Hebrew or pagan vessel to the central myth of Christianity. In doing so, he followed, either deliberately or by accident, the lineage of temple mysteries that brought the presence of the Divine into direct contact with humanity. Where before the temple itself had been the means by which humankind spoke with its creator, now the sacred vessel (represented upon every altar in Christendom) became the way that offered access to God.

The Earthly Paradise

All of the foregoing leads to the idea of an earthly paradise, a perfect state of being in a realm as close to the idea of heaven as it is possible to get, and a perfect home for the Grail. The myth has been around for a long time.[43] Some of the oldest written references we have refer to gardens of delight, walled enclosures filled with exotic creatures and plants…an overflowing of creation and fullness…a mirror of heaven. And of course we have, in the West, the idea of Eden, the garden where humankind first awoke and where they dwelled in a place of perfect harmony and delight until one of them sought to access greater wisdom. In the process of becoming even more human, they transgressed against the laws ascribed by their god and were expelled. The very name *Eden* became synonymous with the idea of loss and exile, and—along with the equally evocative myth of the fall—it became a central tenet of belief from the earliest days within Judaism and Christianity.

From this ancient myth grew the idea of a place within the realm of earth that could be reached by seekers after perfection. Amongst the earliest maps in existence, we find references to this, with the earthly paradise marked with confidence—if towards the edges of the map— as a real place. Heroes of all kinds, from the Mesopotamian Gilgamesh and the Greek Alexander the Great to the knights of Arthur, went in search of paradise. Most did not find it, and those who got as far as its walls were often turned away. Only the best of the best, the perfected ones whose belief was unshakable and whose faith absolute, could enter. This became, not surprisingly, part of the Grail myth.

Both Wolfram and Albrecht refer to the area around the temple as Salvaterre (Sacred Earth), while the Mountain of Muntsalvasche (Mountain of Salvation) becomes a beacon of

---

43. The word itself entered the English language from the French *paradis*, which in turn received it from a long line of languages—Latin, Greek, Hebrew, Persian, etc.—most of which meant a walled garden or a sacred enclosure.

hope and sacredness. A recent commentator has wisely noted that the Grail country is the expression of a perfect realm, in the centre of which is the temple, and in the centre of this the Grail itself.[44] Descriptions of the area surrounding the castles and temples where the Grail resided—sometimes within walls, sometimes outside them—were clearly attempts to evoke a paradisal state. And what more appropriate place to find the most famous relic of all, the Holy Grail? As we shall see in the following chapters, much of the imagery, especially that relating to the semi-mythical figure of Prester John, who becomes a guardian of the Grail in *The Later Titurel*, derives entirely from the idea of a perfect place in which everything was as it should be, where peace reigned, love abounded, and God smiled on his creation.

But just as the Grail was hard to find and could only be reached after a long search, often accompanied by great hardship and loss, so too the way to the earthly paradise was fraught with danger and rejection. Thus in what is usually considered the third continuation to Chrétien's *Conte del Graal*, ascribed to Gerbert de Montreuil (mid-thirteenth century), we find Perceval, shortly after his visit to the Grail castle, reaching the gates of paradise. Following the road away from the Fisher King's castle, Perceval finds himself outside a wall that is coloured one half red and the other white. Puzzled by this, he follows the wall until he reaches a gate, upon which he hammers. The gate remains firmly shut, but within he can hear sounds of merriment and music so sweet that he forgets every trouble he had ever had "since the moment he was born." Desperate for an answer, Perceval draws his sword (which had been recently given to him by the Fisher King himself) and hammers on the door with its pommel. At once thunder rolls and lightning flashes and the sword breaks in two. Perceval is horrified to see this, but as he stands frozen with distress, the gate opens a crack and a white-haired man looks out at him:

> "What do you want, young man, yelling and bawling, battering at our gate?…Now your blade needs mending—it's broken in half, I see! You've added seven whole years and a half to the toil you'll endure before you see the bleeding lance! And you can be sure of this: you'll not learn the secrets of the grail until you've done enough to earn forgiveness for all your sins and misdeeds…"
>
> "Ah, good sir," said Perceval. "Open your wicket gate wide! I can see a shining light inside—a radiant light; it looks a glorious place to be: everyone's laughing with joy!"
>
> There was no anger now in the worthy man's reply, as he said: "You'll see no more till you return, young sir. But if you can find your way back here you may well witness all our joy, and know for sure the perfect truth about the grail and why the lance bleeds—those secrets that have caused you so much toil."[45]

44. Wilson, "The Grail Utopia in Southern Germany."
45. Bryant, *The Complete Story of the Grail*, 340.

✦ ✦ ✦

Here Perceval, whose search for the Grail is to continue for a great deal longer, glimpses what is clearly the entrance to the earthly paradise. Though not allowed in, he is given a promise that if he can find his own way back, he may be permitted more than a glimpse of the mysteries within. As we shall see again and again throughout this book, the home of the Grail, if not actually within the garden of paradise, is close at hand.

Dwelling Places of God

The symbolism of the temple within the earthly paradisal realm takes us back thousands of years before Chrétien and Robert composed their enigmatic works, to a time when human beings first began to create buildings that were seen as both a dwelling place for their gods and a means of inviting deity into a space between worlds. Thus, when the high priest of the Temple of Solomon entered the Holy of Holies, he was seen to be communicating directly with God—just as, centuries later, those who stood before the Grail in a building that recalled the Solomonic temple were able to look into the vessel itself and perceive there "the secrets of the saviour."[46]

The earliest traditions relating to temple building depict them as liminal spaces, where the creators, invited to enter their house, could choose to communicate with their creation (humanity). The earth upon which the temple stood was itself sacred, either through its being placed at that spot or by a hallowing touch of the Divine that designated the building as a marker for those in search of the sacred. Thus it became a temenos, a place set apart, where an invisible border showed that here was sacred space, a reflection of heaven on earth. A key statement in the Lancelot-Grail relates that

> those who possessed the Grail thereafter … were by this very fact able to establish a Spiritual center destined to replace the lost Paradise, and *to serve as an image of it.*[47]

It is this image that is represented by the temple of the Grail, as described in Chrétien, the work of Albrecht in *The Later Titurel, Sone de Nansay,* and the Cistercian compilers of the Lancelot-Grail. All of these writers described a place where God and his creation could meet and converse as they once had in paradise.

It is as though the temple builders, by inviting God to descend into the temenos, were asking not only to be guided along the path towards unity and perfection, but also were anticipating that God would actually evolve through contact with them. Since God is spirit and humanity is

46. Matarasso, *The Quest of the Holy Grail.*
47. *The Lancelot-Grail: The Old French Arthurian Vulgate and Post-Vulgate in Translation,* our italics.

matter, and since the two states of being cannot evolve separately, they are linked like two inter-locking circles, which are only complete when superimposed precisely one upon the other—at which moment they become one. All the temples we will examine here were intended as physi-cal glyphs to be read by mankind and their gods, mirrors reflecting images of the temporal and Divine upon each other.

To quote the third-century Greek philosopher Plotinus:

> … those ancient sages who sought to secure the presence of divine beings by the erection of shrines … showed insight into the nature of the All [perceiving that] though the Soul is everywhere, its presence will be secured all the more readily when an appropriate receptacle is elaborated, serving like a mirror to catch an image of it.[48]

In its most complete and complex form, this cosmic mirror for the reflection of God becomes also an initiator into the divine mystery of creation, the most perfect object of the quest.

The imagery of the Grail Temple is notably consistent. It is usually situated at the top of a mountain, which is in turn surrounded either by impenetrable forest or deep water. Access, if any, is by way of a perilously narrow, sharply edged bridge, which became known as the Sword Bridge. To make entrance even harder, the whole temple, or the castle that contained it, would often revolve, making it almost impossible to gain entry by normal means. Once within, more perils awaited, and for those few who succeeded in reaching the center, where lay the Chapel of the Grail, the experience could, as in Lancelot's case, be both chastening and parlous. Nor was the castle without its human guardians; at an early stage in the mythos, a family of kings, sup-ported by a specially chosen body of knights, appeared to serve and protect the sacred vessel.

The most completely developed description of the medieval Grail Temple is to be found in the two thirteenth-century romances we shall be exploring in this book, especially in the Middle High German poem *Der Jüngerer Titurel* ("The Later Titurel")[49] attributed to Albrecht von Scharffenberg. Here the lineage of the Grail Kings, first mentioned by Robert de Boron, is traced back to Solomon, and the temple of the Grail founded upon structures dating from more ancient times.

Let us look, now, at the first of these works.

---

48. Plotinus, *The Enneads*, as quoted in Crichlow, *Soul as Sphere and Androgine*, 23.

49. See footnote 101 on page 107.

2

SONE AND THE GRAIL

The Grail romances may … have preserved
for the West a Christian initiatic tradition.

✦ ✦ ✦

S. R. Wilson, "Rene Guénon and the Heart of the Grail"

There are two medieval romances that preserve detailed accounts, both descriptive and interpretive, of the Grail Temple. They were written close to each other in time, one in France, the other in Germany. Both reflect the belief in the Grail as an actual relic and the building that housed it as a physical place. They have been largely ignored by Grail scholars and only brief excerpts have been translated into English.

The first of these texts is *Sone de Nansay*, an epic romance that exists in a single manuscript found in the Royal Library of Turin, Italy (Ms. 1626) as part of a collection of chivalric and Arthurian tales, including Chrétien de Troyes's *Cligès*. Written in medieval French, the copy was made sometime during the mid-fourteenth century, but the poem of *Sone* itself dates from somewhat earlier, between the end of the thirteenth and the early fourteenth centuries. It consists of some 21,321 lines, with a lacuna of some 2,400 lines, the result of fire damage, the contents of which can be inferred from the remainder of the work. Just two editions of the work have appeared to date: the first by Moritz Goldschmidt in 1899 and a more recent edition by Claude Lachet in 2014. Lachet's modern French edition was published in 2012. *Sone* is said to derive from the German name *Sueno*, while *Nansay* is probably *Nanbsheim*, near Neuf-Brisach in northeastern France.

The story has received little attention until now, due in part to its length and the dismissive comments of the first scholars to notice it, who termed it prolix and lacking in skill, as well

✦ ✦ ✦

as failing to grasp the nature of the Grail material, which was seen as having been "inserted" into the romance in a clumsy way. In fact, a great deal of the poem is taken up with the Grail story, with its titular hero's life being compared to that of the first Grail guardian, Joseph of Arimathea. It also adds many important details to the Grail myth, especially in its description of the building where the sacred relic is kept. This is the only part of the poem to receive any attention until now, although it will quickly be seen, as we continue our exploration, that there are many subtle references within the work that add significantly to our understanding of the Grail myth.

The only full-length study of the poem in English to date is by Kruger Normand in a PhD dissertation submitted in 1975 to the University of Pennsylvania. Normand categorizes the work as "ancestral and biographical" since it describes the life of the hero from birth to death and deals both with his antecedents and successors. We must be grateful to Dr. Normand for providing the fullest and most detailed summary of the work, which made our own task lighter, but unfortunately there are a number of errors within this that make the reading of the poem significantly different, while the overall study of the romance is limited and lacks a detailed understanding of the Grail tradition in particular.[50]

Given the length of the poem, we decided to include only those passages that are of particular relevance to our argument. We believe these to be the first complete translations of these passages into English—with the exception of the visit to the Castle of the Grail (lines 4271–5020) that were partially translated by R. S. Loomis in 1963.

Much of the poem falls outside the scope of this book, but to make the arc of the story more understandable, we have placed the translated sections within a complete summary. In preparing this we have followed the breakdown of the text into sections suggested by Normand, not including the prologue, which he omits, and some additional details from a shorter summary by Pierre Langlois in his book *La Societe Francais au XIII Siecle*, published in 1904. The sections Gareth has translated into English are set in bold type to set it apart from our summary, which is not a direct translation. A detailed exploration of the meaning of the text follows in chapter 3.

The prologue begins with a curious prelude attributed to one of Sone's descendants. It continues with an overall tour of Sone's family history, chronicling both his ancestors and successors, placed within a pseudo-historical framework.

50. Normand, *A Study of the Old French Romance of Sone de Nansay*.

❖ ❖ ❖

SONE DE NANSAY
translated by Gareth Knight

1: Prologue
The Beginning of Sone
(LINES 1–352)

In the name of Jesus Christ, the Holy Virgin who bore him, and all the saints, may the writing of the work that I begin this day exalt the faith and courage of all valiant knights who sustain the Holy Church against miscreants throughout time. As Lady of Beyrouth and Chatelaine of Cyprus, my patrimony by the grace of Our Lord, I have the true history of my ancestors in diverse accounts that tell how they founded and sustained the Holy Church over more than a hundred and forty years. I would like them to be united into a single history that pleases me to evoke and to hear, and be remembered after me through my clerk Branque, at my command, to whom I have entrusted these histories.

Fane of Beyrouth

♦ ♦ ♦

I, Branque, clerk to the Lady of Beyrouth over the past forty years, a master in logic, medicine, canon law, and astronomy, and knowledgeable in geometry, have never obtained a benefice in the Holy Church nor ever sought one; and though a hundred and five years old and one who has ever done his best to study, I would not claim to be more than half a clerk, yet at my lady's command I will tell the history of her ancestors.

I begin with Count Anselm of Brabant, who, as well as being the most handsome, was one of the bravest knights of his time, also renowned for the wisdom of his counsel at courts of law in France and Germany, where none of his peers dare oppose him. He married Aélis, daughter of Ernoul, count of Flanders, a good, beautiful, and pious lady, by whom he had two sons, the elder named Renaut and the second Henri.

When she died, the countess was buried at the monastery of St. Gertrude at Nivelles, and God performed several miracles through her. Her mother then sought to have her remains removed to Gand, where she had been born, and as

♦ ♦ ♦

neither count nor abbess objected, this was done, although it has been said that it may not have pleased Our Lord.

The count died in 632. Renaut became an accomplished knight, and, according to the records of the time, possessed a domain worth two thousand pounds on the borders of Alsace, which he gave to his brother, Henri, who paid homage to the emperor for it. The emperor thought well of him and knighted him, as he had many fine qualities. At Leyde, a city near Germany, he presented him with Ydoine, daughter of the Duke of Mélone, in marriage.

The wife of King Floire of Hungary was the sister of this duke and therefore the aunt of Ydoine who had married Henri. She was extremely tall, even for Germany, where knights were generally tall, but she was well made for her size and so beautiful that no one knew any other who combined such beauty with such high morals. Henri sent her to his castle of Nansay, where she was much loved and honoured by all and bore her husband two children.

The older one was a dwarf, so small that they were astonished to compare him to the lady who bore him and the father who engendered him, who were both very tall and good looking. But he was noble hearted and was named Henri, after his father. The younger son was called Sone, a German name, and had a very different appearance.

Their father and mother died on the same day, so after they were buried, others brought up the children until the age of reason. Sone quickly learned to read and write and bent all his efforts to learning. He grew much and progressed well, being knowledgeable, courteous, and handsome, and assuredly one of the finest-looking boys in the world, with many virtues. He learned with such application in infancy that he left four of his tutors behind, who were astonished by his intelligence.

Eudes of Douchery—not Douchery-on-Meuse but the castle—had served the emperor well, who now knighted him. For the celebration, Eudes invited ladies, maidens, and knights from all around. Sone turned up at this magnificent fête and after the meal there was round-dancing, in which Eudes's young sister took part. All who saw her said they had never seen such a beautiful girl. Sone was seized with such passion for her that he had to leave the fête and return to Nansay, but was so taken with love for her that she became the object of all his desire. He returned to the young lady several times to seek her love but found her so proud that he was unable to see how he could stay. So at the age of twelve and a half he entered the service of the Count of Santois, who was a very fine knight.

✦ ✦ ✦

Sone won his first prize at a tourney at Châlon-sur-Saône, as you will learn later in the tale of his great deeds. He won his second at a round table tournament reserved for squires that took place between Lyons and Cluny in Bourgogne, and here, as you will learn in the course of this story, he championed his lord's daughter, who, after he had won fifteen horses, was crowned queen of the event. On his return his lord wanted to marry him to his daughter. But Sone still loved Yde so much that he could not keep away from her and went again, seeking her love. But the fair Yde treated him badly.

He was greatly hurt by this, and leaving his brother, rode toward the coast and went to England, then to Scotland, and from there to Ireland, where the queen bore him a son, who later became King of Sicily. Finally he passed from Ireland to Norway where he increased his exploits, as you will learn. He married the daughter of the King of Norway where he was crowned king in his turn, and fathered three sons.

It was at this time that the Pope demanded that he join him to become emperor and so Sone had to leave. His son Houdient, just eighteen months old, was crowned King of Norway and later married Matabrune, the worst woman in the world, on whom he fathered King Oriant, who in turn married Élouse, who bore him triplets, each of the three boys born wearing a little gold chain round his neck.

Because she hated Élouse, Matabrune stole the gold necklet from one of the boys, who transformed into a swan, so she dare not try this again. The swan flew towards the river that ran at the foot of the wall of Galoche. This was the swan that accompanied his brother Élyas—known as the Knight of the Swan.

Élyas killed the Saxon champion at Nimègue and married Béatrix, the heiress, who gave birth to Yde. Despite forbidding her to do so, Béatrix could not resist asking Élyas his identity; at which he replied: "After today you will never see me again, as you did not obey my conditions," and blew his horn. His swan brother was ready with the little boat. Élyas stepped into it and arrived at Beyrouth, the port of my lady, who still lived there and also had three sons.

They were at the great battle that took place at the port of Acre where 120,000 Christians and 300,000 pagans were killed and no miscreant escaped death. The battle lasted for five days and five nights, and Élyas was cut to pieces. His brother the swan brought him back by sea to die in the arms of my lady. Nor did anyone witness such grief as that shown by his brother the swan. Nothing could console him. He threw himself into the waves and perished.

◆ ◆ ◆

I have brought this matter up at the start because the story does not say any more about it. Sone went off to Rome with three of his sons. One was King of Sicily, the second King of Norway, the third, King of Jerusalem (father of Fane of Beyrouth, who asked for this story); the fourth became Pope of Rome.

2: Sone's Early Adventures in Chivalry and Love
(LINES 353–2918)

Sone now journeys to the court of the Count Vandémont-en-Saintois, who is well known for his dedication to chivalry. On learning of Sone's family history, the count willingly takes him into his household, and Sone thereafter accompanies his new master everywhere—including to tournaments. At one of these he rescues the count from a mêlée. For this he is counted a hero. But his mind is still on Yde and he begs to be allowed to leave to go and see his friends. He departs for Doncheri, much to the sorrow of Luciane, the count's daughter, who is secretly in love with him.

Back at Doncheri Sone finds Yde even more beautiful. He declares his love in front of a room full of people but is greeted scornfully by Yde, who suggests he has learned his "art" of courtship from "Chateau Landon," a place known for its ill-bred people, where "in praising one, they blame another."

Shocked and distressed, Sone prepares to leave. Yde, seeing how upset he is, relents and hands him his gloves, which he had dropped, whispering that it is a friend who returns them. Sone is far too sorrowful to notice this small kindness and departs to return to Saintois.

Luciane is desperately happy to see him, and the count and countess honour him and offer the hand of their daughter in marriage. But all Sone can think of is Yde, while back in Doncheri, she reviews her recent actions, wondering if she has been too harsh. Wavering between humility and pride, she decides to keep silent but wishes Sone well wherever he goes.

Soon after this, a tournament is to be held at Saintois, to which each baron sends a squire to test his skills. At his master's bidding, Sone attends, bringing Luciane and her women with him, each wearing a new red dress; but secretly he sends a message to Yde, begging her to attend.

The tournament is a splendid affair, with many knights and nobles attending. In the midst of a field next to the lists is a tent containing a chair for the lady who will be crowned as queen of the tournament according to the prowess of her champion. Sone is fighting in Luciane's name, but in his heart it is Yde he champions.

On the first day Sone wins eight jousts and receives the acclaim of all, but he wears plain armour and carries a blank shield so that no one knows who he is. Next day Sone continues to fight bravely and at the end wins the crown for Luciane. All of this is observed by Yde's servants, who are also in attendance.

Back at Vandémont-en-Saintois, Sone receives news that his brother is ill and returns to Nansay. Henri is soon better and tries to keep Sone from leaving by offering him land and riches. But nothing will deter the young man, who sets off for Doncheri. There, once again, he declares his love for Yde, who has heard of his success in the tournament but still rejects him, telling him that he should love the one for whom he jousted and who was crowned in the tent—in other words, Luciane.

Hurt and angry, Sone returns to Nansay, where he finds a maiden reading a lay composed for him by Luciane. Distraught, Sone determines to leave again immediately. He saddles his good horse, Moriel, and departs, heading for England.

3: Sone's Journey to England and Scotland
(LINES 2919–3150)

Sone had gone off towards England and did not stop until he came to the sea. Having reached port, the youthful company boarded a ship that took them across the sea. Arriving in England, they hardly paused before crossing to the salt sea on the other side of the country. Passing Berwick, they were soon in Scotland and lodged in the town of Liendlousiel.[51] They were closely watched by the Scots, who remarked on the striking beauty of Sone, passing this information on to the court, where the queen was awaiting her husband.

After they told her, she was eager to meet Sone and invited him to come to court along with his warhorse. Sone replied that he would gladly bring the horse and had it saddled up while he put on his sumptuous squire's attire. They brought the horse, which he mounted and rode to court accompanied by a favourite page.

They arrived at the bridge while the queen awaited them in the great hall. When Sone arrived along with such a horse, which seemed as if it must be the finest in the world, a lady in waiting remarked to the queen, "Never can you have seen, madame, such a young lord. If it pleases you, go down and see

51. Possibly Galashiels.

how well he sits in the saddle. It is as if he were enchanted. He hardly seems a member of the human race but more like an angel come down from heaven to inspect us."

Thus praising the young man to the queen, they led her down to meet him. When the queen saw him, she declared that they had certainly spoken truly. Sone dismounted on seeing the queen and her suite, passed his horse to a servant, and approached her, kneeling at her feet for a moment before, finding him so pleasant to look at, she invited him to stand, looking upon him with as much pleasure as she had looked upon his horse.

Leading him up to the reception hall, she asked his name and country. "Tell us your name and where you were born, if you please, and what brings you here. The journey must have been tiresome."

"Madame, my name is Sone and my country is called Alsace. I am a son of the Lord of Nansay, but my parents are dead and my brother is lord of the domain. And that is the truth!"

But a knight was present, just returned from Saint Jacques de Compostella,[52] who had been present at the Table Round tournament where Sone had successfully jousted. Having seen him there, the knight also recognized the horse on which he had fought. Recalling all this, he told the queen about it, the crowning of the young girl, and the honors awarded them, to the confusion of the young man before them, as the knight affirmed that throughout the whole world there could not exist, in his opinion, such a squire able to handle such arms and such horses.

"In those respects he is greatly experienced," he added. "Keep him if you want. The king will let you know if you may do so."

The queen reflected that Sone's great beauty would not engender any suspicion in the matter for she was not in the habit of so diverting herself.

Sone remained standing, intently observed by all because he was such an extraordinary being, but they did not, for all that, honour him. So Sone decided to ask to take formal leave of the queen and her court and return the way he had come. All gave their leave but without exchanging a word of farewell, nor did Sone insist upon it.

---

52. St. James of Compostella.

4: Sone's Arrival in Norway
and His Service to the King
(LINES 3151–3410)

Sone sets out from Norway in a hired ship. The king of that land, whose name is
Alain, hears of his coming.

The king sent a messenger to the ship to ask what merchandise it had
brought. The sailors replied it was enough wheat for a large population to live
on for a long time. "Then welcome, your cargo will be sold at a profit." When
the messenger saw Sone preparing to disembark, along with his servants, his
packhorse, and his good warhorse Moriel, he returned to his lord and told him
what he had seen.

Having heard this, the king rode to the ship, saluted Sone, and invited him
to come and dine with him, adding: "It would be helpful to tell us your name.
You would be very welcome, and I would like to know if you are a knight."

"Sire, I am called Sone, but I have not yet been dubbed a knight."

The king took him by the hand and led him to his castle, and to honour his
visitor ordered his servants to carry Sone's baggage and that of his squire.

When Sone entered, the great hall was lit up by his beauty. It was like the
moon appearing in the midst of the stars, so did Sone shine, disconcerting the
rest of the world. The king's sons, Houdiant and Thomas, welcomed him with
great marks of respect. Their sister, Odée, came down from her room as soon as
she saw Sone in the hall, asking her brothers if this young man was a messenger
or envoy from the King of Ireland. "Sister," replied Houdiant, "we know nothing yet of the reasons for his coming."

At this they asked for water to be brought to wash their hands. The king was
very courteous and sat them along with his barons at the table of honour as the
hall filled with knights who sat at tables where they could, for they were very
numerous. The king's sons paid particular attention to Sone as the dishes were
brought in along with ale and wine, as was their custom. They stayed so long
at table that it could have been irksome to anyone not used to it. In fact, they
drank so much that each told stories that no one else listened to and were so
keen to talk that no one could hear anything. A third of the day passed this way.

Each knight wore a hauberk with shield hung round his neck and sword at
hand. All Ireland would be massacred, according to everyone as they drank,
and on his arrival the King of Scotland would be the first to be killed and his
brother never leave prison.

◆ ◆ ◆

Sone, unfamiliar with these customs, looked on in a stupor. He would have preferred the company of his horse. One of the king's sons amiably prayed Sone not to be angry: "It is the way they pass the time, to drink, eat, talk, threaten the absent; it is the custom of the country, and if you were the first to rise, they would be greatly offended."

As they conversed on many subjects, the king's daughter, Odée, approached them, holding a great goblet. She drank from it first and then, kneeling, passed it to Sone, saying: "Dear sir, drink deep by the faith that you owe me."

Sone, who did not know this custom, replied that he would not drink while the young girl remained kneeling. The king's son intervened: "Drink, or you will be blamed by everyone. It is our custom. She does you great honour. Accept it without any more talk. Remember that she is the king's daughter and we are both her brothers."

When Sone heard this custom, he thought it very foolish but took the cup that the girl offered. It contained a drink that did not much please him but he said nothing of what he thought and thus "howled with the wolves." Having drunk, he passed the cup to those with whom he had eaten. His companion drank and then passed the goblet on to his brother, who completely emptied it. The girl then rose before declaring: "My lords, I thank you for having well drunk as you have done."

She returned to her room but did not forget them. Having taken three shining swords and three lances with sparkling iron tips, she offered them to the young men to whom she had brought the drink. The first she took to Sone, who did not refuse them, and each of the brothers were given the same.

The eldest, Houdiant, was very keen to instruct Sone, if he could, in their customs. First they took up the tablecloths that were fashionable in their country but after the meal did not wash their hands. Almost all present carefully observed Sone and said they had never seen anyone so handsome; all the same, they could not divine what necessity had brought him here. Then the king rose and took Sone and his sons to one side.

He said to Sone, "Welcome among us, dear sir. And if it pleases you to stay, that would be useful in the perilous situation in which we find ourselves. I promise to pay you to your liking, for I have need of friends. The King of Ireland is driven with a desire for war and will be attacking with armed forces to put us in prison. He swears he will seize my two sons despite all my efforts to protect them and will marry my daughter to a peasant. But if it pleases God, in whom I believe, he will not have such power over me. Dear sir, will you agree to be the protector of my children?"

◆ ◆ ◆

Then the queen came, holding her daughter by the hand. She courteously greeted Sone and gave him a magnificent gold ring, saying: "I give you this jewel through affection for you, but with this present I pray you, through friendship of a sincere heart, to keep company with my two sons. In times of danger, do not go without them, but remain with each as a faithful friend." She added, "My daughter prays for that too."

"Willingly, madam," said the young man, "and welcome. I will help with all my power."

They all thanked him, assured of his help.

5: War and Single Combat
(LINES 3411–4270)

Back in Scotland, the king of that land returns, hears of Sone's decision to fight on the Norwegian side, and learns of his tremendous prowess. The king begins preparations for war, conscripting men from the court.

In Norway cities and castles are provisioned in readiness for war. Hearing that the kings of Scotland and Ireland have landed at the harbour of St. Joseph with 60,000 poorly equipped and half-naked men, Sone and the king's sons, Houdiant and Thomas, arm themselves and lead a force against the invaders.

Arriving at St. Joseph, they surprise the invading army and slaughter 10,000 of the Irish, taking many more prisoners; but in the maelstrom both of King Alain's sons are killed.

The King of Scotland now proposes a single combat to decide the outcome without further deaths. The King of Norway accepts and the date is set twenty days hence. The Scots choose Aligos, an eleven-foot giant, to be their champion. Sone volunteers and is accepted as champion of Norway.

6: The Visit to the Grail Castle
(LINES 4271–5020)[53]

Because of his dangerous mission, the king determined to prepare Sone well, to take him to a holy place to make his confession, hear the word of God, and gain confidence in defending his cause. They set off in a party of only twenty men, and the king kept Sone close beside him.

Crossing Norway they discovered many strange places. On one high mountain an eyrie of rare falcons no longer found in Christian lands. On another, animals called elks that can appear quite large but are really quite small, with thin bodies, looking like rapidly moving camels. Other beasts included mountain wolves with hair so long that it trailed on the ground. They too can seem big because their hair picks up and drags along loose branches. King Alain kept some and described their nature.

They passed through valleys and mountains for a couple of days in a country so strange it can hardly be described, proving very difficult until they came to a grassland at the foot of a mountain that all declared the most beautiful place they had ever seen. This took two more days to cross, but one could not say how far because it ran alongside a rugged coast.

When they had crossed it, the king struck camp and the party rested for the evening. Rising at midnight, they travelled on until noon, making for the sea and the place they sought. Here at some time in the past a raised roadway had been built, leading into the water. It was difficult to find, and many brave knights must have come to grief before doing so or even catching a glimpse of it. But the king, who owned these lands, knew them well and took them directly to where two rocks formed a gateway that led into the sea.

The king drew his horn and sounded a call, after which they saw a boat approaching, propelled by two monks. As they arrived between the rocks, it could be seen that they were weeping. The monks appeared reluctant and hardly pleased to see them and asked who they were. The king replied that they

---

53. The following section, as translated, assumes a personal quality that feels very much as though the writer was present at an actual site. This is not of itself unusual within medieval romance literature, but the sudden switch from impersonal to personal in the narrative is. It was this that suggested to some who have studied the text that this part could be an interpolation. However, the style and setting are so precise when compared to the rest, before and after, that is seems unlikely to be the case. It is more likely that the author wanted to add veracity to the story he was telling, making it a reminiscence rather than an imaginative telling. Equally, he may be repeating an actual traveller's account.

ought to be happy enough when they knew, and when they recognized him, they were overjoyed and ceased their crying.

"Welcome, sire, we had keenly hoped for your coming, having heard you had suffered great grief and misfortune. Is there anything you need? Have you come to stay with us?"

"One could wish for nothing better," replied the king.

"Then step aboard," said one of the monks. "The ferry will be along to pick up your men and horses."

And so the king and Sone stepped into the boat, and the monks rowed them across to the castle.

Never had anything more beautiful been seen. It stood in the open sea at a distance where no machine could hurl anything to harm its crenelated walls that rose up out of the living rock. On its outer wall were four towers that looked the finest in the world, and in the centre, midway between them, a greater one surpassing the others. This contained the palace; surely nothing more sumptuous had ever been built.

In every direction it was a hundred feet wide because it was perfectly circular. At the centre of the central tower was a fireplace that rested on four gilded pillars that supported a pure copper pipe, four feet high, decorated with gold coloured mosaics that crossed the reception hall. I am sure no more wondrous place had ever been built.

Any who carefully studied its detail would never be puzzled by it if truly loved by God. Here was the basis of faith; the beginnings of religion, of the angel who was sent by God to greet the holy Virgin, of the comportment that God observed in his earthly life, of the way he died and descended into hell to lead out the faithful, and the way we must act to enter paradise. All the good things, of which you may have heard, if it pleases God, were figured there in abundance, rendered in fine gold.

The king having disembarked with Sone, the monks instructed servers to lead them into the palace. The king entered first and the others willingly followed. As they passed inside they were observed by the monks, who wept as they did so, their hearts melting into tears.

And when he was asked, in the name of God, why we had come, King Alain told them about Sone, saying, "He is a great warrior whom God has sent to help us. He has already avenged my two sons and I pray you to honour him when he represents us in single combat." At which the monks felt greatly relieved.

+ + +

Then the abbot said to the king: "Sire, it is past noon and a meal is ready. If it is your pleasure, shall we have it brought in?" And the king agreed that they do so.

Tables were placed in a sheltered area that overlooked the outer wall and gave onto the sea. It was bounded by a carved balustrade of white marble upon which no bird, animal, or fish could not be found represented, including ten leopards, each with a gaping mouth, whose heads turned ever to face the wind to produce agreeable harmonies. Whoever wished to contemplate the sea could find no better place.

In the other direction lay woodlands of laburnum, cypress, sycamore, alisier, [54] almond, olive, and other beautiful trees flourishing by the sea. To see stags and deer at play, swans, peacocks, moose, birds diving into fresh or salt water, though with wings that cannot fly far. Some who have seen them say they can be as big as badgers, though not any smaller, and similar to bats in that their wings are covered in fur. They have hair, pointed features, and make such a racket that the woods resound with it. [55]

Three streams of water meet at the castle that well up from the rock and flow into the sea, mixing the fresh water with the salt. There are so many fish gathered here as could never be destroyed by fishing. Search the whole world and you would never find so solid a castle provided with such riches. Whoever built this one was certainly no apprentice!

The abbot, the king, and his knights were seated at tables of honour, while Sone took his place to one side where a seat had been reserved for him. The guests had a profusion of dishes to eat, enough to exhaust even those who served them. After the meal, when all had washed their hands, the monks left for church to give thanks for all the blessings so generously dispensed by God.

Talking to the abbot, the king said that next morning early he would like to see the reliquaries opened up to make their confessions, after which they would leave. "Including Sone, for we have great need of him."

"We will hear your confessions willingly, sire, and intend to pray for you overnight; the perilous situation calls for it and you will find us ready in the best way we know how to fight—by invoking Jesus Christ."

54. *Sorbus Torminalis*, or service tree, native to England and Wales.

55. These strange creatures may possibly be raccoon dogs, who are neither dog nor raccoon but have long fur and pointed faces and are quite noisy.

✦ ✦ ✦

Sone met the holy community and took an old monk by the hand to confess, repenting and weeping hot tears. Absolving him, the good monk emphasized he would be fighting to maintain the peace of the kingdom.

He concluded: "Dear brother, you will be fighting in the name of God, as you will discover. And tomorrow the abbot will preach the necessary virtues you need to bear."

Sone went to bed very thoughtfully, for he had been well instructed that day.

◆ ◆ ◆

Next morning the dawn bell was rung. The monks had performed their overnight vigil as promised. King and knights heard Mass at the church, the abbot in person chanting it. Then, in his priestly garments, he stood before them to preach.

"Hear this, O King, as well as those you have brought with you. As you may know, this castle was founded by a saint, who rests in one of the coffins you see before you.

"On his death bed, he asked for the story of his life to be written, and it is right that I should speak of it from the beginning, for we can take great profit from it. It is astonishing how those who live on earth can sometimes choose to act—seemingly without fear of losing their reason or their life.

"Originally from Arimathea, Joseph worked as a bailiff for seven years in the house of Pilate, but ever revered Jesus Christ, who had preached the new religion. Thus after seven years, on conclusion of his service, he asked if he might have the body of Jesus as a gift.

"Pilate liked Joseph but thought him mad not to have asked for something better, though he did not refuse. For his part, Joseph felt well paid, for he believed Jesus to be a true king whom he adored in body and soul. Keen to remove it from the cross, he extracted the nails and placed the body in a sepulchre—for which he was accused of going against the religion of the country.

"Far from denying this, Joseph continued to call upon God, in whom he believed in all sincerity. But when these accusations were brought to Pilate, although he respected his former bailiff, he did not hesitate to render justice on him. For admitting his Christian faith, Joseph was cast into a deep pit 20 toises deep[56] and swarming with snakes, toads, and spiders that greatly harassed him. Enormous stones were rolled across the top, which was sealed with cement.

56. About 120 feet.

◆ ◆ ◆

"Being imprisoned in this terrible place troubled Joseph greatly until Jesus appeared to him and offered him a wonderous vessel. You can safely believe me for you will very soon see it!

"It consoled Joseph greatly, for it removed the vermin, caused the stench of the place to disappear, and softened the rock, which from now on was easier to lie on than a fine woolen mattress. The place became fragrant with the true blood of Christ that spread a light as bright as the sun. And when Joseph put the vessel to his lips, he suffered neither hunger nor thirst.

"For forty years things continued thus, and he suffered no further torment. Vespasian, the Roman emperor, was a leper. He had once been handsome but was now hideous, until Veronica cured him with her miraculous veil with which she had comforted Jesus on the way to the Crucifixion.

"Vespasian proclaimed that he now believed in God and Jesus Christ, as he had recovered his health thanks to him. And as God and Jesus Christ had cured him, so he would now fight for him with his army. He thus led his troops towards Jerusalem, and night and day attacked the city and those who dwelt there. At least one starving mother ate her children, and when the city was abandoned, thirty Jews could be bought for a denier.[57]

"When all were gone, Veronica and the high priest, Ananias, told Vespasian how Joseph had been incarcerated in the bottom of a cavern forty years ago. 'Let us at least have his bones, sir,' they said, 'for his flesh will have rotted by now.'

"'Take me there,' replied the king. 'I have heard about this.' Ananias led him to the cavern, and the emperor had the stones removed and the opening completely cleared. From the cave came a light as bright as if the sun had risen and such a sweet fragrance that all were overcome.

"Vespasian looked in and saw Joseph, hailed him in the name of God, and addressed him as a friend.

"'God and Saint Mary be praised!' cried Joseph, 'I have heard your voice before, and if you believe in God and Jesus Christ, let it ring out again.'

"'My friend, I am a Christian king and wish only the best for you if you have been walled up for believing in God and Jesus Christ.'

"'Yes,' replied Joseph, 'I believe in him and would not wish for any other religion.'

"The emperor arranged straight away to have him pulled up.

"Joseph still carried in his arms the vessel given him by God. It was gazed upon by all the people, who desired to kiss it. Any of the sick that touched it

---

57. A small silver coin.

were returned to perfect health, exalting their faith. And so Christianity was assured, and its bounds increased.

◆ ◆ ◆

"Now when Joseph was imprisoned, he already had a son, named Josephé, who became a very fine clerk and was the first Christian bishop; a very wise and virtuous man, he led a saintly life, and the faith was greatly increased thereby. Vespasian was also joined by his son, Titus.

"Joseph of Arimathea still had the wonderous vessel in his possession, and now he knocked down a wall and took out the holy lance with which Longinus had pierced the side of God, who later forgave him. Joseph had previously hidden the lance in the wall, which was how he knew it was there. Now he honoured it and kept it with him.

"He later spent some time in Syria. God told him to cross the sea and increase the divine faith there. He found a ship awaiting him near Ascalon with nothing within it.

"'Come aboard, fear not,' said a voice, 'let God act according to his will. He will lead you well, as he pleases.' Following this order, Joseph quickly boarded the boat.

"He was deprived of nothing, for the holy vessel was his friend, and he had the holy lance for companion, thanks to which Longinus received his pardon. The boat was good and solid that carried Joseph and his precious objects, although as yet he had no followers. He willingly accepted whatever God did, and so it was that as he boarded the boat, it left port as fast as any other craft could, despite lacking mast or sail—a sight the inhabitants of Caesarea found miraculous.

"Joseph's boat was guided by God until it arrived at Gaète,[58] where Joseph disembarked to find a horse standing by with armour fine enough to suit the most valiant warrior.

"By his progress, Joseph increased the faith and caused it ever to advance. But I cannot tell you all ways by which God allowed him to work. God liked him to do it thus and Joseph also loved it. He crossed many countries as a valiant knight and friend of God until he arrived in Norway, from which he drove the Saracens.

"He killed the king who ruled there and who had the most beautiful daughter in the world. Joseph was greatly taken with her—in body, heart, and will,

58. Either a city in Italy or a township in Holland.

◆ ◆ ◆

but acted foolishly. For he had the young girl baptized, who had no call for it, for she did not believe in God or Jesus Christ. Indeed, she hated Joseph more than anyone because he had killed her father and most of their friends.

"Joseph did not want to renounce his intention to marry her, and when they were wed he loved her with all his heart. But God, who greatly loved Joseph, decided, through her, to tempt him; he wounded him in the reins and below, from which Joseph endured terrible suffering.

"Finding himself like this, he repented and sought support from all his vassals, by whom he was truly loved. Because Norway was a kingdom, he felt he ought to wear a crown; his barons approved and crowned him king. And his wife, having borne a child, was also crowned.

"He had this child brought up by able-bodied friends while kept by God in this state whereby he could not serve, use his limbs, feed himself, or move about, but remained lying down. But he thought constantly of Jesus Christ so that his whole heart beat for him. He led a saintly life, and the Holy Church was thus exalted.

"During the time he remained thus wounded, the castle that Sone now observed was built. One could not find a better fortress, situated in the open sea, free from assault. No ship could reach it by sea for fear of being cast on hidden rocks. And as the fresh water flows and strikes the walls here, there is always a profusion of fish of all kinds.

"The good king had a boat in which, after celebrating Mass, he went fishing, aided by a sailor who guided the boat to wherever he wanted to go. The fishing and the company of the sailors pleased him. Here he could forget his terrible suffering, for such pain could kill many a man. And because he thus fished, his popular name spread everywhere: he was called the Fisher King—a name that is still well known.

"He led this life for many days until a knight came that could cure him; and afterwards he was so powerful through the practice of arms that he destroyed the miscreants. Although his young son sinned and lies in the other coffin, the king himself lived a very long time, during which the faith was exalted.

"When he was on his deathbed, he appointed thirteen monks to serve in the tradition of the named apostles, and we remain thirteen in this castle.

"I have told you quite frankly the true story of his life. In that time the country was called Logres, a name of suffering, renowned for its tears and weeping. It very much merited being renowned for suffering since one can grow neither beans nor wheat, no child be born, no young girl find a husband, no tree bear leaves, no grass regrow, no bird have chicks, no beast have young since the king

◆ ◆ ◆

was mutilated and until he had expiated his sins, for Jesus Christ was strongly opposed by the actions of Joseph and the miscreant [whom he had married]. By the example of Adam, you can see that one must never transgress a divine command. Joseph and his wife, the transgressor, realised it through suffering.

"I speak to you also of this country that has been called Norway since then. Sir King, you hold it from God and have no other lord. Those who defend it serve God who grants all recompense, but whoever makes war on it will meet no agreeable end. You can see an example with the Irish who have come to die here. And know for sure that whoever fights against Sone will die.

"Do not worry, Sone! God will come to your aid, I know that for certain truth but will not reveal all I know about you—and nor will you learn about us. But I love you in complete loyalty and know very well that I must."

Here, the holy abbot wept hot tears from the bottom of his heart so that the chasuble he had put on again became quite wet.

"Sone, come to my side and take advantage from it, whatever your sins, as I show you the vessel that was once called the Graal and is still called that today. Be valiant and loyal, for I do not seek to hide from you that it is necessary to endure pain. I will not preach to you any longer but will show you the holy vessel. Repent your sins, for each must fight his own guilt!"

He called for all to kneel in turn and take the holy cross. It contained a sliver of the sacred wood on which the body of God was hung. The abbot then gave his blessing and accorded his plenary indulgence, then opened an ivory reliquary ornamented with sculpted scenes and took out the holy Graal.

The vessel was like no other. The holy man, friend of God,[59] placed the Graal on the altar, next to the Cross. He went next to bring the holy lance of which you have heard me speak. The abbot and the monks wept so copiously one could say they dissolved into tears. The iron of the lance was magnificent and brilliant. At its point, to the fore, formed a drop of red blood, at which many of them marvelled. The abbot showed them two coffins, in one reposed the body of Joseph and in the other Adam, his son, was found. Joseph had only two children. The eldest was called Josephé and he was the first consecrated bishop.

Protected by these relics, the abbot honoured God first and the relics afterward. The monks and he served them with zeal. When the abbot had shown all, he removed the robes in which he had sung the mass, took the young man by the hand, and said to him: "Come now, my friend, you have fasted too long. It has rung noon. Go to restore yourself, for you will have much need of it."

59. i.e., Joseph.

◆ ◆ ◆

The monks brought the king to the board, for the meal was ready. The abbot and the king washed their hands and were installed at the table of honour. Sone sat in the company of a clerk who told him much about the monastery. The meal lasted a long time and the dishes came very often, until the king, once reseated, said he wished to leave.

The abbot did not wish to stay him, for he had much to do besides. He declared: "Sire, you may leave but will take a solid comfort from here; for night and day we will pray for you."

Sone and King Alain now set out to return to Norway, where…

…the abbot, not wishing to forget Sone, sent him the sword with which Joseph of Arimathea had protected the realm. With the holy community, he had sung three high Masses in the name of God and of his saints because the monks were desirous of praying for the love of the king who loved them in good faith.

The abbot had the sword, which had never been lent before, in his keeping. He asked that Sone should send it back to him when God had consoled them.

The sword was very long and big. Sone drew it from the scabbard, he seized it and lifted it into the air; he had fallen deeply in love with it and said many times that he wished to hold it and did not want to be separated from it. He turned it every way, examining it carefully under the eyes of the people and the king. He held himself a fool to love it so. And when he had looked it over to his satisfaction, he replaced it in the scabbard. He placed it in the keeping of one of his servants in whom he had full trust, who guarded it as a treasure.

7: Sone Receives Knighthood, Fights in Single Combat, and Is Loved by Odée
(LINES 5021–5499)

The day for the single combat dawns, and Sone receives knighthood from King Alain. The battle commences. After a long struggle Sone uses the sword of Joseph of Arimathea to defeat the eleven-foot giant Aligos, cutting off first his sword arm, then his head, which he takes to the Scottish king. Knowing he has lost the battle, the king departs for home with his battered army. Sone returns to his hosts, where he is praised and honoured—especially by Odée, King Alain's daughter.

◆ ◆ ◆

The story now turns to Yde, who is beginning to regret her stubbornness and refusing Sone's love. She speaks with her servant Sabine, who tells her that everyone else thinks she should have accepted Sone and that she has no good reason not to.

8: *The Abbot Requests the Sword; A Storm and Journey to Ireland*
(LINES 5500–6916)

The abbot now requests the return of Joseph's sword, but Sone is reluctant to give up the great weapon. His thoughts returned to Yde, and on the pretext of needing to test his mettle as a new knight, he determines to return to France to take part in any tournaments he can find.

Odée is so besotted she determines to keep the sword of Galoche[60] for Sone, despite her father's objections. On the pretext of bringing him a message, Odée boards Sone's ship and at that moment a huge storm drives them out to sea. They are tossed about on the water for three days, finally arriving in Ireland at a city called Alexandria.

When word of Sone's arrival spreads, he is hated for having killed the Irish king. The ship's crew offer to help him if he will give them Odée. Sone refuses and is attacked. Odée produces the sword and encourages Sone to use it. He defeats his attackers and takes refuge with Odée in a Templar church, where they are surrounded by angry townspeople. Sone explains that he defeated the king in fair combat. The people, still not happy about this, declare that he may leave if he fights two of their champions at once. Before he can leave, the Queen of Ireland requests a meeting. She falls in love with Sone on sight and tries to persuade him to stay. When Sone proves reluctant, she requests the help of the master of the Templars, who comes up with a plan. As night falls, the Templar master takes Sone to the queen's chamber on the pretext of making peace between them. The queen says she cannot help hating Sone for killing her husband; the master tells him to kneel before her and ask forgiveness. Sone does so, and at that point the master departs quietly, leaving Sone and the queen alone.[61]

---

60. An alternative name for the sword of Joseph of Arimathea.
61. It is later revealed that Sone fathers a child on her this night.

9: *The Shipboard Fight and*
Return to Norway
(LINES 6917–7226)

On the ship returning to Norway the crew mutinies, seeking to kill Sone and take Odée to claim a reward. Odée overhears them plotting and tells Sone, who successfully defends them both. He receives a wound in the thigh and Odée one near the heart, but they successfully drive off the mutineers, holding them at bay until the ship arrives in the port of St. Joseph. Odée now declares her love for Sone and says she will die if he does not return her feelings. The people of St. Joseph come out to welcome them home with great jubilation, and Sone and Odée are taken home to rest and recover from their wounds. The remaining mutineers are all hung.

10: *Sone's Recovery from Wounds*
and His Departure
(LINES 7227–8208)

A struggle now begins to keep Sone in Norway. Odée proclaims her love again, telling Sone he owns her, body and soul. Her parents offer him the kingdom if he marries their daughter. But Sone refuses all the offers and is determined to leave. Nevertheless, he embraces Odée and promises to return. That night a feast is thrown in his honour, and Odée presents him with a casket full of gold. That night she comes to his room but does not stay long. Next day he departs and Odée, watching sadly, convinces herself he will indeed return.

11: *Sone's Return and Rejection of Yde*
(LINES 8209–8868)

Sone sails back to Doncheri via Wales, Scotland, and Denmark. He goes from Finland to Logarde,[62] then Bruges. From there he sends a letter and a ring to Odée, promising to keep his word. He also writes to his brother Henri, warning him of his arrival. Everyone rejoices, especially Yde, but when Sone arrives she cannot face him or find any way to tell him of her feelings. After some awkward moments Yde says she has heard all about Odée and tells Sone he should return to her. She then storms out. Hurt and angry, Sone returns to Nansay swearing to forget Yde.

62. Possibly a town in Portugal.

12: *Tournament and False Knight*
(LINES 8869–9646)

An invitation comes to a tournament at Chalons, arranged by the Countess of Champagne. Sone pretends to decline but in fact goes along in plain armour. He distinguishes himself well and wins the prize on the first day. After, as he is unarming himself, a minstrel named Romenans enters his tent. Sone's brother recognizes him as an honourable and chivalrous man and welcomes him. Sone speaks of the torments meted out to him by Yde, and Romenans weeps for the pains of love.

Wishing to remain incognito, Sone changes armour the next day and having fought well, takes himself off in the evening. A nameless knight, noticing Sone's departure, decides to pretend that he was the victor in the tournament. He acquires plain armour and beats it up to give the impression of having been in the tournament. He then appears before the countess and claims to be the victor.

Completely fooled, the countess awards him the prize and honors him before all. At this point Romenans appears and slowly and devastatingly reveals the fraud. The false knight is forthwith taken off to jail.

13: *Tournament at Machau*
and Some Symbolic Lances
(LINES 9647–11516)

Determined to bring Sone out of hiding, the countess announces another tournament, to take place at Machau. She sends messages to Sone, Yde, and her brother Eudes. Sone pretends to refuse but goes anyway, again in disguise. He challenges every knight whose shield is displayed near where Yde sits, defeating them all. He also defeats Eudes. Romenans is present also and finds out from Henri that the anonymous knight is indeed Sone.

At the end of the day, the countess seizes Sone before he can escape and takes him to her pavilion, where he is taken care of by her own squires. At the following banquet, Sone is seated first with Yde next to him, but they scarcely speak. At the end of the evening, the countess takes Sone's and Yde's hands and tells them they should be kind to each other.

Also present at the feast is Sone's uncle, Reynaud of Brabant, who hears of Sone's love for Yde and her failure to respond. He tells her she should be kinder to his nephew, and she promises to do so.

✦ ✦ ✦

Next day Yde prepares five special lances of different colours: white, green, blue, red, and gold. She displays these close to her seat and tells Renault of Brabant she is doing as she had promised.

When Sone sees her and the lances, he falls into a kind of stupor and has to be woken from his dream by a herald. He then comes for a lance and Yde sings to him from a ballad that tells him the white lance is for her beloved friend.

Sone, as ever, defeats every opponent, winning each lance from the hand of Yde. The count asks her for the meaning of each one, and she answers that the white refers to the love (for Sone) she has kept secret, the green signifies the flowering of that love, the blue is the royal colour which brings comfort, the red means she will give her love totally, and the gold represents the long-term feelings she has had for Sone.

Yde explains why she has acted so harshly until now; as the godchild of Sone's mother, the church forbids the union. Hearing this, Sone is utterly disconsolate and departs the field without taking his leave of anyone or claiming a prize. At the banquet that night, the count now decides to woo Yde—for himself. She refuses and prepares to leave. The countess is once again left without a victor to award the prize—a golden stag—and the count advises her to send it to the queen, then sets out to Doncheri and asks Yde's brother for her hand. Eudes agrees, but she refuses point-blank. The count returns to Brabant in a lovesick mood.

14: A Tournament in France; Sone and Henri at the French Court
(LINES 11517–11672)

The French king and queen hold court at Paris. The golden stag, intended for the best knight in the recent tournaments, is brought to them. They hear of the mysterious knight who should have been awarded the prize for his prowess. On hearing a description of this knight, the queen recognizes him as her cousin Sone. The king proposes another tournament at Montargis to follow in a month, with the stag to be awarded to the best knight there. This will be followed by a round table tournament at which the prize would be a statue of a white lion. The announcement is made, and Henri and Sone hear of it when they encounter a messenger on the way to Nansay. Sone recognizes him as Gratian and learns that the King of Norway (Alain) had died three months before and that the Norwegians would like Sone to rule over them. He thinks of the kindness of the king and queen and of the gentleness of Odée. He sends a white horse and a gold ring to her, promising to return shortly.

◆ ◆ ◆

Gratian returns to Norway with the gifts and informs the queen that Sone will come soon. Overhearing this, Odée thinks that her mother wants Sone for herself and swears she will die if this happens. Gratian reassures her and gives her the horse and ring. Mollified, Odée decides to send Sone a message.

Meanwhile, still trying to forget his feelings for Yde, Sone receives a letter from his cousin, the Queen of France. Gratian then tells him of the plan to marry Yde to the Count of Machau, who is over eighty years old.

Sone regrets not having taken formal leave of the count and countess, and also for his treatment of Yde, especially considering her father's kindness to him.

Sone and Henri travel to the town of Bar, where they meet with Luciane and her parents. Luciane reminds Sone of his promises to her. She tells him her father did not want to give her to another while there was a chance that he might fulfil their desire to see the couple married. Sone replies gently but firmly that he has no desire to disinherit her father.[63] On hearing this, Luciane knows that she and Sone will only ever be friends. Both parents try to persuade him to stay and marry her, but Sone refuses, preparing to depart so as not to add to Luciane's sorrow.

Sone sets out for France with Henri, arriving at Senlis, where the king and queen are holding court. Word of Sone's exploits have preceded him, and he is made welcome by both the king and queen (his aunt). When asked to tell of his adventures, Sone blushes. The queen notices this and gives him a hard look.

There are a number of courtiers who do not like the queen, including the seneschal, and when they see how glad she is to see Sone, they make a point of ignoring him. Sone is offended by this and decides to leave. When she hears of this, the queen is furious and, taking a large stick, goes into the hall and strikes first the seneschal and then a knight who had joined with the others in insulting Sone. The king himself has to take the stick away from his wife.

Back in Nansay, Sone feels melancholic and sends two horses to Luciane and Yde in the hope that they will still be his friends. Odée, meanwhile, is thinking of the forthcoming tournament she believes Sone will attend and wonders what message to send him. Having considered for a time, she decides to put her thoughts into the form of a lay. She singles out a girl named Papegay, who sings and plays the harp beautifully. Odée teaches her the lay, then sends her with a lady named Countess Orvale, famed for her ugliness, to France.

---

63. The suggested meaning for this is that whoever she marries will become the lord of her father's lands on his death.

◆ ◆ ◆

Meanwhile, Sone begins to throw off his melancholy and decides to attend the tournament, again incognito. Henri orders several suits of clothes for him in variable styles.

15: Souvrain Mesnil; Sone Prepares for the Tournament
(LINES 12673–13220)

Near the forest of Montargis lies a fortified house named Souvrain Mesnil. Partially ruined, it is the home of a noble family who has fallen on hard times due to the lies of the bailiff with a powerful influence on the king.

When Sone arrives he finds an older lady in bed, attended by her daughter, who is in rags that barely cover her. Sone at once has his squire bring her a better garment. Godefroy, the master of the house, now appears and greets his visitors humbly. He looks undernourished and is poorly dressed. He is embarrassed to be seen in this way but offers his guests the best that he has.

Moved by his host's state, Sone himself provides food for the entire household. While they eat, Godefroy tells his story. At one time he was lord of 100 liegemen and had castles, towns, and property. His wife was nobly born and much admired, one of the four daughters of the Count of Flanders. Her aunt was Aelis la Belle, also known as St. Aelis of Nivelle.

Godefroy's fall from grace was partly due to his own desire to appear a great man. He used always to travel with a retinue of thirty knights, but the cost of this was great and in the end he borrowed money from usurers, one of whom falsified his accounts, changing a sum from £2,000 to £100,000. The king's bailiff, Clabaud, had supported this claim, and Godefroy lost everything.

Listening to this sad tale, Sone realises that Godefroy's wife is actually his cousin. He sends out at once for the best materials to make new clothes for the whole family. Dressed again in fine clothes, the lady and her daughter, Nicole, weep for joy.

Sone now decides that he will take part in the tournament and represent Godefroy and his family as their champion. As ever, he wants to be in disguise. Godefroy suggests he set up a temporary camp in the forest near the tourney field so that he can retire there and change his armour after each bout.

Henri meanwhile talks to the lady of Souvrain Mesnil and tells her his grandmother was Aelis of Nivelle. This makes both he and Sone her cousins, which is very pleasing to the lady. Dressed in her new finery, she greets her husband and Sone on their return from setting up camp. She now firmly believes that Sone's

+ + +

championing of their cause will restore their fortunes and hopes that Sone will fall in love with her daughter and rescue her from poverty. Sone promises to do what he can and sets off for the tournament dressed entirely in white.

16: The Four-Day Tournament
(LINES 13221–15541)

Sone sends a squire ahead to find out who is at the tournament. He learns that the king and queen are there, along with Romenans, who is explaining the shields to the queen. Also present are the Countess of Champagne, the Duchess of Bourgogne, the Countess of Bar, and numerous ladies and nobles.

As usual, Sone acquits himself well in the lists, beating everyone he encounters. Just as he had entered mysteriously, so he departs, changing his white armour first for red and then for green. Romenans, watching him, feels certain he recognizes the mysterious knight's style of fighting, but keeps silent so as not to give away his friend.

At the end of the day, Sone retires to Souvrain Mesnil. He sees a boy watching from the woods and thinks he might be a spy. He sends a knight named Tubes to question him. Learning that Tubes is a poor knight that has taken part in the tournament, the boy departs. His mistress is the Countess of Champagne, who had sent him to find out the identity of the mysterious champion. She now believes it to be Tubes.

Meanwhile, the court is discussing the relative merits of the various knights—white, red, and green. Each one seems more powerful than the last, but no one realizes he is the same person, except for Romenans. That same night Romenans is attacked by twenty knights whom he had chided for their boastfulness and determination to kill Sone the next day. Seeing this, the queen interrupts the braggart knights, and Romenans leaves at once for Souvrain Mesnil to relay word of the imminent attack and the insulting behaviour of the knights to the queen. He also relates how the bailiff who caused Godefroy's problems has done the same thing to several other good men.

Next day Sone dons blue armour with a golden eagle on his shield and sets out for the tournament field with Godefroy. Once again he defeats all comers, changing to white armour and carrying a shield with three *croissans* (crescents), easily defeating six more knights.

At the end of the day, the golden stag has still not been claimed and the court is subdued. The queen, however, is happy, despite an exchange of insults between herself and the bailiff.

✦ ✦ ✦

The third day dawns. Romenans informs Sone that the boorish knights have hung their shields in opposition to him. Romenans then returns to the Countess of Champagne. The poet now tells us that she had married a young baron who died soon after and that she had not remarried, despite having many suitors.

Meanwhile, Sone proceeds to overcome all his opponents, defeating five knights once again with ease. The sixth is clearly a better man because he succeeds in wounding Sone, immediately calling to his friends to continue the attack upon him. Despite his wound, Sone fights off all twelve of them. At this point, a herald named Plumelen identifies the mighty knight as Sone de Nansay, and at once the queen rises from her seat, mounts a horse, and rides into the centre of the melee. She rides right up to Sone, seizes his horse's bridle, and demands that he name himself. Sone refuses, saying he will only do so when justice is done.

Sone then leaves for Souvrain Mesnil. The queen orders Plumelen to follow him and report back to her. Once she learns of his whereabouts, she sends the knight named Welerans,[64] well known for his wisdom, to ask Sone to return. Again he refuses, declaring he will not come because the court disinherited Godefroy. When he learns of this, the king promises to return Godefroy's estates and houses and prepares to punish the bailiff, who flees.

When he learns of this, Sone and Godefroy, dressed in fine clothing, journey to the court. Sone is now honoured, and the king orders him not to leave his side. That night at table Sone is the centre of attention, and the conversation revolves around love, its pains, and its delights, much to his secret distress.

Next day the tournament (now a Round Table event[65]) continues, with many knights arriving from England, coming to joust for the white lion. All day Nicole sits with the queen and hands Sone each new lance that he uses. On this day he finally wears his own armour and carries a shield with his ancestral device: three rampant lions on a field of gold.

Yet again Sone is triumphant, but his wound grows worse throughout the day and that night he is cared for by the countess and her ladies. The countess takes the opportunity to tell Sone that, if he wishes, she is his, but he responds in his usual vague way.

The king and queen now seek to bring Sone to the court, but he is still reluctant until his cousins are fully restored to their original position. The king prom-

---

64. Possibly Gawain, whose name is sometimes spelled Walewein in several texts from this period. However, one of Sone's children is later given this name.

65. Round Tables were elaborate events set up to emulate the descriptions of tournaments in Arthurian romances.

ises to do this, and though still weak from his wound, Sone appears at court. The lady of Souvrain Mesnil has saved all the changes of clothing with which Sone had disguised himself as the red, white, and green knights. With his identity revealed, he receives both prizes—the golden stag and the white lion. He gives the former to his aunt and the latter to the Countess of Champagne.

That night, at the banquet to celebrate the great tournament, the plan is that every knight present should sit either with his wife or his love. Thierry, Count of Alsace, has fallen in love with Nicole and wishes to marry her. Knowing this to be a great marriage and having secured her consent, Sone agrees to the match providing Thierry's sister, Felisse, should marry his brother Henri. All is agreed, and a double wedding is celebrated.

17: Arrivals from Norway and the Lay of Odée
(LINES 15523–16572)

The king entered the meadow exactly at the place of the jousts, followed by the barons and ladies of noble lineage. After their arrival the great gates were closed, but they had prepared meals outside where each one had food in abundance. Those invited to the full court washed their hands. The king seated the most powerful barons at his table. Within the enclosure other barons of renown were seated at tables. Then began the circulation of those who served, bringing the plates of food.

It was then that those sent by Odée, bringing the falcon, presented themselves at the gates. The guards, armed with great axes, let no one enter.

Papagay, a maiden of great beauty, spoke first: "My lords, pray let us in. We bring rare gifts for the king."

Those who carried the falcon were allowed to enter. Along with them came a burly Breton who had heard their authorization and joined their company, mixing in with the barons and closely following she who carried the falcon. Papagay advanced to where the king was to be found at the table of honour.

She noticed Sone near the king and she flushed. And when Sone saw her, he too changed colour. It was on account of their great natural beauty, although those who looked on assumed it might be proof of some amorous liaison. But she was very beautiful as well as honourable. With her was another lady, named Orvale, whose ugliness surpassed any living, along with a deformed body.

Sone saw this ugly woman and politely asked the king to honour her, as she was the daughter of a count and a peer. "Willingly," the king replied and

♦ ♦ ♦

commanded a knight to give her a seat at table. He approached Orvale and said: "Madam, there is nothing to be done but to do as I say, for the king wants you to come and eat at his table."

"I will come," replied Orvale, "but first I must have some water." And they brought some for the lady to wash her hands.

Everywhere knights were seated eating with their ladies. As could be seen, everyone saw Orvale wash her hands, but her looks were such that all were astonished. There was not a knight in the whole place, however tall, who could not have sheltered under her arm. She was equally proportioned apart from having a hump behind and one before that supported her chin. From the lump of the rear she had fashioned an ear for her head. She thus had her head raised behind and leaning on something in front. She was blacker than ink and had a great beard and teeth so long that her upper lip was two fingers distant from the lower. She had eyes bigger than a warhorse, and above them eyebrows three fingers wide. The sides of her head were wrinkled, her arms long and fat with big hands. She had features too ugly to be describable. They prepared a napkin for her to drive herself. Then a knight brought her to Sone, who greeted her nobly and sat her beside him with great welcome before saying: "And how is that perfect woman, my good lady, the queen? And Odée, my fiancée?"

"She often wets her cheeks," replied Orvale, "like a tender friend, on account of you, who have behaved so badly. You have taken her heart that she accorded you in good faith, along with her body and her money, with which you have acted unwisely. You could do much better if you accepted my advice."

"I will," replied Sone. "I never believed you could think such ill of me. Your father, the count, loved me most sincerely, and I was greatly esteemed. I ask with astonishment—what could be the cause of this anger towards me?"

"It is not with me but with Odée that you have acted so disloyally, to your great shame."

"My dear friend," continued Sone, "eat, don't be angry. I will put to rights all the wrongs I have committed."

"If you right your wrongs," concluded Orvale, "I think you will greatly profit from it."

Orvale sat to eat, for she was in great need of it and was perfectly served, thanks to the attentions of Sone. However, everyone was surprised to see her eating at the king's table.

The meal continued a long time with an abundance of dishes. Ladies, young girls, and knights amused themselves during the feasting. Then they raised the tablecloths and those at the table of honour washed their hands.

❖ ❖ ❖

The great Celot[66] entered the enclosure when they brought in the falcon, with two bucklers[67] and two swords hidden about his person, along with a batten of medlar wood with which he could give violent blows. Celot was big and strong and came before the king with a buckler and sword. He gave such rapid strokes with the sword that birds would not have been able to fly around him without being struck with the whirling blade. When he had shown his tricks, he addressed the king in these terms: "Sire, Sir King, I will take on any three of your men, and when I have beaten them, give me whatever price I claim."

"You will get," replied the king, "whatever you deserve."

Mirant, a very impetuous royal champion, wanted to know what handicap he required. Celot replied: "Take this very sharp sword and choose one of these bucklers and give me the little club; I would not want to fight with any other weapon. If you can cut my head off, then do the worst you can."

Each one adjusted their clothes and returned for a buckler. "Now we will see how brave you are," said the king to his champion, before adding: "Cut off the head of this good-for-nothing!"

At that moment Sone summoned his squire and whispered: "Bring me my best sword, quickly." Far from making him wait, the squire soon brought the sword to his master, concealed under his clothes, and awaited his orders.

Celot the Breton had returned and now raised his arms in the air. He was extraordinarily big and well muscled. He had his buckler on his arm, and the club with which he proposed to fight was small and heavy looking, while the sword with which Mirant prepared to fight was solid and very sharp in his right hand. He knew little of handling a buckler, being used to larger and heavier shields. As he held his buckler and sword, Celot threw himself upon him; maneuvering behind his buckler, he struck Mirant with many blows of his club, so fast that Mirant, clumsy with the buckler, did not know how to protect himself. Celot gave him such a blow on the forehead as to crack the bone, then attacked again with the club and broke the right arm of his opponent, who was forced to drop his sword. Thus the fight was over.

Celot stood before the king the second time and declared: "Sir King, bring on those who want to fight me."

The king ordered no one, and none of the barons approached Celot, who turned to the king and said: "King, all the members of your suit have returned to their nests for protection, and no one can make them come out. There is no

---

66. The Breton warrior who had entered the castle with Papagay.

67. A small round shield, also known as a targe.

longer a warrior among them brave enough to fight me—all are beaten without a blow being struck. But I promise you that when I leave here, I will tell in all the other courts what I found in yours: that all have admitted themselves beaten."

These words so greatly irked the king that he blanched. The barons were annoyed by the insults of this fool. Some rose and stood before the Breton and declared: "Fool, you will suffer greatly by criticizing the barons thus."

"It is to your ill fortune that you think that," replied Celot. "You who have reproached my folly, I can see you want to fight, but it is your blood I will spill. Run far from me before you seize a buckler. But if you like fighting, take this short sword and whatever buckler you want. You'll meet death from this club, and I would not wish for any other weapon."

"If that is your will," replied Sone, "take your own buckler and sword, and I will fight with mine."

Sone was now approached by his squire, who gave him his steel blade, which he held in his right hand. Then furious battle commenced.

The onlooking barons feared the death of Sone, who all the same was very fierce; in fact, his face seemed quite disfigured, for he bared his teeth with a most threatening look. He was as red in the face as burning embers. His ardent look never ceased to fix Celot in trenchant manner, fixed so as to make anyone sick with fright. Never had anyone seen a face of such beauty so deformed.

Celot asked himself with astonishment how Sone could have become such an expert with his sword. He greatly feared for his life, as Sone rained many blows upon him, cutting his buckler into pieces, so that they flew through the air, neither wood nor metal able to resist. Realizing that his buckler would fail him, Celot attacked vigorously with his sword, convinced that one of them would soon die. The two adversaries multiplied their efforts without remit and made their swords fly so quickly that it was impossible to count the exchanges. The battle lasted long without the flesh of either being wounded.

Sone pressed Celot strongly and cut his buckler in such pieces that the other only with great difficulty could protect himself and feared greatly for his death. He tried to fight body to body, for he was exhausted from trading blows. Sone realised his adversary's desire to close with him and held his buckler before him, preventing Celot from approaching. The latter was unbalanced when Sone, after calm reflection, attacked his most unprotected side. He struck him in the throat so violently that he cut off his head, which flew out of the field of battle. Sone then kicked his adversary in the chest and turned him over onto his back.

◆ ◆ ◆

The king had the body of Celot removed, clearing the place of he who had spoken so foolishly and received an appropriate reward. Like a mad dog he had enjoyed a short journey!

Orvale then gave her the falcon. No better bird existed this side of Cornwall. Papagay regained her spirits and took the falcon on her fist gracefully and elegantly. She came before the king and declared: "Hear, O King of France, you are the greatest of sovereigns and have just title to protect the faith that God has given us. We have come to you from afar and found you, thanks be to God, and have brought you this falcon, the best that ever flew. If you have someone to put it to the test, you will soon learn the truth about that. The daughter of the King of Norway offers it to you. Accept it, King, and judge with deliberation your opinion that she should legitimately have her man after having heard her cause."

"I accept the falcon," replied the king, "and will hear her cause. When I have heard what my barons gathered here judge of the affair, I will lose no time in making it known."

"Then pay attention," continued Papagay, "and let your barons be silent."

The good king received the falcon from her, and she took up her harp, the finest that had ever been strung. Papagay was so beautiful that everyone marvelled. She turned towards the king and said: "Sire, you will now hear a lay composed from the truth, telling the adventures of my lady, which is why we have assembled here. Then we will hear your judgement." She struck the harp-strings and began the words of the lay.

Listen to the story in the following verses.

[The lay takes from line 15984 to line 16143. It is omitted here.]

These words ended the song that was attentively heard, along with many tears before the end of the poem. They in fact realised it to be the truth. They saw Sone blush and great tears run down his face.

Papagay declared: "Sire, dear King, that is the just cause of my lady. Much more could I have sung, but it is not courteous to tell all. After what I have told, judge truly if your friend should be married to so loyal and tender a queen, who would lose her life if she lost him. And since if he comes to her he will have the crown at his disposition, the kingdom and all the country want no more then the lady and her champion. Judge then, dear King; from now on you will not hear me plead more."

After some consideration, the court declared that Sone and Odée should marry. Sone admits that he is the person described in the lay and agrees to abide

❖ ❖ ❖

by the decision of the court. He will marry Odée and become King of Norway. When she hears this, the Countess of Champagne is distraught but hides her feelings.

Sone prepares to depart for Norway, but before he goes he has one last task to perform. Thierry d'Alsace dies unexpectedly and Sone is able to obtain from the Emperor of Cologne permission for his brother Henri, who is of course married to Thierry's sister, to become the new count. Stones from the walls of the old castle of Nansay are used to build a new, much stronger castle, and Henri is established there. The region becomes known for its fine wines, which are widely exported.

18: Return to Norway and Sone's Marriage to Odée
(LINES 16573–17114)

Odée, Sone's loyal fiancée, thought of him day and night, and ardently wished for his homecoming. Oppressed by the pangs of love, she would climb up into the tower, dressed in her most sumptuous attire, to scrutinize the distant horizon for his galley speeding on its way. She did not want to move from the place until his ship arrived and had even equipped galleys to meet the ones that were arriving.

Sailors on an eighty-oared galley leading the rest sought the arrival of Sone and his party, whose presence would soon rejoice her. The sailors on the ships knew what to do, for they had all been trained together. Those in the leading one from the town asked the arrivals if they had brought their lord with them, who loudly cried: "Yes! Rejoice!"

Sone, who heard the noise, returned to the city, making for it as quickly as birds could fly. Reaching port, they informed the town of the coming of the valorous Sone, which all so greatly desired. As the news spread, Odée knew for certain. She had ordered all the sailors across the city to stay close and in great barques, nefs, galleys, sloops, transport barges, large and small fishing boats, all were ready to serve. Three hundred vessels had left port, filled with musical instruments. Trumpets, drums, symbols, tambourines, flageolets, sarrasan horns, and those that were sounded for guests of honour. Great cornemuses, harps, psalteries, vielles, rotes, and other instruments encouraged the dancers, while conjurors performed magic tricks. Each showed the greatest possible joy in their performance as they awaited the galley that carried their lord.

As soon as it arrived, they nobly greeted it, the arrivals saluting in turn. The instruments started up again, sounding joyously as new instruments joined in and the inhabitants of the city rejoiced. They had decorated the streets with banners, ornamented the doors, and carpeted the roads with flowers. Agile young men were equipped for jousting. All the bells rang throughout the town. Not even white-haired old women failed to feel their hearts beat with joy as all, great and small, ran to the port in jubilation.

As Sone's galley pulled in, he leaped from the ship and mounted a horse brought by barons overjoyed to see him again. Without cloak or hood, so all could see him, he entered the city in triumph. The inhabitants heartily welcomed him, and he greeted them in turn. The people bowed before him and prayed, hands joined in supplication, begging him to become their true lord and protect their kingdom.

Sone passed on to climb toward the castle, which he entered and found all well arranged. The queen mother came to meet him, held him in her arms, and kissed him on the mouth, which touched him to the heart. Odée arrived after her mother and behaved with great wisdom, without revealing all she felt. She welcomed her friend with her eyes and greeted him simply, saying: "Sir, you are welcome as our sovereign if it pleases you to accept that title, and to command all as our lord. I do not wish to hide that I have called you my love with a true heart, and from now on will act according to your will."

"We will act in such a way as not to encourage reproach," declared Sone, and retired to a room where they took his equipment and brought him scarlet clothes and ermine fur with which he was adorned, while a girl with a comb dressed his hair. He was then taken to the people as the bishop arrived, who greeted him in the name of God.

The noble queen rejoined them to explain why she wanted to remit the kingdom to Sone to govern and defend. The bishop bade them sit and listen carefully as he said: "My lords, your King Alain, so wise and courteous, is dead; we cannot bring him back to life. And as a woman is not able to protect the land, my lady will give her daughter to Sone, whom she has sought for this marriage, and he will govern the land." And to Sone, "If you are pleased to accept it as lord, I believe you will do it well; in fact, you know already what valor that requires."

All who heard replied to the bishop: "By the grace of God, we pray him to accept us as his vassals. He has given complete satisfaction, and so if he wishes and the queen agrees, we will all be joyful."

"I proclaim, Sone," resumed the bishop, "that you are our lord and will marry the princess and be crowned. Commit yourself to her before us all, and she will

◆ ◆ ◆

do the same for you." They did as the bishop proposed, who announced their solemn engagement before the barons, and all rejoiced.

Odée was overjoyed; she now possessed her man. She could forget the painful torments she had for so long endured in their adventures together when threatened by pirates and the insults thrown by those who said that Sone had already slept with her. Joy could now replace regret.

For his part, Sone felt greatly honoured. The barons had met him, and following his good advice sent a galley to Galoche, sumptuously equipped, and charged with a sealed message. The ship left port, the rowers making numerous detours to avoid the rocks, but maintaining their speed as far as Galoche, where they moored.

The faithful captain Gratien, by whom they had sent the letter, went up to the castle and was directed to the abbot, who had seen the messenger coming. The sailor gave him the letter that the bishop read, and rising from his seat happily entered the church where he rang a little bell. The monks assembled and the abbot read the letter to them. There is no point in repeating all, but they showed their jubilation in the name of God because of the message from the queen. They compiled a reply, sealed it, and sent it by the sailor, whom they pressed to leave immediately according to the instructions contained in the missive. Without delay, Gratien rejoined his crew and made them row so hard that the galley bounded over the sea by day and night and returned to St. Joseph, where he climbed up to the castle and delivered the letter.

Happily all had soon read it and shown great joy because the abbot had let it be known that all would soon be ready for the ceremony. The queen had convoked the great barons of her realm to come without delay to Galoche to offer their service. Sone would be crowned there, according to everyone's desire. The news was spread immediately. The queen made all the necessary preparations, putting great riches on board the galleys.

The barons showed unmistakable joy. Odée had not yet come fully to believe that she was loved by Sone. She loved him in fact so passionately that jealousy was mixed with love and she would have liked to have come into his rooms and keep him company, but Sone awaited the day when they could proclaim their love openly. And thus they made their way as far as Galoche.

At the port the queen was very happy surrounded by her barons. The abbot came down from the castle and boarded a boat with experienced men that brought them to port quickly. He went to greet the queen and calling Sone to one side said to him, "Lord, when you have become king, I advise you to make your confession before being anointed and crowned. You must show yourself

◆ ◆ ◆

particularly worthy since you will be entrusted with guarding a large part of the holy cross upon which hung the body of God.

"You will also guard the holy lance that pierced his side, and be the guardian of the holy Graal. You must thus take care to act in a saintly way; thus your soul will be saved, for the holy king who brought the Graal here took care of it in a very saintly fashion. You must also take an oath to govern the kingdom according to the just customs that rule it. Do not deprive the towns or the barons of the rights to which they are used, but maintain them loyally; you will take an oath on that subject. If you want to know the truth, official documents will be brought to you, and thus you will be reassured in maintaining us according to our customs."

"I would like to see these writings, since I will need to have counsel," declared Sone.

The abbot brought the texts of the law instituted by Joseph of Arimathea and instituted himself with the powers of a tribune in company with the knights, queen, and the barons. He revealed the precepts of the law introduced by Joseph, contained in these documents. After having killed the pagan king, Joseph had converted the people to the religion prescribed by Jesus Christ, who had given the Holy Scriptures to St. Peter when he ascended to heaven, leaving St. Peter on earth, which was the moment when Joseph received the Holy Scriptures. Thus the abbot revealed the faith and all present willingly listened and regretted their sins, weeping at the recall of the Scriptures. They also well understood the secular law that they respected.

When the abbot had eloquently recalled to Sone that he must swear by God and the Holy Scriptures to rule the land according to the customs he had recalled, Sone replied, "I will swear to it, if it pleases God, and carry it out loyally. For the present, write out the law so that I am unlikely to commit any injustice."

When the abbot had so written and Sone had sworn to rule the land like Joseph and never to transgress the law, the oath was pronounced. The abbot went to Sone and said, "Lord, confess yourself now, and then go to the castle. After your marriage, for which all is ready, you will be anointed and crowned along with your spouse."

The abbot called a monk, a religious man endowed with great kindness, who took Sone to one side and confessed him, avowing all the sins by which he thought he might have annoyed God. The holy man, having seen a repentant Sone beat his breast and cry, absolved him of his sins. Sone was thus put to rights and went aboard the galley with the most powerful barons.

✦ ✦ ✦

They arrived at Galoche and climbed up to the castle. The great lords entered by a little door that was locked, and less eminent persons remained outside. The clerks intoned their chant while the abbot dressed again in his priestly robes, there also being present an archbishop and three bishops, all wearing priestly vestments. Thus they began the Mass that the archbishop chanted. Sone was clad in a white robe in which he married Odée. They led the young couple to the main altar where they prostrated themselves, after which they placed over them brand-new rich white silk material over white linen.

When all was ready, the archbishop chanted over them. The newlyweds had the sacraments put before them, which they received piously, and when told descended from the altar. Having observed the ritual and been anointed with holy oils, they were crowned. The abbot chanted the rest of the Mass with gifts of gold, incense, and myrrh, and the queen presented her offerings.

The divine service once ended, the Graal was brought and exposed to the view of all, also the lance with which God had his side pierced and received death to redeem our sins, along with a cross containing a large fragment of holy wood on which Jesus Christ was hung and put to death to pay for our sins. There was a golden candelabrum carrying five candles, the one in the centre burning with an inextinguishable flame. It was held in high esteem for it was present at the birth of God, as Joseph witnessed in a sealed writing.

When God was born of the Virgin, the holy angel performed his service by bringing three candles; there were two of them before the tomb of Mahomet, and Joseph had the third in his possession. It was given him in his lifetime, when he had recovered his health, after having been ill a long time. He went overseas and acted as a valiant knight, and it was on his return to his own country that the candle was given him. All his life he honoured it, and it burned there on this candelabrum. The four candles around it burned in its honour.

The abbot kissed the Graal, then the king [Sone] carried it in his arms at his breast and the holy lance was placed before, preceded by the cross blessed by the holy wood. The candelabrum went before with the lit candles. Such was the procession. A holy bishop of great renown sang the Mass, and all brought their offerings.

At the end of the office, the abbot took the Graal and put it in an ivory reliquary. The holy lance and holy cross he placed appropriately and finally the candelabrum to a place chosen by Joseph. When all had been put in its rightful place, the abbot said to the king, "Now we must go to the island to observe the festivities prepared there."

"So be it!" replied the king.

+ + +

19: *The Visit to the Square Island*
(LINES 17115–17524)

All cried "To the ships!" and many vessels were prepared. The archbishop had boarded a specially prepared boat accompanied by the three bishops, and the first had already left port and disembarked on the island. Without waiting any longer, Sone boarded the galley with Odée at his side. The barons had embarked on another ship and all landed on the island, but I have not yet described it or tried to explain the purpose it served.

It was situated half a league out to sea and one could never find a more beautiful one in the world. It was such a perfect square that it was impossible to tell which side was the longest. The pagan king who had built it was called Tadus. He was very wise and generous, for he had heard tell of the Christian faith and had written up the words he had heard, truly believed them and converted all his people. His son Baudemagu was wise and intelligent and the most courtly of his times, but his son Meleagant was most perfidious and the worst of all the lords of the island.

It was beautiful, magnificent, well fortified, and surrounded by the sea. It had very high sandstone walls that faced the sea, built on the rocks and crenelated at their tops which were so wide that two wagons could easily pass. At the four corners of the walls, four edifices were built that faced the sea. On the side facing the interior of the island, the walls rested on sumptuous pillars of porphyry, and the arches were so well made that they supported the rest. Each edifice was finely carved and perforated, facing each other, and when one wanted to close them, one could drop a great door sustained by great pulleys that pulled it up or down. Near this, at an arched doorway, was a great causeway in the sea that came up to the walls where, according to witnesses, the Sword Bridge could be found. It is here alleged that many heads had been cut off when Meleagant had been lord of the island, a cruel traitor who did evil wherever and whenever he could and died a violent death that perfectly merited his end.

On the island was a cemetery where the bodies of notables were buried, each possessing their own sepulchre, with the tombstone inscribed with the name of the baron who reposed there.

In the cemetery there were now many different kinds of tree, giving off a sweet and attractive fragrance, whilst in the very centre of the island a spring flowed through a gold plated copper horn, producing a very great quantity of cool fresh water. There was only one entrance to the island, which was closed everywhere else, but which no one had seen one more sumptuous.

✦ ✦ ✦

Once all the barons had entered, Sone went to the place that had been prepared at the table of honour, his queen at his side. Each wore a crown with white vestments according to the custom of previous sovereigns. The abbot had changed and abandoned his religious garments for others of scarlet vermillion to the astonishment of many. But this was the rule because he was at the same time an abbot and a count. He was served before the king and given the first dish. All was prepared within.

Having given his orders, the abbot looked all round him and saw the sky was covered with clouds to such an extent that one could hardly see anymore. Then lightning flashed and it began to thunder so violently that all thought the sky was about to fall on their heads. Such a storm was unleashed that it broke and tore the great trees situated inside, whose fragments struck the walls. The sea was so rough that it threw waves over the walls, covering the island with water in which goods floated. People would all have been drowned if they had not rushed to the walls. The storm became stronger and stronger, without the least respite, provoking terrible suffering such as the old had never seen before.

Sone climbed to the top of the walls, with Odée at his side, but such a downpour of water fell on them that they were nearly washed off into the sea. They spent a day and a night without the hurricane ceasing for a single minute; it was so violent that all were close to perishing. The queen would have died had she not been in the arms of her husband, who thus brought her great comfort. The storm lasted for three days and three nights during which they ate or drank nothing, nor slept or rested, but endured more suffering than could be told. With the new dawn the lightning struck brusquely in the cemetery, producing a clap of thunder that shook the whole island. The people at the top of the walls no longer expected any help and were on the point of being knocked down. But when God willed, the storm ceased to torment them a little.

The lightning accompanying the thunder ceased, the hurricane was carried out to sea, and the sky above cleared. This was needful for those survivors who found themselves on the island. The sun appeared and the light brought much good. The hurricane had gone, but the ships were lost; the storm had broken their rigging and sunk them. The island was inundated with water thrown over the walls, now flowing off in great streams.

The island was thus a mess but there were so many conduits in the walls that it was rapidly emptied. When the water had gone and the land had cleared, a smell so foul spread that the hearts of everyone ceased to beat. It came from the cemetery, where the lightning had fallen. The people high on the walls were

◆ ◆ ◆

tired, having passed three days without sleep or rest, with nothing to eat or drink. They were exhausted and close to death if God did not help them.

However, those who had stayed in Galoche and seen the hurricane had raised the moorings of the boats, barques, and galleys in the port. They hastily mounted on board and made towards the island. Arriving there, they were not able to approach as the smell was so strong, and they had to retreat. All the same, Gratien loved the king and was his faithful sailor. He understood that if God almighty did not help them, they would all be lost as they had suffered so much. Although astonished by the smell, he forced himself to penetrate the isle and go toward the infected place. In the cemetery he saw a hole had been struck by the lightning and thrown up a tomb enclosing a corpse. The gravestone was completely broken, but the corpse, with flesh and body intact, lay with open mouth that exhaled this infection.

Gratien was in a very bad way, but all would have been worse if he had left the body there. He dragged it to the ship and put himself to great trouble by breathing in this terrible smell; then he threw it to the bottom of the sea within a fjord. Be sure that there is no one in the world like a mariner when in danger, for enduring such pain without anxiety and acting with praiseworthy courage, Gratien had eliminated this terrible smell by returning to the island. The day was fine and clear, the infection disappeared, and the people were greatly comforted.

The king held the queen in his arms but did not know if she were alive or dead for she frequently fainted. He looked at the queen who had endured so much suffering and sighed, but others had played their parts as well. Gratien, the faithful sailor, feared that the king, who loved him and whom he had served many times, might be dead. But he was mounted high on the walls, holding the exhausted queen in his arms, whom they then passed from one to the other, Gratian calling, "Madame, keep enough courage to board a ship."

The queen observed him attentively and recognized him. Then she had looked at her husband, who had put his arms around her neck, saying: "My lords, let us leave here as quickly as possible."

"My dear sweet love," replied the king, "do not let ourselves fail now." They descended to the foot of the walls and embarked in a galley where Gratian installed them at their ease and took them as far as Galoche.

Seeing them arrive, the monks were pressed to open the doors. They carried the queen mother very gently as far as the great chamber where they laid her on a bed for she was exhausted. At her side, the king climbed with several of their

✦ ✦ ✦

friends. The abbot who had known plenty of misfortune was most desirous that the seneschals prepare a meal, for everyone was starving.

When the seneschals had done their task and all had eaten at least a small amount of nourishment, the old queen suffered severe pain, and, overcome by the smell, died that day. A number of people who remained on the island never came off it. If they received no help from others, they would rot away forever, to be buried in the cemetery where the corpse had been for so long, which still stank enormously. The survivors had stayed in the forest to recover their health, for one could find no better place in the world to benefit from venison in quantity and all kinds of fish. Here they stayed for a long time until cured.

The king remained at the castle, which greatly pleased him, seeing the beauty of the place. All honoured him, and the queen was soon cured who had endured such pain; she had forgotten all because now she was assured of the love of her husband.

One day the sovereign found himself at Galoche with the abbot, who took the king on one side and declared, "Sire, let us go and see what has happened on the island." The king willingly agreed and they asked Gratien to prepare a galley. They had hardly landed, accompanied by all the barons who desired to come, when, arrived at the cemetery, they saw the great hole caused by the lightning. Gratien had taken the corpse that had lain exuding its smell.

The abbot walked towards the tombstone and read the inscription. He had known the storm was to do with the wife of Joseph, who had once been the king of this land, and it was remembered that she had never loved Jesus Christ. As a result, these great sufferings—the stain and this terrible smell—had overwhelmed and affected the people so that many had died.

For his action, Gratien received many marks of gratitude, and the king awarded him with many favours.

Sone and Odée, accompanied by the abbott, now set forth on a progress through the kingdom, seeking the promise of fealty from the people. Sone refused all the many gifts offered to him so as not to cause anyone to suffer poverty.

20: Visitors from Ireland; Odée Gives Birth to Twins
(LINES 17525–17689)

Soon after this, a boat arrives at the harbour of St. Joseph. On it is the old Templar master, Margon, accompanied by a woman with a baby. The Templar master tells Sone that when she heard of his marriage, the Queen of Ireland could not be

◆ ◆ ◆

comforted. She put the baby at his door and together with the woman who had escaped by night. Sone sent the child to Odée and requests Margon to remain as his advisor. Margon tells Odée about the child. Soon after this she gives birth to twins, named Houdians and Henri, the latter after Sone's brother. The other baby is named Margon (after the Templar?) and the three boys are raised together.[68]

21: A Message from the Pope;
Sone Fights the Saracens and Becomes Emperor
(LINES 17690–18007)

A message arrives from the Pope requesting Sone to take up the sword of St. Peter and fight for Christendom. That same night Odée gives birth to another son, who is named Milon, after the Pope, and whom he will one day succeed.

A second message now arrives from Rome. This time the Pope writes that the emperor is dead and that he will excommunicate Sone unless he comes to the aid of the church. Sone goes to see the Abbot of Galoche, taking his one-and-a-half-year-old son Houdians to be knighted and crowned as King of Norway in the event of his father's death. He leaves the child with the abbot to raise and teach him how to be king.

[At this point there is the lacuna of some 2,400 lines, which must tell of Sone's journey to fight the Saracens, followed by his coronation as emperor of Rome. From later references we gather that he killed seven Saracen kings and took possession of three of their gods—presumably idols. In return, the Saracens have abducted Odée.]

22: Emperor Sone Rescues Odée and
Fights Three Saracen Kings
(LINES 18008–18546)

Sone is now emperor and wages war against the Saracens in Southern Italy. Odée has been abducted by a Saracen king, and Sone is now advised by Medus and Vande, whom we have not met before. The Saracens are willing to exchange Odée for the return of their three gods, presumably won by Sone in previous battles. Sone arrives at Otrente[69] with a fleet. One of the pagan kings, Madoc, known to be wise and kind, speaks with two other Saracen kings, Simonins and Andala,

---

68. Clearly this is Sone's child by the Irish queen, but the author is shy of saying this exactly.
69. Likely Otranto.

about the great losses Emperor Sone has caused them. At his advice they send him to see Sone in person, to plead for their rights to the lands they inhabit.

Armed with an olive branch, Madoc arrives in the emperor's camp and speaks at length about the history of the world. He lists Africa, Asia, and Europe, which he claims to be the Saracens' heritage. Julius Caesar, Clovis, Pepin, and Charlemagne are all named as having caused great pain and suffering to the Saracens.

Madoc now throws down the gauntlet. If Sone will not leave their lands, he must stand against three kings in single combat. If Sone wins the fight, he can do with them as he will, but if he loses, he must withdraw and leave Europe to the pagans.

Having taken council with Medus and Vande, Sone elects to exchange the three gods for Odée. After this he will fight the three kings, as he has no intention of withdrawing.

Odée has been treated well and with great honour by her captors. She is now released and sent home, dressed in gold and riding a mule in the company of numerous ladies. She promises to pray for her captors.

23: Sone Fights the Three Kings
(LINES 18547–19008)

The day of the combat with the Saracen kings draws near. Sone prepares for battle advised by Medus of the fighting style of his opponents. He puts on a mail hauberk and a silk tunic which, when wet, prevents wounds. Odée laments his certain death.

Sone goes out to meet his foes. Madoc repeats his threats, which Sone dismisses. The fight begins. Sone defeats Andala. Meanwhile, Odée goes to pray for him and puts on rags to show her penitence. While she prays, Sone fights Simonins, killing him. As he watches, Madoc begins to lose faith in his gods, and when Sone strikes him down, he surrenders and begs for baptism.

Sone grants he enemy's wish, sending him to Odée, whom he finds in the chapel. He offers her his sword and she gives him knighthood. He is then baptized and given a new name by Sone.

24: Sone's Crusade
(LINES 19009–19312)

Sone now embarks on a crusade to clear out the pagans from several cities. He sends messages via the newly converted Medus to Otrente and Trapes, offering them the teachings of Christ. When they refuse, he takes the cities and has the

◆ ◆ ◆

people put to death. Only one, Bladon, the ruler of Trapes, escapes without a fight. Sone sends men to take over the city and castle.

25: Sone's Fame Spreads
(LINES 19313–20194)

Sone's fame spreads through the Empire. He is lauded for his bravery and generosity. The Pope commends him. His nobles love him. He gives away all his material goods, keeping only his horse and his sword.

When the pagans come near to the site of the Holy Sepulchre, Sone comes to the rescue. His mere presence causes the Saracens to sue for peace. Sone meets the Sultan of Baghdad and agreement is reached. All prisoners are released, and Gratian becomes the bailiff of Damas.[70] Sone continues to spread the word of Christ throughout his realm.

26: Sone's Son Henri Dispenses Justice
(LINES 20195–20348)

Henri, Sone's second son, proves to be just as good and generous as his father, giving away his possessions to others less fortunate than him. When he learns how the bailiff of Mechines[71] is siphoning off all the wealth of the city, he makes his way there. A brief sea battle follows in which Henri is slightly wounded but is victorious. The bailiff is captured, the emperors see all taken from him, and he is condemned to be torn apart by four horses.

27: Sone's Son Margon and the Lady Giloine
(LINES 20349–20511)

Sone's son Margon surpasses all of his children in beauty and goodness. He falls in love with Giloine, one of the two daughters of King Ourses of Sicily, who has been brought up by Empress Odée. Giloine begs the emperor and empress to allow her to marry Margon and that they should reign together over her lands. Sone and Odée agree, and the pair are married with great ceremony.

70. Almost certainly Damascus.

71. Mechlin?

◆ ◆ ◆

28: Henri Becomes King of Jerusalem
(LINES 20512–20711)

A message arrives from Rome asking Sone to send his son Henri to the Holy Land to help the Templars and Hospitallers defend them against the Saracens. Henri goes to Baruth[72] with a large force. While there he falls in love with Hermione, daughter of the late ruler. The Templars and Hospitallers support them, offering riches if they marry. Sone agrees, and they are married soon after. After this Henri becomes king of Jerusalem.

29: Sone's Son Becomes Pope
(LINES 20712–20746)

All is well with Sone. His lands are at peace. Three of his sons are crowned kings and the fourth becomes a holy cleric. Milon becomes a cardinal and is finally elected pope.

30: A Family Reunion
(LINES 20747–21080)

Sone never ceased to love the Holy Virgin who, in return, protected him in all his combats. She delayed his death so he could meet up with his sons. Messengers went to Norway, where King Houdiant had married Matabrune of Bohemia, a very cruel woman. He left for Rome, where the other sons had gathered. Odée was very pleased to see her children, although it was Sone she loved the most. On the day of Pentecost Sone crowned his sons, who in turn crowned their mother, while their brother Pope Milon sang the Mass. The festivities lasted four days, and on the fifth Sone announced the principles of good government: to love God, keep the commandments, and serve the people in their care as a good ruler should. After this he divided all he had between his sons. To Houdiant he gave the sacred vessel, the sword of Joseph of Arimathea, and his sense of reason; to Henri his valor and the sword of Brudon; Margon received his oliphant,[73] his carbuncle, his charm and his courtesy, and his warhorse, Flori. Finally, to Milon, the favour that was always his own: to be ever regarded with affection.

---

72. Beirut.

73. This is probably a hunting horn made from elephant ivory.

◆ ◆ ◆

31: Henri and Welerans, the Sons of Sone's Brother, Are Tested
(LINES 21081–21223)

Sone now summons the two sons of his brother Henri, Welerans and Henri (the Younger). He tells them one of them will be emperor after him, but they must fight each other to the death to achieve this honour. He then sends them to separate rooms to consider.

After a time Welerans, the elder of the two, returned to say that he was willing to kill his brother to be emperor. Sone then sends for Henri, who comes in weeping. Despite being mocked by Sone, he declares that he could not kill his brother for the sake of the empire. Sone embraces him and sends Welerans away, saying he never wants to see him again. Calling all his sons together, he commands them to crown Henri emperor after his death.

32: Sone's Death
(LINES 21224–21321)

His illness getting worse, Sone is confined to bed. A dispute about succession breaks out between Welerans and Henri, which Sone proposed should be settled by single combat. Welerans remained the most aggressive, while Henri would not oppose his elder brother, whom Sone now banished from the court and ruled that his nephew Henri should succeed him after his death. Sone then called Odée and asked her not to be anxious about his death, for he left her among their sons. Seeing his death was nigh, the cardinals reconciled the emperor. After he had received communion, the pope absolved him and purified him of his sins.

Sone then asked that the wood of the True Cross should be brought to him. Taking it in his arms, he kissed it a hundred times. Rendering up his soul, he left his body, though his colour seemed unimpaired.

Odée, who could not bear to be parted from her husband, lay on his breast and gave up the ghost as well …

Placed in a copper coffin, the couple were buried before the altar at St. Peter's in Rome; the four brothers crowned Henri emperor and were present at his marriage to Gille, the sister-in-law of Margon, before returning to their respective countries.

◆ ◆ ◆

Explicit Sone de Nansay

Thus ends the extraordinary story of Sone. Judged alongside other romances of the time, it is every bit as engrossing as any and filled with details that appear in no other source. For this reason alone, it is worthy of study; for the purpose of our understanding of the temples of the Grail, it is of enormous importance. Let us now look more deeply at aspects of Sone's story that reveal the Grail and its environs with increasing clarity.

❖ ❖ ❖

3

ISLANDS OF THE GRAIL

Any who carefully studied its detail would never be
puzzled by it if truly loved by God. Here was the basis
of faith; the beginnings of religion … and the way we
must act to enter paradise.

◆ ◆ ◆

Sone de Nansay

Even the most superficial reading of the *Sone* text demonstrates a number of elements
within the story that are unique to the Grail myth. Some are familiar—such as the
wounding of the king, the existence of a wasteland, and the story of Joseph of Arimathea.
These can be found (amongst others) in the *Conte del Graal* of Chrétien de Troyes, the *Joseph*
of Robert de Boron, and the anonymous *Quest del Saint Graal* and *Perlesvaus*. But the combination of these elements with some highly original additions makes this an extremely important
and unjustly neglected work. As we shall see, the description of the Grail castle and the mysterious Square Island bring an entirely new dimension to the story, which gives a unique insight
into the Grail mysteries.

We should be aware from the start that *Sone* is not truly an "Arthurian" romance. None of
the traditional figures are in it (with the exception of two minor characters, whose roles we
shall examine below) or are even mentioned; there are no references to Arthur's court or the
Round Table fellowship. However, the links to the Grail cycle and through these to the Matter
of Britain[74] are still present.

---

74. The overall title used to describe the Arthurian legends.

◆ ◆ ◆

Our commentary follows the same division of the text as those in chapter 2, making it convenient to look back and refresh your memory regarding the individual sections of the poem. We have not commented on those parts that are not related to the central theme of this book; for this we refer the reader to the work of Claude Lachet, the premier scholar of the work, listed in the bibliography at the end of this book.

The Prologue

From the start we have a sense of a different approach to the subject to that normally expected in a medieval romance. To begin with, the prologue is unusual in that it begins in the first person in the voice of a woman, who is directing the author of the text to write an account of her own ancestor, Sone. This gives a level of veracity to the text, though the "historical" aspects of the story are very clearly fictional. The name of the woman—Fane of Beyrouth, the chatelaine of Cyprus—suggests factors to which we shall return later. We also learn that the author is a clerk of the Lady of Beyrouth, named Branque, who is 105 years old and learned in a variety of skills, including logic, medicine, canon law, astronomy, and geometry. Nothing further is known of him, though it is assumed that he is an invention of the anonymous author, but Branque may well be intended to recall another mysterious source of Grail lore: Flegetanis, the Arabic scribe mentioned in the *Parzifal* of Wolfram von Eschenbach as being "learned in star lore" as well as many other things. He, according to Wolfram, passed on the mysteries of the Grail to a troubadour named Kyot, who is in turn the source of Wolfram's own poem.

Such ancient masters are not unusual in medieval works. The authors often liked to give their stories veracity and weight by claiming an older and more mysterious source. Thus Geoffrey of Monmouth, who penned one of the first properly Arthurian works in his *Historia Regum Britanniae*, published in 1136, claimed that he had been lent a "certain ancient book in the British tongue" by his friend Walter the Archdeacon of Oxford. The fact that no such book has yet been discovered does not, of course, mean that it did not exist, but Geoffrey's use of it, as with Wolfram's invoking of Flegetanis and Kyot and the *Sone* author's Branque lend a suitably "ancient" feel to their stories.

Though the introduction to the poem is short, it contains sufficient enigmatic information to cause Moritz Goldschmidt, the first academic to attempt its publication back in 1899, to include the prologue at the end rather than the beginning of the text.

The prologue is presented in two parts, beginning with an overall tour through Sone's family history, chronicling both his antecedents and successors, all set within an elaborate pseudo-historical time frame. The shorter part purports to be written by an aristocratic lady who

◆ ◆ ◆

describes herself as the Lady of Beirut and chatelaine of Cyprus—an unlikely sounding combination; both locations still exist but remain far apart, one as a coastal town in Lebanon, the other as an island tucked in the northeast corner of the Mediterranean.

However, any history of the First and Third Crusades that claims to cover 140 years, as the prologue seems to do, will feature them both. The town of Beirut was taken by the crusaders on May 13, 1110, in a mopping-up operation a decade after the fall of Jerusalem, only to be lost back to the Saracens on August 6, 1187, after the disastrous Battle of Hattin sparked the Third Crusade. (Of the Second Crusade, the less said the better, since it fizzled out following a domestic row between Eleanor of Aquitaine and her husband in 1148.)

During the period of almost eighty years of Crusader occupation, there was time enough for the predominantly French ruling classes to award themselves various titles, which they retained as titular honorifics even after being physically deprived of them. Hence, perhaps, the lady's claim to be "la dame de Beyrouth" more than a hundred years later.

As one of his first acts during the Third Crusade, Richard Coeur de Lion captured Cyprus, even though it belonged to the Byzantine Empire, and in 1192 he sold it to Guy of Lusignan. After Guy's death, his brother Aimery swore fealty to the Holy Roman Emperor Frederick II in exchange for being regarded as a king. And when, by force of circumstance, minor relatives became heirs to the throne, the powerful Ibelin family was first in line to provide regents, and it so happened that they, like Fane, could also claim titular connections to Beirut.

There was also an otherworldly element in that Guy's family, the Lusignans, could boast descent from the faery Melusine, which may have encouraged Fane to claim relationship with the legendary Knight of the Swan, along with her eponymous hero Sone de Nansay and the initial rulers of the Crusader Kingdom of Jerusalem, Godefroy and Baudouin de Bouillon.[75] There could be some doubt about this, but at least she produced an intriguing family tree in an attempt to prove it.

One of the most interesting aspects of the prologue is the name of the lady herself. *Fane* can be translated as "temple" or "shrine," from the Latin *fanum*, often found in a Late Middle English context. Although not in the Hebrew Bible, *Baruch* is found in the Septuagint and the Vulgate Bible, as well as the Ethiopian Orthodox Bible, and also in the version of the Old Testament arranged by the Hellenistic Jewish scholar Theodotion, who compiled a Greek version of the texts around AD 150. It is also a title—according to both the *Parzifal* of Wolfram von Eschenbach and *The Later Titurel*, Parsifal's father, Gamuret, is himself described as having served the

75. We shall examine this lineage at greater length in appendix 1.

◆ ◆ ◆

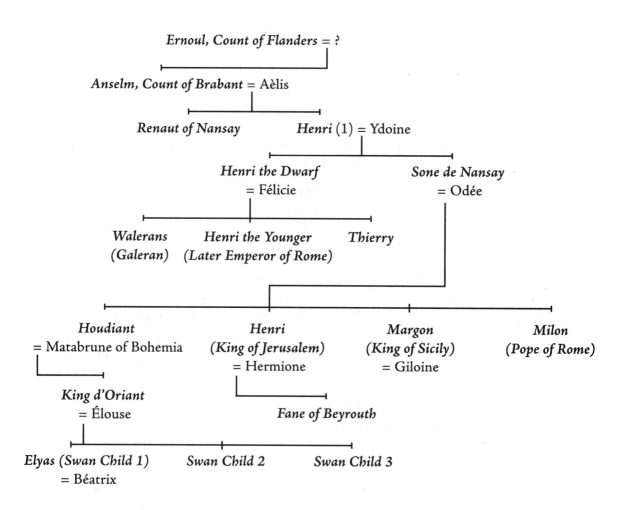

Figure 1 ◆ Sone de Nansay's Family Tree

◆ ◆ ◆

"Baruch of Bagdad." However, according to Arabic scholar Paul Kunitzch, the word is not Arabic but Hebrew, *baruk* meaning "blessed." This means that Gamuret served "the blessed one." With this in mind, it seems more than possible that the author of *Sone* was making a punning reference to the theme of the sacred temple within his work. *Fane of Baruch* may well be translated simply as "Temple of the Blessed One."

The presence of these exotic references, along with others to be discussed later, show the level of learning and awareness of other cultures possessed by the anonymous author (or his alter ego Branque). Beyrouth is almost certainly the modern Beirut in present-day Lebanon. The fact that Fane names herself chatelaine of Cyprus is also not without significance. The ancient culture of this island kingdom, a striking blend of Christian and Muslim, again testifies to a strand of multiculturalism that extends throughout *Sone*. As we saw in chapter 1, there are aspects of the Grail story as told by Chrétien that seem to have been borrowed from Hebrew traditions, while in *Sone* we learn that two of the candles which illumine the Grail once burned before the tomb of Mohammed in Medina.

The remainder of the prologue deals with Sone's family and his earliest experiences. He is, we learn, the grandson of Count Anselm of Brabant, who marries Aèlis, daughter of Ernoul, Count of Flanders, by whom he had two sons, Renaut and Henri. The latter marries Ydoine, the daughter of a German lord of Mélone, and Sone is the younger of their two sons. The elder, also named Henri, is a dwarf—despite, we are told, both parents being of normal height, while Ydoine is unusually tall. We learn that Sone himself received an excellent education, having four tutors—something that at once marks him out as coming from a very rich and powerful family. He learned chess, mathematics, geometry, fencing, and everything about dogs and birds, presumably as part of the noble pursuit of hunting. He also had a beautiful singing voice and at age twelve sang better than most.

The presence of the name Ernoul, designated Count of Flanders, Sone's maternal grandfather, is of particular interest. Under an alternate spelling of this name—Arnoul—we saw in the *Chronicle* of Lambert d'Ardres how another man with this name was responsible for the creation of a Grail Temple in the heart of France in the twelfth century. The similarity may be no more than coincidental, but it is equally possible that the author of *Sone* knew of Arnoul's copy of the Solomonic Holy of Holies.

Meanwhile, at the tender age of thirteen—when to the medieval world he would have been considered a man—Sone visits the castle of Doncheri, home to the Baron Eudes. Here he meets and falls head over heels in love with Yde, the sister of Eudes, becoming so enamored of her that he is unable to eat or sleep. Unfortunately, the lady shows no interest—or at least shows a kind of high-handed response, which would, in other texts, have earned her the title Orgellous, or "haughty." Returning home, Sone's sadness is noticed by his brother, who enquires after the reason. Not for the last time Sone refuses to speak of the matter but instead declares his intention of distracting himself by seeking service with someone skilled in arms. He sets out despite all his family's efforts to dissuade him, recalling the simple Perceval, who leaves home to seek service at Arthur's court in Chrétien de Troyes's *Conte del Graal*. The prologue ends with a flourish, with Branque declaring that he has brought these matters up here "because the story does not say any more about it." He then lists a number of Sone's descendants, including kings of Sicily and Norway, a king of Jerusalem, and a pope of Rome.

2: Sone's Early Adventures in Chivalry and Love

Sone's search for a suitable tutor in arms leads him to the court of the Count Vandémont-en-Saintois, famed for his devotion to chivalry. Once the count learns the young man's excellent pedigree, he is happy to welcome him into his household—in fact, so impressed is he that he insists Sone accompany him everywhere, including tournaments. At one of these Sone rescues the count from a melee, this making himself even more popular, especially with count's daughter Luciane, who becomes the second of Sone's many romantic conquests. But Sone is still thinking only of Yde and begs leave to go and visit his friends.

Back at Doncheri, Sone finds Yde even more irresistible. He declares his love to her in front of a room full of people but is greeted so scornfully that Sone leaves again, returning to the count's home at Saintois.

Naturally, Luciane is desperately happy to see him, and seeing which way the wind blows, the count and countess offer him the hand of their daughter in marriage. But all Sone can think of is Yde, who meanwhile is considering her recent actions as perhaps too harsh. Wavering between humility and pride, she decides to keep silent, though her thoughts remain with Sone and she wishes him well.

Soon after this a tournament is to be held at Saintois, to which each baron sends a squire to test his skills. At his master's bidding, Sone attends this, bringing Luciane and her women with him, each wearing a red dress. At the same time he secretly sends a message to Yde, begging her to attend.

The tournament is a splendid affair, with many knights and nobles attending. In the midst of a field next to the lists is a tent containing a chair for the lady who will be crowned as queen of the tournament according to the prowess of her champion. Needless to say, Sone is impressively successful in the jousts, and Luciane is duly crowned as queen of the games and seated in

◆ ◆ ◆

the tent in her red gown. This is duly noted by Yde's servants, who attended the jousts in order to observe Sone's prowess and report back to their mistress.

This episode is reminiscent of Chrétien's story of *Erec and Enide*,[76] where the eponymous hero takes part in a contest against a faery knight named Mabonagrain. There, too, is a woman in a red tent, seated upon a golden chair, surrounded by a garden full of apple trees and a fence decorated with the heads of fallen champions. This whole episode is known as the Joy of the Court, and aspects of it reoccur later in *Sone* during the visit to the Square Island.

Most of the story of *Erec and Enide* is taken up with an account of the relationship problem between the eponymous hero and heroine. But the last part of the story takes a different turn. In the version found in the Welsh collection of myths known as the Mabinogion,[77] where the hero is called Geraint and his wife Enid, they come to a place called Raven Castle, ruled over by Earl Owain. Everyone on the road warns Geraint not to go there, for all who did so must play a perilous enchanted game if they accept hospitality from Owain, whose mother's kin were of otherworldly stock. This only made Geraint spur forward more eagerly, while Enid trailed patiently behind. Owain greeted them warmly. After supper, he saw how Geraint was pale and withdrawn. "Say but the word and you shall not have to enter the enchanted games," he offered. But Geraint responded firmly: "Show me what I have to do."

Owain showed him a high hedge with stakes about it. On each of the stakes was a man's head. Beyond the hedge all was blanketed in thick mist, beyond which lay a fair orchard where fruit was always available, even in winter. There also was set a red tent next to an apple tree, from which hung a horn. Geraint went through the mist and inside the tent found a woman sitting in a golden chair with a vacant seat beside her. She warned Geraint against sitting in it because its owner never permitted this. However, he sat down and at once a well-armoured knight appeared and challenged him. They fought, and Geraint overcame his adversary. As he was about to behead him, the knight begged for mercy, promising to do Geraint's will. "I wish these games to cease for all time and for the mist to be dispersed!" cried Geraint. The woman of the tent bade him blow the horn, and when he had done so, she told Geraint that he must "announce the Joy of the Court to the world. Seek your lady's forgiveness and be as true to her as you have been strong in your deeds." And this Geraint did.

The faery knight had once been a mortal champion of great strength called Mabonagrain. He had served in the world of Faery for twenty years, and now the blowing of the horn caused

76. Translation by Carlton W. Carroll in de Troyes, *Arthurian Romances*.
77. Davies, *The Mabinogion*.

✦ ✦ ✦

him to regain his mortality. He had entered the enchanted gardens as a young man; now he was past his prime. Geraint accordingly took him into his service and made him steward of his lands.

This story appears in a slightly different form in other romances of the period, including an anonymous prelude to Chrétien's Grail romance known as *The Elucidation*.[78] The Joy of the Court probably derives from a confusion (or a deliberate pun) to the French words for horn (*cor*), body (*corps*), and court, so that it could be translated as "joy of the horn," "joy of the body," or "joy of the court." The woman in the garden has been shown to represent an aspect of Sovereignty,[79] a goddess who holds the burden of the land in her remit. This story falls largely outside the scope of the present book, but its presence here suggests that not only was the author of *Sone* familiar with Chrétien's work (there are other references, as we shall see), but that he was pointing ahead to the importance of Sone's family as guardians of sacred relics, which included the Grail, and all of which are linked to the power of the land. The fact that in the garden fruit grows at all times of the year shows that it is a type of earthly paradise, common to most descriptions of the setting for the temple of the Grail.

Back at Vandémont-en-Saintois, Sone receives news that his brother is ill and heads back to Nansay. Henri is soon better and again tries to keep Sone from leaving, this time by offering him lands and riches. But nothing will deter the young man, who leaves for Doncheri as soon as possible. There he once more declares his love for Yde, who has of course heard of his success in the tournament. But she still rejects him, telling him that he should declare his love for the one who was crowned in the tent—in other words, Luciane. Perhaps here again we may see the author hinting at Sone's relationship with Sovereignty, as his future life will attest.

Sone returns to Nansay, where he finds a maiden reading a lay composed for him by Luciane. Sone leaves again immediately, saddling his good horse Moriel and heading for England.

3: Sone's Journey to England and Scotland

Sone arrives in England but passes through to Scotland. There he is well received by the queen because of his lineage and prowess in the recent tournament, as witnessed by one of the Scottish knights. However, the rest of the court behaves boorishly, and Sone determines to leave again. He asks if there are any wars being fought at the time, and the queen tells him that one is brewing between the kings of Ireland, Scotland, and Norway, in which her husband will sup-

78. Matthews et. al., *The Lost Book of the Grail: Restoring the Courts of Joy*.
79. Matthews, *King Arthur and the Goddess of the Land: The Divine Feminine in the Mabinogion*.

port Ireland. She asks Sone to remain until the king returns, but he is offended by the uncouth courtiers and departs.

The section describes Sone acting as a *sudoyer*—a paid mercenary—a common enough occupation for younger sons of families at a time when eldest sons generally inherited all. It also happens to be the occupation that Joseph of Arimathea held under Pontius Pilate, according to the romance—one of a number of parallels underlined by the author between Sone and Joseph.

4: Sone's Arrival in Norway and His Service to the King

Sone now sets out for Norway. The king of that land, whose name is Alain, hears reports of his coming and goes forth to meet him. Liking what he sees, he invites Sone to the court to join in a great banquet, given as part of the preparations for war with Scotland and Ireland. The description of the hall and the actions of the king's daughter Odée, who is to become Sone's greatest love and his future wife, offer some intriguing possibilities to our understanding of the poem. The fact that the King of Norway is called Alain is interesting, as this is also the name of one of the most prominent Grail kings. Sometimes called Alain le Gros, he is listed amongst the ancestors of the Grail knight Perceval and as a descendent of Joseph of Arimathea.

To begin with, Sone is somewhat confused by the behaviour of the court, who are noisy and boastful. However, it has been pointed out that this scene, in which table manners of the Norwegians causes Sone some discomfort, could be a more or less faithful image of a *heit-strenging*—a sumptuous feast given by the king on the eve of a battle in the course of which the warriors in arms pronounce solemn vows and boasts.[80]

The scene in which the king's daughter offers a cup to certain knights, including Sone, and afterwards brings forth swords and spears, which she hands out to the same men, seems to prelude the later revelations of the Grail. It is also reminiscent of a scene of Geoffrey in Monmouth's *Historia Regum Brittaniae* ("History of the Kings of Britain") who was the first author to introduce the story of Arthur into the literature of the Middle Ages. In this scene Rowena, the daughter of the Saxon leader Hengist, offers a cup to the British King Vortigern. It is the beginning of a planned seduction that ends with Vortigern marrying Rowena and thus ensuring a claim to the British throne by the Saxons. In *Sone* the gesture seems to echo the Grail feast (though no one there is offered a drink from the sacred vessel save for the Wounded King)

---

80. K. Nyrop, "Sone de Nansai et la Norvege," *Romania* 35 (1906): 555–569.

◆ ◆ ◆

and indicate that in due course Sone will himself marry into the Norwegian royal family and become a guardian of the Grail.

5: *War and Single Combat*

Both Scotland and Ireland are preparing for war, while in Norway castles and cities are provisioned. The Scots and Irish arrive at the harbour of St. Joseph with 60,000 poorly equipped and half-naked men, and Sone, together with the king's sons, Houdiant and Thomas, leads a force against the invaders. They surprise the invading army and slaughter 10,000 of the Irish, taking many more prisoners; but in the maelstrom both of King Alain's sons are killed.

Having lost so many of his allies, the King of Scotland proposes a single combat to decide the outcome of the war, thus avoiding further deaths. Mourning his dead sons, King Alain accepts, and the date is set for twenty days hence. The Scots choose Aligos, an eleven-foot giant, to be their champion. Sone immediately volunteers and is accepted as champion of Norway.

6: *The Visit to the Grail Castle*

We now come to the heart of the poem, in which much will be revealed concerning both the Grail and the place where it is kept. There are references both to more familiar strands within the Grail romances and to some hitherto unknown aspects that show the author of *Sone* taking the Grail story into different waters.

The description of the Grail castle (as it very clearly is here) is both similar and different to that of Chrétien's account of the visit by Perceval. It also very clearly makes reference to the First Temple of Solomon, which, as we saw in chapter 1, is a major source for the depiction of all subsequent Grail Temples. It is also, as noted previously, a point at which the author (or perhaps the clerk Branque) steps to the fore, apparently describing what he sees:

> Never had anything more beautiful been seen. It stood in the open sea at a distance where no machine could hurl anything to harm its crenelated walls that rose up out of the living rock. On its outer wall were four towers that looked the finest in the world, and in the centre, midway between them, a greater one surpassing the others. This contained the palace; surely nothing more sumptuous had ever been built.
>
> In every direction it was a hundred feet wide because it was perfectly circular. At the centre of the central tower was a fireplace that rested on four gilded pillars that supported a pure copper pipe, four feet high, decorated with gold coloured mosaics that crossed the reception hall. I am sure no more wondrous place had ever been built.

◆ ◆ ◆

The description has a number of highly original details not found in any other Grail romance and adding significantly to our understanding of the building created to house this most sacred relic.

It is made clear that the journey to the island is to help prepare Sone for his coming battle with the giant Aligos, but the way there is described as difficult and the king's party has to journey though mountains and valleys for two days until they reach the coast. There they encounter a road that leads into the sea and is described as having been built "at some time in the past." Many knights are said to have come to grief in searching for it, but the king knows the way and they arrive at a place where "two rocks formed a gateway that lead into the sea." Here the king sounds a horn and a small boat approaches, manned by two weeping monks, neither of whom seem at all pleased to see their visitors. The king tells them they will be happy when they see who has come, and when they recognize him, they are "overjoyed."

This suggests that one of the reasons for the sorrow of the monks is the absence of the king. Although there are other reasons, as we shall see, and despite the fact that there is an abbot ruling over them, ultimately the king is the guardian of the sacred relic they keep watch over, so that his absence can be seen as a kind of abandonment. This is interesting in itself as it has been noted before that Arthur, who rules over the kingdom in which the Grail appears in later romances, knows nothing of the Grail and sends his knights in search of it rather than going himself. For this reason he has been named a *roi fainéant*, a faint-hearted or do-nothing king, and the eventual destruction of his kingdom can be seen as being brought about by the presence of the Grail and as a cause of the Wasteland.

With increasing delight, the monks row the party across to the island, the author waxing lyrical in his description. He also makes it clear that just to visit there is itself a blessing:

> Any who carefully studied its detail would never be puzzled by it if truly loved by God. Here was the basis of faith; the beginnings of religion, of the angel who was sent by God to greet the holy Virgin, of the comportment that God observed in his earthly life, of the way he died and descended into hell to lead out the faithful, and the way we must act to enter paradise. All the good things, of which you may have heard, if it pleases God, were figured there in abundance, rendered in fine gold.

This is an important point, as it tells us clearly that to enter the castle shows how we must act if we are to enter paradise. The castle, or temple, of the Grail is located, more often than not, within an earthly paradise, and there are aspects of the description here that suggest the island itself is the memory of such a place. The details of the measurements of the building and the fireplace with its four gilded pillars and the copper pipe recall descriptions of the Solomonic temple and other sites created to house the Grail.

Entering the castle, the monks are delighted to learn that the king has brought his new champion to see them. A meal is laid ready and a lengthy description of the building is given in elaborate detail. This is worth repeating here, as it is an important indicator of the way in which the home of the Grail is closely associated with other depictions of the earthy paradise.

> Tables were placed in a sheltered area that overlooked the outer wall and gave onto the sea. It was bounded by a carved balustrade of white marble upon which no bird, animal, or fish could not be found represented, including ten leopards, each with a gaping mouth, whose heads turned ever to face the wind to produce agreeable harmonies. Whoever wished to contemplate the sea could find no better place.
>
> In the other direction lay woodlands of laburnum, cypress, sycamore, alisier, almond, olive, and other beautiful trees flourishing by the sea. To see stags and deer at play, swans, peacocks, moose, birds diving into fresh or salt water, though with wings that cannot fly far. Some who have seen them say they can be as big as badgers, though not any smaller, and similar to bats in that their wings are covered in fur. They have hair, pointed features, and make such a racket that the woods resound with it.
>
> Three streams of water meet at the castle that well up from the rock and flow into the sea, mixing the fresh water with the salt. There are so many fish gathered here as could never be destroyed by fishing. Search the whole world and you would never find so solid a castle provided with such riches.

This is very clearly a derivative of descriptions of Eden or Eden-like places—of an earthly paradise that borders on the very doors to heaven. The proliferation of creatures—most not native to Norway—along with the three rivers and the sheer golden glory of the place, all point to this. As we saw in chapter 1, there are a number of medieval romances that contain descriptions of such places, and these are a central part of the mythical kingdom ruled over by the mysterious Prester John, who becomes a guardian of the Grail in another of the romances we shall examine later. The placing of the Grail in such a setting happens with greater frequency from this point on.

Having dined, the king requests the opening of "the reliquaries" stored there. They prepare to make their confessions before going to bed, and Sone, in particular, knowing that his life may well end during his fight with the giant, is happy to do so. The relics are not described at this point and may be a reference to the more usual type held in churches throughout the West, such as the bones of saints. The sense of this passage seems to say that the relics will bear silent witness to the confessions of the king and his party.

❖ ❖ ❖

Next morning they attend Mass, sung by the abbot himself, and when it is time for him to preach to all present, he begins by reminding them that the castle was itself founded by a saint, whose body rests in a coffin before the high altar.

He then announces that this saint is none other than Joseph of Arimathea, whose relationship to Jesus was widely accepted throughout the Middle Ages. A variety of tales dealing with Joseph's part in the Grail myth itself, mostly revolving around his request to Pontius Pilate for the body of the crucified messiah, the subsequent capturing of Jesus's blood during the deposition from the cross, and the preparation of the body for burial in Joseph's own tomb. We shall examine these legends further in chapter 6; for the moment, it is sufficient to say that the links between Joseph and the sacred vessel are traceable to within a few hundred years of the events of the Crucifixion, displaying a remarkable consistency of detail.

The version relayed by the abbot differs in a number of details, however, suggesting either that these were the creation of the author of *Sone* or that he had access to documents no longer extant. Once again, it is worth repeating parts of the account given by the abbot so that we may examine it in more detail.

> Originally from Arimathea, Joseph worked as a bailiff for seven years in the house of Pilate, but ever revered Jesus Christ, who had preached the new religion. Thus after seven years, on conclusion of his service, he asked if he might have the body of Jesus as a gift.
>
> Pilate liked Joseph but thought him mad not to have asked for something better, though he did not refuse. For his part, Joseph felt well paid, for he believed Jesus to be a true king whom he adored in body and soul. Keen to remove it from the cross, he extracted the nails and placed the body in a sepulchre—for which he was accused of going against the religion of the country.
>
> Far from denying this, Joseph continued to call upon God, in whom he believed in all sincerity. But when these accusations were brought to Pilate, although he respected his former bailiff, he did not hesitate to render justice on him. For admitting his Christian faith, Joseph was cast into a deep pit 20 toises deep and swarming with snakes, toads, and spiders that greatly harassed him. Enormous stones were rolled across the top, which was sealed with cement.
>
> Being imprisoned in this terrible place troubled Joseph greatly until Jesus appeared to him and offered him a wonderous vessel. You can safely believe me for you will very soon see it!
>
> It consoled Joseph greatly, for it removed the vermin, caused the stench of the place to disappear, and softened the rock, which from now on was easier to lie on than a fine woolen mattress. The place became fragrant with the true blood of Christ that spread a light as

◆ ◆ ◆

bright as the sun. And when Joseph put the vessel to his lips, he suffered neither hunger nor thirst.

For forty years things continued thus, and he suffered no further torment. Vespasian, the Roman emperor, was a leper. He had once been handsome but was now hideous, until Veronica cured him with her miraculous veil with which she had comforted Jesus on the way to the Crucifixion.

Vespasian proclaimed that he now believed in God and Jesus Christ, as he had recovered his health thanks to him. And as God and Jesus Christ had cured him, so he would now fight for him with his army. He thus led his troops towards Jerusalem, and night and day attacked the city and those who dwelt there. At least one starving mother ate her children, and when the city was abandoned, thirty Jews could be bought for a denier.

When all were gone, Veronica and the high priest, Ananias, told Vespasian how Joseph had been incarcerated in the bottom of a cavern forty years ago. "Let us at least have his bones, sir," they said, "for his flesh will have rotted by now."

"Take me there," replied the king. "I have heard about this." Ananias led him to the cavern, and the emperor had the stones removed and the opening completely cleared. From the cave came a light as bright as if the sun had risen and such a sweet fragrance that all were overcome.

Vespasian looked in and saw Joseph, hailed him in the name of God, and addressed him as a friend.

"God and Saint Mary be praised!" cried Joseph, "I have heard your voice before, and if you believe in God and Jesus Christ, let it ring out again."

"My friend, I am a Christian king and wish only the best for you if you have been walled up for believing in God and Jesus Christ."

"Yes," replied Joseph, "I believe in him and would not wish for any other religion."

The emperor arranged straight away to have him pulled up.

Joseph still carried in his arms the vessel given him by God. It was gazed upon by all the people, who desired to kiss it. Any of the sick that touched it were returned to perfect health, exalting their faith. And so Christianity was assured, and its bounds increased.

Much of this comes directly from the story told in two apocryphal gospels, excluded from the canon of the Bible by St. Jerome circa 405. The most familiar of these, and the first to expand the brief mentions of Joseph of Arimathea into something like a biography, is the *Evangelium Nicodemi* (Gospel of Nicodemus), which also includes a further apocryphal document, the *Acta Pilati*, or Acts of Pilate. The former is presented as a Hebrew gospel written by Nicodemus, who is mentioned in the Gospel of St. John as a follower of Jesus. We shall examine these more fully in chapter 6.

✦ ✦ ✦

Other details not found in either of these texts but present in *Sone* are the pit of spiders, snakes, and toads. This is more usually described as a room within or beneath a tower, where Joseph is imprisoned and the key thrown away. The large stones, sealed in concrete, may be intended to recall the stones placed before the tomb of Jesus.

The appearance of Christ in this noisome place is in line with earlier and later accounts, but the driving away of the vermin, the sweet smell of the Holy Blood overcoming the stink of the place, as well as providing light in the darkness, not to mention the softening of the stones lining the walls and floor of the pit so that they become as comfortable as a woolen mattress, are unique to this text.

Of course the most important aspect of the story is the gift of the sacred vessel to Joseph. Not only does the vessel give forth light and a sweet scent, it also keeps Joseph alive, since to merely touch it with his lips ensures that "he suffered neither hunger nor thirst."

This miraculous state of suspension lasts forty years, until the Roman emperor Vespasian (AD 9–79) conquers Jerusalem. This did indeed happen in AD 69, when the emperor crushed a Jewish rebellion. When he arrives in Jerusalem, the high priest Ananias tells him how the man who had been given care of the body of Jesus and had given up his own tomb for the messiah had been thrown into a pit. Ananias then asks of he can have the bones of the long-dead man, and Vespasian agrees. He goes in person to the place and has the stones cleared from the entrance. To the amazement of everyone, a great light and sweet scent comes from within, and there is Joseph, hale and hearty as the day he was incarcerated.

Two things in this account suggest some kind of previous connection between Joseph and the emperor, though there are no references in the text or elsewhere. Vespasian says that he has heard the story before, and when the prison is opened, Joseph says he has heard the emperor's voice before. Whether this refers to a now-lost text or was simply an addition of the author of *Sone* remains unclear.

At the emperor's command, Joseph is brought out of the pit. He is carrying the sacred vessel and all there who saw it at once desire to kiss it. On doing so, any who were sick are immediately healed. The first appearance of the sacred relic here thus begins with a series of miracles.

Again, there is no conclusive evidence whether Chrétien de Troyes or Robert de Boron and the author of *Sone* were independently drawing upon a common source. It seems likely that Chrétien had access to texts that have since vanished, while Robert seems to have drawn upon Christian apocryphal texts then in circulation, including the Acts of Pilate and the Gospel of Nicodemus. The author of *Sone* almost certainly knew Robert's *Joseph*, but the variations between the two texts suggest an independent source.

✦ ✦ ✦

Perlesvaus

A third medieval story, often described as one of the most unusual and even uncanonical accounts of the Grail, may also have been known to the author of *Sone* since it contains episodes that appear nowhere else. This text is known as *Perlesvaus*, attributed (within the text itself) to an author named Josephus, to whom the story was dictated by an angel. The author sets up not one but two significant sources—the angelic and the historical. We are presumably intended to believe that "Josephus" is the Jewish historian Titus Flavius Josephus (AD 37–100), who lived during the reign of Vespasian. Initially an opponent of the Romans, he later became the emperor's slave and interpreter but was given his freedom when Vespasian became emperor in AD 69. He wrote several important books, including the *Antiquities of the Jews*,[81] in which he claimed that the prophecies of a messiah in fact referred to Vespasian!

If we were to follow the suggestion of the author/scribe of *Perlesvaus*, this would make Josephus the composer of the first and earliest Grail text. Although this is most unlikely, there are, as we shall see later, some curious correspondences between these historical characters and the story narrated in the *Apocrypha*, *Sone*, and *The Later Titurel* (see chapter 6).

Also known as *Li Hauz Livres du Graal* (*The High History of the Holy Grail*, the text was probably composed during the first ten years of the thirteenth century, though much disagreement rages on this detail.[82] It purports to be yet another continuation of Chrétien's unfinished *Perceval*, though is generally seen as separate from the works of the other continuators because of its many variations from the canon of the Grail romances. It survives in just three manuscripts, two additional fragments, and two sixteenth-century editions. It has had a varied reception from the scholars who have studied it. Some have found it confusing, while at least one described it as "a sort of symbolical New Testament, canonical and apocryphal, employing a system of knightly substitutes for biblical characters."[83]

When the story opens, all is not well in the kingdom of Arthur. Always a noble and honourable knight, the king has fallen victim to a strange malaise that causes him to withdraw from court life, becoming something of a hermit. Only the urgings of Queen Guinevere drive him forth on an adventure in which he is blessed by a vision of the Grail, after which he hears the story of the failure of a certain knight to ask an important question, which caused the Wasteland. Then a Black Knight who carries a flaming lance attacks and wounds Arthur, who is left

---

81. Whiston, *New Complete Works of Flavius Josephus*.

82. Bryant, *The High Book of the Grail*.

83. Carman, "The Symbolism of the Perlesvaus."

for dead. A maiden arrives and heals the king, but rebukes him for his negligence when she learns his identity.

This part of the story is unusual and the only time in which Arthur becomes actively involved in the Grail story. It suggests that at one time a now-lost story told that he was himself the Wounded King, which would make the land over which he ruled the Wasteland of the Grail romances. However, in *Perlesvaus* the story quickly turns to the adventuress of Gawain, Lancelot, and Perceval. Lancelot, in fact, undergoes a form of the Beheading Test, also found later in *Sone*, as well as elsewhere. Gawain's many adventures are outside the range of this book. Perceval's, however, offers some intriguing parallels to our text. However, it is Arthur himself, still caught up in the repercussions of his kingly failure, who comes to the Grail castle, which Perceval has already begun to restore to its former glory.

The description of the building leaves us in no doubt of its ultimate origin:

> Behind the castle, the story says, there was a river, by which the castle was supplied with all good things; it was a beautiful river indeed and rich in fish, and Josephus tells us that it came from the Earthly Paradise and ran all around the castle and flowed on into the forest … There its course ended and it vanished into the earth, but wherever it flowed there was a great abundance of all good things.
>
> In the rich Castle … nothing was lacking, and it had three names, the story says. Eden was its first name, another was the Castle of Joy, and another was the Castle of Souls … because the soul of anyone who died there went to Paradise.[84]

The castle is named Eden, watered by a river that flowed out of an earthly paradise. We are also told that the bells that ring every day to call people to celebrate at the altar of the Grail were made by Solomon—another reference that adds to the accumulation of evidence connecting the biblical king with the Grail. Arthur is also shown the tomb of Joseph of Arimathea and richly entertained in the castle, as are King Alain and Sone.

Again and again, we are reminded of *Sone* and the description of the Grail castle. Though the one in *Sone* is on an island, it too is fed by a river out of paradise, contains the tomb of Joseph, and is the home of the Grail. Other parallels between the two texts will emerge in a later section of the poem.

The next part of Joseph of Arimathea's story, narrated by the abbot, is astonishingly original and differs from all other surviving versions. Freshly released from prison, Joseph breaks down a wall and retrieves the Lance of Longinus,[85] which he had concealed there previously. Thus

---

84. Bryant, *The Complete Story of the Grail*, 195.

85. The terms "lance" and "spear" are used interchangably from text to text.

armed with two sacred relics, he sets out for Syria, where he spends some time. One day a mysterious ship appears and a voice instructs him to go aboard, bringing the vessel and the Lance with him. This is another correlative with the later Grail romances where a ship built by Solomon at the behest of the Queen of Sheba becomes a kind of floating temple (see chapter 7).

The ship takes him to Gaète, possibly identifiable as a Dutch province of Brabant or a city in Italy. There he finds a horse and armour awaiting him and proceeds on a series of adventures more appropriate to a knight than a holy disciple. Though the author of *Sone* says he is unable to tell us how, Joseph "increased the faith" of Christianity wherever he went. Finally he reaches Norway, then still a pagan land, and drives out "the Saracens." This last term is most often used to refer to Muslim opponents of Christianity, but here it may be seen as a more general description of the followers of other gods.

In the context of the poem, we must assume that Joseph has become a renowned warrior, leading an army against pagan forces. Having killed the king of the land that will eventually be known as Norway, he then diverts radically from the norm by marrying the pagan king's daughter, who was apparently extremely beautiful. Here it seems that Joseph is motivated by human desire rather than the cause he has followed to date. He has the girl baptized—against her will, we are told—but she continues to hate him for killing her father and pays only lip service to Christianity, in which she has no real belief.

God, we are now told, had decided to tempt Joseph with the Saracen princess, and was so displeased with the outcome that he punished his warrior by wounding him "in the reins and below"—a term referring to the kidneys and genitals—after which Joseph "endured terrible suffering."

All of this differs profoundly from the more familiar story told in the work of Robert de Boron and the anonymous authors of the Lancelot-Grail cycle. In *Sone* Joseph is a warrior rather than a saintly follower of Jesus, and when he succumbs to the beauty of the pagan princess, he is punished with an unhealing generative wound such as that endured by all subsequent Grail kings—though seldom because of their failure to remain celibate. Before he is thus emasculated, Joseph fathers a child by his newly baptized wife, but he gives the infant into the care of others to be raised since he himself is no longer able-bodied.

From here on Joseph "could not … use his limbs, feed himself, or move about, but remained lying down." However, he possessed

> a boat in which, after celebrating Mass, he went fishing, aided by a sailor who guided the boat to wherever he wanted to go. The fishing and the company of the sailors pleased him. Here he could forget his terrible suffering, for such pain could kill many a man. And because

❖ ❖ ❖

he thus fished, his popular name spread everywhere: he was called the Fisher King—a name that is still well known.

After this bold excursion into unfamiliar waters, the author brings us back to Chrétien's story of a king wounded so grossly that he spends all his time fishing. He tells us that it was during this time—while the king remained in a state of woundedness—that the castle was built,

> situated in the open sea free from assault. No ship could reach it by sea for fear of being cast on hidden rocks. And as the fresh water flows and strikes the walls here, there is always a profusion of fish of all kinds.

Thus the king leads a life of suspended animation until, we are told, "a knight came that could cure him; and afterwards he was … powerful through the practice of arms." After this the king "lived a very long time, during which the faith was exalted." Finally, when on his death-bed, Joseph "appointed thirteen monks to serve in the tradition of the named apostles, and we remain thirteen in this castle."

The number thirteen is not without significance. This is, as stated, the number of disciples who sat with Jesus at the table of the Last Supper. It is also the original number of Knights of the Round Table and of the later Grail knights—though there were at first only twelve, with an empty place for the seat of Judas, until the coming of Galahad, who will in time replace Perceval as the achiever of the Grail.

The abbot concludes with another striking passage:

> In that time the country was called Logres, a name of suffering, renowned for its tears and weeping. It very much merited being renowned for suffering since one can grow neither beans nor wheat, no child be born, no young girl find a husband, no tree bear leaves, no grass regrow, no bird have chicks, no beast have young since the king was mutilated and until he had expiated his sins …

There is a certain degree of confusion over the name of the kingdom ruled over by Joseph in *Sone*. It is not clear in this passage whether the abbot is here saying that Norway was once called Logres or whether this is simply a scribal error and is actually supposed to refer to Arthur's kingdom. The poet tells us that Normandy was formally called Logres, suggesting that the setting of the story may at one time have been Britain. Norway often features as an otherworldly place in medieval writings, and this may have contributed to the confusion.

Making Sone King of Norway also ties the story in with the reference at the beginning of the *Quest del Saint Graal,* where the author of the text, having seen Christ in a vision, is

◆ ◆ ◆

instructed to follow a strange beast to the land of Norway, where he will find the book of the Grail. This is not followed up in the Arthurian quest but shows that a link existed between the Grail story and Norway.

The particular description of the suffering land—very clearly the Wasteland described as surrounding the Grail castle during the period of the king's wounded state—corresponds almost exactly to another text, intended as a prequel to Chrétien's Grail poem. Known as the *Elucidation*, this text is another largely overlooked account, which offers variations on the *Conte del Graal*. It also includes references to the Joy of the Court. Here the anonymous author describes the wounded kingdom of Logres as being

> laid waste,
> With no wells nor tree in leaf;
> The meadows and the flowers dried up,
> And the brooks diminished;
> Nor could be found from now on
> The court of the Rich Fisher … [86]

It is difficult at times to establish a timeline in *Sone*—especially as it relates to the more familiar Arthurian and Grail romances. Here we are told that Joseph of Arimathea was not only the first guardian of the Grail but also the first wounded Fisher King, and that his sad state continued "until he was cured by a knight." This must refer to either Perceval or one of the other Grail knights, whose principle task it is to cure the Wounded King. We are told that after this Joseph "lived to a great age and founded a community of twelve monks," from which the current protectors of the Grail and the Spear are descended. This would place the entire Wounded King episode, including the Wasteland, which we are told affected the kingdom of Logres as long as King Joseph remained wounded, before the more normal period of the Grail quest in Arthurian times—in which case it makes *Sone* a prequel to the main body of Grail romances.

As we shall see, there is a considerable amount of material relating to Joseph of Arimathea and his descendants, which pushes this particular aspect of the Grail back several hundreds of years (see chapter 6). But *Sone* is unique in taking the life of Joseph into a chivalric period and setting as well as making him a Grail King who suffers a wound that incapacitates him and forces him to seek refuge in fishing.

---

86. Matthews et. al., *The Lost Book of the Grail.*

♦ ♦ ♦

The fact that the Island of the Grail is called Galoche (a corruption of Wales) suggests that the author may have mixed up accounts of the Island of Gwales off the coast of Wales, which possessed Grail associations, from the account of Merlin hiding the twelve treasures of Britain there (including a Grail-type relic) with an island off the coast of Norway. As we shall see when we examine the nature of the two islands, there are several connections with the older Celtic mythology that underlies many of the Arthurian legends. In particular, the idea of the island where the Grail is housed echoes several references of Celtic tradition in which a sacred vessel is found on an island. The fact that Joseph of Arimathea is presented as the patron saint of Norway (St. Olaf is not referenced) may be seen as a further attempt to establish the country as a suitable resting place for the Grail.

Numerous attempts have been made to correlate the various versions of the Wounded King, the Grail procession, and the Wasteland, but all have failed to observe the most striking parallel present in *Sone*, *Parsifal*, *Titurel*, and *Perlesvaus*. This common factor is the description of the Grail castle/Temple/Chapel. The specific nature of this ties the romances together and points both to physical sites as well as the mystical reality of the Grail Temple.

When it comes to the Wounded King, the variations in virtually every version of the Grail myth are minor and the essential meaning is the same: the wounding of the king is reflected in the land. The king is no longer perfect in body, and the land suffers accordingly. The parallels between the cause of Joseph's wound in *Sone* and that of the various later Grail kings are many. But here—and only here—does Joseph of Arimathea fulfil the role of the Grail King (Fisher King), rather than simply being its guardian. The time element is important also, as it creates a timeline in which the Grail is held by Joseph from the time of Jesus into the thirteenth-century setting of *Sone*. The point is—was the author of the romance trying to make parallels between mystical time and historic time? The last third of the poem suggests that he was.

Throughout *Sone* Joseph is seen as an immediate successor to Christ and ultimately as one of the most senior founders of Christianity—second only to St. Peter—as well as being the first to hold the Grail and be its guardian. He is also perceived as the first person to bring Christianity to Europe. The very distinctive establishment of Sone as Joseph's successor is even more remarkable. It is further emphasized in the description of his wedding to Odée. To begin with, everyone is dressed in white, signifying purity and innocence, and during the celebration of the Mass (sung by no less than an archbishop and two bishops) Sone offers gold, incense, and myrrh, the three sacred substances offered by the Persian magi at the birth of Jesus. Immediately following the service, the Grail and the Spear are brought out, along with a piece of the True Cross and a golden Candelabrum in which are five candles.

◆ ◆ ◆

The significance of this last object is considerable. In virtually every description of the Grail procession, a Candelabrum containing several candles—the numbers vary from three to ten—is born before or immediately after the Grail itself. In every instance their light is brilliant, said to be brighter than the sun. Here, the light that comes from the Grail itself illumines the entire island. We also learn that "according to the writings of Joseph of Arimathea," one of the candles had witnessed the birth of Christ, while two more had "burned before the tomb of Mohamed"—a striking and unusual reference to find in a highly Christianized work.

The importance of brilliant light in Christian myth is beyond the scope of this work, but it should be noted that the oldest surviving Christian documents refer to the face of Jesus as bright and shining,[87] while we are constantly reminded, throughout the Gospels and in the theology of both Western and Eastern churches, that Jesus is "the light of the world." Icons dating from the first days of Christianity show Jesus with a light around his head that is more than a simple halo. It has been suggested that the origin of this brilliant corona lies in older mythologies, such as those of classical Rome itself, where the sun god Helios is inevitably portrayed emitting rays of light. The presence of this light around the Grail is a significant reminder of the holiness of the relic and its powerful and continuing association with Jesus of Nazareth.

As noted above, at this point in the narrative when a procession is formed, the four sacred things (again, this number is consistent through most of the Grail romances) are carried in order—the Candelabrum first, followed by the piece of the True Cross, the Spear that drips blood, and finally the Grail, carried by Sone, every inch a Grail King.

This section of the poem ends on a high note, with the abbot promising Sone that God is on his side and that he cannot fail to defeat whoever fights against him. He then summons everyone present to view the Grail and the Spear, which are unearthed from reliquaries. At once

> The whole place lit up. At that moment the monks loudly sang, in tears, the *Te Deum Laudamus*. The vessels no longer existed. On the altar, by the cross, the Graal was replaced by the holy man, friend of God.
>
> [The abbot] went next to bring the holy lance of which you have heard me speak. The abbot and the monks wept so copiously one could say they dissolved into tears. The iron of the lance was magnificent and brilliant. At its point, to the fore, formed a drop of red blood, at which many of them marvelled.

The mysteries of the Grail and the Spear are thus revealed. The phrase "the vessels no longer existed" does not appear to refer to the Grail itself but to the chalices used to celebrate the

87. This is explored further in the work of David Elkington, currently unpublished. We give our thanks to him for sharing his research.

✦ ✦ ✦

Mass, which the sacred vessel replaces. However, the Grail itself is "replaced by the holy man, friend of God." Does this refer to the spirit of Joseph of Arimathea himself, or even to Christ? In the Lancelot-Grail, and later the *Morte d'Arthur* of Sir Thomas Malory, during the celebration of the Mass *with* the Grail, Jesus himself appears, and the miracle of the transubstantiation is shown in actuality. Joseph of Arimathea is also present, acting as a psychopomp to the risen lord.[88]

◆ ◆ ◆

Sone now heads back to Norway and is received with a tumultuous welcome. Having accepted the invitation of the people to become their new king, he declares his intention of being crowned on the Island of the Grail. This is a very significant decision, as it establishes Sone not only as King of Norway, but as King of the Grail also. The abbot confirms this himself by telling Sone he will be the guardian of the Spear and the Grail.

He also awards Sone with the guardianship of the sword belonging to Joseph of Arimathea (also referred to as the sword of Galoche), with which the saint had defended the land against the pagans.

Sone is the only character in the entire Arthurian corpus, other than the Grail maiden and members of her family, who is described as carrying the Grail in his own hands in the procession of the sacred relics described later in the poem. In fact, since Sone passes on the guardianship of the relics to his children at the end of the poem, he is in fact establishing a new Grail "family" separate from those who appear in other Arthurian romances.

In the following section (7), wielding the sword of Joseph of Arimathea, Sone defeats the eleven-foot-tall giant Aligos. His bravery earns him a knighthood and the love of the king's daughter Odée. Sone is still thinking of Yde, however, and decides to prove himself as a knight errant. He declines to return the sword of Joseph despite the abbot's request and instead gives it to Odée to keep for him. This she does without telling her father. Sone now sets sail for Ireland. The next few hundred lines (sections 7–16 in our numbered sequence) do not advance the story of the Grail to any degree, except for a curious detail found in section 9, which recounts the mutiny of the sailors aboard the ship carrying Sone and Odée back to Norway. In the ensuing battle—which ends with the overcoming of the crew—the royal pair are both wounded. Sone receives a wound in the thigh, Odée one near the heart. Neither are fatal, but there is a suggestion here that Sone is being given a modified Grail wound, while that of Odée is perhaps a reference to the eternal struggle between human and sacred love.

88. Malory, *Le Morte d'Arthur.*

◆ ◆ ◆

Sone is now established as a hero par excellence, while much of the story here deals at length with his complex relationships with women.

Section 13 deals with a tournament at Machau organized by the Countess of Champagne, who has taken rather a liking to Sone. She also invites the troublesome Yde, who has continued her rejection of Sone's advances. Having decided to attend, Yde prepares five lances, each one of a different colour: white, green, blue, red, and gold. She displays these close to her seat at the tournament.

When Sone sees her and the lances, he falls into a kind of stupor and has to be woken from his dream by a herald. He then comes for a lance and Yde sings to him from a ballad that tells him the white lance is for her beloved friend.

Sone, as ever, defeats every opponent, winning each lance from the hand of Yde. She explains the meaning of the lances in symbolic terms, indicating that the white refers to her love for Sone, the green the flowering of that love, the blue a royal colour which brings comfort, the red meaning that she will give her love totally, and the gold the long-term feelings she has had for Sone. Having thus given Sone some hope that his love is returned, she then explains that her resistance to Sone's love is because, as the goddaughter of his mother, the church forbids their union.

Sone is devastated. He departs for France, where he encounters Luciane and dashes her hopes of capturing his heart. More adventures ensue, each one designed to increase Sone's fame and to help establish his family through dynastic marriages.

17: Arrivals from Norway and the Lay of Odée

The story picks up its pace again here as Odée, still in love with Sone, writes a lay in which she describes her feelings. She then seeks out a girl named Papagay, a famous singer and harpist, and sends her to France in search of Sone.

Attending this lady is a hideously ugly woman named the Countess Orvale, who seems to be a type known as the loathly or hideous lady. The presence of this character here is intriguing. Originating in Irish myth as a representative of the Goddess of Sovereignty, and later found in Arthurian romances including *The Marriage of Sir Gawain and Dame Ragnall*, she makes a more extended and familiar appearance in several Grail romances, including Chrétien's *Conte du Graal* and Wolfram von Eschenbach's *Parzival*. In these she acts as a severe agent of the Grail, reminding the heroes on the quest at crucial points when they are about to take a wrong turn or neglect their sacred undertaking.

✦ ✦ ✦

The presence of this figure at this particular juncture of the story is interesting. Though the Countess Orvale does not have a specific purpose here, beyond her accompaniment of Papagay, the fact that her appearance is followed by a version of the beheading test gives one pause for thought. Did the author of *Sone* know the stories of Gawain, who also undergoes the beheading game in *Sir Gawain and the Green Knight* and encounters a loathly lady in *Gawain and Ragnall* or was he simply borrowing from *Perlesvaus*, where Lancelot faces the same test? In either case, he seems to be suggesting Sone as a Knight of Sovereignty, who passes the beheading test and perhaps that of the loathly lady, thus establishing a link between the pagan story of the Green Knight and the Christian Grail myth.

The text is ambiguous on these matters; however, there are some striking similarities between the description of the loathly lady in *Sone* and those in the much later fifteenth-century poem of *Gawain and Ragnall*.

> Her face was red, her nose snotty withal,
> Her mouth wide, her teethe yellow over all,
> With bleared eyes greater then a ball;
> Her mouth was not to lack;
> Her teethe hung over her lips;
> Her cheeks were wide as women's hips;
> A lute she bare upon her back.
>
> Her neck long and thereto great;
> Her hair clotted in a heap;
> In the shoulders she was a yard broad;
> Hanging paps that were an horse's lode;
> And like a barrel she was made;
> And to rehearse the foulness of that lady,
> There is no tongue may tell, sincerely...

The description also recalls the earlier Irish story of Conn of the Hundred Battles, where the hero encounters a woman of hideous appearance who tests his fitness to become king and who turns out to be the Sovereign Goddess of Ireland. Given that these events take place immediately before Sone himself becomes King of Norway, one cannot help but wonder if the author of the romance was not thinking of this ancient theme.[89]

---

89. For a complete breakdown of this theme, see Elizabeth Brewer, *Sir Gawain and the Green Knight*.

❖ ❖ ❖

The words in which the Countess Orvale upbraids Sone for his previous failure to accept Odée are strikingly modern to our ears: he has stolen her heart, used her body—and her money—and now is the time to behave like a gentleman and marry her. As the loathly lady berates the Grail knights in both Chrétien and Wolfram's romances, here she castigates Sone for his failure to respond to his love. But it is the lay sent by Odée and sung by the beautiful musician Papagay that is most persuasive. A solemn and lyrical statement of her love for the hero, it causes the French court to decide that Sone should marry her. Finally admitting his own feelings, he agrees.

Sone now returns to Norway amid great rejoicing—especially on the part of Odée, whose love for him knows no bounds and is finally reciprocated. Their wedding takes place in elaborate splendour on the Island of the Grail, and the couple are joined in the presence of the holy relics. The abbot, who performs the ceremony, now tells them that further festivities have been prepared on a second island that lies nearby. Thither they must go.

The striking variations we have seen between the description of the Grail castle in *Sone* and those found in more familiar texts are not the only surprises this remarkable work has in store for us. As if the author seeks to suggest a mirror-like image of the perfect Island of the Grail, he now presents us with a shocking alternative: the Square Island.

19: The Visit to the Square Island

Sone and the wedding party repair to this other site, apparently in the innocent belief that they are attending a splendid feast. We are told that the island lies just half a league across the sea and that it was built by a pagan king named Tadus. Although the text seems to imply that this figure built the island itself, we can safely assume that the reference is to the huge walls that surround it, which recall the vast walls of the magician Gundebald in the Latin text of *Historia Meriadoci* (see pages 104–5).

Tadus is a curious choice of name. There is a reference in the Gospel of St. Mark to a Culpius Tadus, who was appointed governor of Judea in 797. This may be no more than an accidental parallel as there is a better-known character with this name who, though he plays no significant role in any of the romances, has a son and grandson who do.

The Tadus mentioned in *Sone* is said to have been converted to Christianity and ordered all of his people to be baptized. Later, the island was ruled over by his son Bagdemagus, and after him by Bagdemagus's own son, Meleagant. Bagdemagus is described as a good and clever ruler, but Meleagant as an evil man. Both of these characters have a history in the Arthurian legends.

❖ ❖ ❖

Bagdemagus (Bagdemagu) is first mentioned in *Lancelot, the Knight of the Cart*, written by Chrétien de Troyes around 1175.[90] There he is described as the King of Gore, a mysterious land connected to Arthur's realm by a sword bridge—as is the castle on the Square Island.

The central part of the story is concerned with his son Meleagant's abduction of Arthur's queen, Guinevere, who is later rescued by Lancelot. However, we can immediately see a number of parallels with the Square Island. Galoche, as we have seen, is probably derived from Wales; Gore is a corruption of *goirre* (glass), which gave rise to the name subsequently attached to Avalon, "the Isle of Glass," in the *Life of St. Gildas* by Caradoc of Llancarfan.[91] This gives us a link with the Grail stories that clustered around the little town of Glastonbury in Somerset from the middle of the twelfth century. In Caradoc's work we find a believable account of the abduction of Guinevere by Melwas (an older variant of Meliagrance). Another possible variant of the name—Meloas, lord of the Isle of Glass—appears in Chrétien's *Erec and Enide*.

This adds to a belief that the author of *Sone* was familiar with Chrétien's writings and indeed borrowed from *Le Conte del Graal* for some of the details of the description of the Grail castle—though this, as we shall see, was by no means his only source, and further evidence suggests a common point of origin for both. Certainly, the cluster of names: Melwas, Meleagant, and Meloas, all of them connected with the Glass Island off the coast of Wales (Galoche), point fairly conclusively to the origin of both islands in *Sone*.

Even the presence of a frieze of severed heads, said to be of Meleagant's enemies, which are arranged alongside of the sword bridge recalls a similar palisade bearing its own ghastly decorations, found in Chrétien's romance of *Erec and Enide*. There, as we saw earlier, the episode of the Joy of the Court concerns the winning of the hand of a mysterious woman who sits on a chair within a tent at the heart of a garden surrounded by the palisade decorated by severed heads. The suggestion that this was an earthly or otherworldly paradise will be seen to echo several of the Grail-themed palaces and temples we shall discuss later.

Bagdemagus, Meleagant's father, appears in later romances. In the Lancelot-Grail cycle he is cousin to Gawain and a friend of Lancelot and condemns his son's evil deeds when Lancelot kills Meleagant. In Malory's *Morte d'Arthur* he has become a simple knight of the Round Table and the father/son relationship is dropped when the story of the abduction and rescue of the queen is retold.

---

90. De Troyes, *Arthurian Romances*.

91. *Two Lives of Gildas* by Cradoc of Llancarfan and the Monk of Ruys, trans. H. Williams (Llanerch Press, 1990).

The presence of the word *magus* in the name of Meleagant's father has lead to speculation as to whether he had at some earlier date been seen as a magician. Perhaps the similarity of the setting to that of the magician Gundebald's castle in the romance of *Meriadoc* may have added to the story.

When we look at the description of the Square Island, we can at once see a number of parallels with Celtic myth. Apart from the shape of the island—which may of course refer only to the square palisade built around it—there are other details that suggest the author of *Sone* was tapping into a much older source than the twelfth-century Grail romances. Celtic tradition is full of references to mysterious islands, some of which are said to revolve of their own volition (a detail we shall return to later when we look at a physical source for the Grail castle and temple) and to contain hallows that parallel those of the Grail.

In one of the oldest surviving accounts of a quest for a sacred vessel, the ninth-century poem *Prieddeu Annwn*, attributed to the sixth-century poet Taliesin and almost certainly containing material from a still older period, Arthur and his warriors, in search of a mystical cauldron that can bring the dead back to life, visit a number of islands, some of which are guarded by powerful negative forces. One of these is termed "The Island of the Strong Door," and we are immediately reminded that in *Sone* the Square Island can only be accessed by a single richly carven door.

> Is not my song worthily to be heard
> In the four-square Caer, four times revolving!
> I draw my knowledge from the famous cauldron,
> The breath of nine maidens keeps it boiling.
> Is not the Head of Annwfn's cauldron so shaped?
> Ridged with enamel, rimmed with pearl?
> It will not boil the cowardly traitor's portion.[92]

Here the cauldron, which derives from the underworld in Celtic tradition, replaces the Grail, but the setting may well have inspired the description of the island in *Sone*. The further mention of a fountain at the centre of the island, with a bronze spout from which cool, clear water issues daily, is once again reminiscent of an earthly paradise, though a very different one to the setting of the Grail castle. Such references are links in the chain leading from Eden to the Temples of the Grail, both real and imaginary.

92. *King Arthur's Raid on the Underworld*, trans. Caitlín Matthews (Gothic Image Publications, 2008).

✦ ✦ ✦

In his early book *Celtic Myth and Arthurian Romance*, Roger Sherman Loomis suggested two further possible sources for this episode. The first is found in a Christianised tenth-century text known as *Imram Snedgusa*, one of a type of tale involving a voyage to various islands, mostly with symbolic meanings. Here we find the hero and his companions visiting an island that bears all the signs of having been rewritten from another source.

> And they beheld a great lofty island, and all therein was delightful and hallowed. Good was the King that abode in the island, and he was holy and righteous: and great was his host, and noble was the dwelling of that King, for there were a hundred doors in that house, and an altar at every door, and a priest at every altar offering Christ's body. So the clerics [Snegdus and his crew] entered the house, and each of them [host and guests] blessed the other: and thereafter the whole of that great host, both woman and man, went to communion that the Mass. [93]

We can see at once the parallels between this and the Island of Galoche. Variants of this descriptive pattern are to be found in several immrama, including the more familiar *Voyage of St. Brendan the Navigator*, where the travellers come to an island on which is a monastery. Welcomed by the monks, just as in *Sone*, their feet are washed and they are given marvelously white bread and wonderfully flavored herbs. The abbot tells them that no one knows the origin of this food, save that it comes from God. Every day the twenty-four monks receive twelve loaves, one between each pair, and on Sundays and Feast Days one loaf each. They have lived there for eighty years, yet neither age nor weakness has affected them. [94]

We may see here echoes of older stories, such as the *Voyage of Maelduin*, where the heroes are still pagan and have very different agendas. [95] The description in *Sone*, both of Galoche and the Square Island, not only demonstrate how long-lived such themes can be, they also hint at older themes hidden beneath the glamorous surface of the medieval romance.

The adventures experienced by Sone and his guests now take a darker turn, telling us that all is not well on Square Island. They have barely disembarked when a violent storm blows up, which drives them inland and reduces their ships to matchwood. The palace to which the party now repairs—almost certainly intended to recall the castle of the Grail in the centre of Galoche—is a very different place. To begin with, the abbot of Galoche, who has accompanied the wedding party, puts aside his normal monkish robes and appears dressed in scarlet. This is said to shock many people, but is described as being in line with the custom of the people. The

---

93. "From Cauldron of Plenty to Grail," trans. A. C. L. Brown, *Modern Philology* XIV (1916): 394.

94. Ibid.

95. See the new edition of C. Matthews's *The Celtic Book of the Dead* (Eddison Books, 2018).

abbot, we are told, is also a count. To further emphasize the topsy-turvy nature of the places, the abbot is served first, before the king and queen. We should perhaps note here that the wearing of scarlet in the Middle Ages was reserved for royalty and very high lords, suggesting that the abbot was of extremely high standing in the world he had left behind to become a monk.

The storm is now unleashed, with blasts of lightning, wind that tears down trees and flings them against the walls of the castle, and giant waves that sweep across the island, carrying all before them and full of goods washed out by the waters. Sone and Odée (hitherto referred to simply as the king and queen) climb to the top of the walls, and Sone holds onto his bride with both arms—without which, we are told, she surely would have died.

The whole scene, described in vivid detail by the poet, seems to be telling us that the very presence of the new Grail King is sufficient to cause a vast upheaval in nature. What happens next confirms this. As the storm abates and the waters recede, a terrible stink overwhelms the whole island, causing hearts to stop beating for a moment. So terrible is the smell that a fleet of rescue ships from Galoche, sent to retrieve the wedding party, is forced to turn back. Only the determined hero Gratian presses on, and on reaching the island seeks out the cause of the foulness. What he discovers is an open grave in the cemetery, apparently struck by a bolt of lightning, with the odor exuding from it. Gratian tosses the body into the sea, and the terrible smell begins to recede. As the rescue ships return, Sone, Odée, and the rest of the party are taken back to Galoche, but the old queen, who had been in their party, dies as a result of breathing in the great stink.

We may, perhaps, be seeing memories of the many plagues that had swept across Europe in the years before *Sone* was composed (though nothing like the Black Death, which would wipe out millions in the next century). But here the writer has another agenda, for as the story unfolds we find that the body which had "escaped" from its grave is that of the pagan princess married by Joseph of Arimathea, who had never truly believed in Christ and in fact hated Joseph for killing her father.

This is revealed when Sone and the abbot return to the Square Island to discover the truth of the matter. The abbot reads the inscription in the tomb and all is revealed. Unfortunately, the story changes direction here as Sone and Odée, accompanied by the abbott, set forth on a progress through the kingdom, seeking the promise of fealty from the people. We do not hear any more about the Square Island episode despite the fact that it plays so intriguingly with the earlier imagery of Galoche and its sacred bounty. It is almost as if the author is trying to set up an idea of a negative version of the Grail Temple, a place rank with the smell of death, plagued by storms and lightning—very different from the light-filled Grail Temple visited by Sone earlier.

◆ ◆ ◆

Again, we find both echoes of older Celtic myths of otherworldly islands where nature is often a personification of gods, as well as some intriguing parallels to *Perlesvaus*, suggesting that either both authors were familiar with each other's work or were drawing upon the same sources.

In *Perlesvaus* we initially find Perceval on board a ship that bears him to waters where none of the crew recognizes either stars or sea. Here the hero finds an island crowned with a castle, on which he and the single surviving sailor disembark.

> They ... entered the castle by the gate facing the sea, and there they beheld the most beautiful halls and most beautiful chambers ever seen. They looked beneath a tall tree with branches spreading wide, and saw the clearest and most beautiful fountain that any man could describe; surrounded it was by rich golden columns, and the sand around it seemed to be of precious stones.[96]

Beneath the fountain Perceval encounters two ancient men sitting, their beards whiter than snow but their faces seeming young. As soon as they see Perceval, they rise and bow before him, kissing the shield he carries. They tell him that they had known the knight who bore the shield before him, and that they saw him many times "before the crucifixion." They then reveal that the shield once belonged to Joseph of Arimathea, and Perceval takes it from around his neck and sets it beneath the tree, which is described as "blossoming with the most beautiful flowers in the world."

Perceval now enters a splendid building and sits at the table where a feast is laid.

> One of the masters sounded a gong three times, and into the hall came 33 men, all in one company; they were dressed all in white, and each bore a red cross on his chest; and they all seemed to be 32 years old. Then they went to wash in a rich, golden wash basin, and then sat down at the tables.

As the feast is served, Perceval is watching everything, having by this time learned not to wonder and keep silent.

> And while he was looking he glanced up and saw a golden chain descending, laden with the finest jewels, and from the middle hung a golden crown ... As soon as the masters saw it descend they opened a great wide pit in the middle of the hall; everyone could see the opening quite clearly, and the moment the pit was uncovered, the greatest and most amendable cries ever heard rose up from below ... Perceval heard this grieving and wondered much what it could be, and he saw the golden chain descend to the pit and hang above the opening

---

96. Bryant, *The High Book of the Grail*, 250.

until the meal was almost over. Then it rose up once more into the air and away, and Perceval did not know what had become of it. [97]

His hosts now hurry to cover the pit, and Perceval asks that these mysteries should be explained. He is told this can only happen if he promises to return to the island when he sees a ship with a red cross on its sail. He promises to do this and is told that the crown will be his and that he will rule over the island, which is called the Island of Plenty. If he fails in this, however, he will be sent to the Island of Need, from whence came the cries of those doomed to be there.

When the day comes, much later, Perceval does indeed enter such a ship and is born away, as are the Grail knights in the Lancelot-Grail and *le Morte d'Arthur*, to a place beyond death—perhaps to the Island of Plenty itself.

The enigmatic *Elucidation*, to which we have referred before, also has its place of lamentation. Here the cause is Perceval's failure to ask the all-important questions about the Grail:

> For three hours, three times in the day, there was such lamentation that no man who heard it would be so hardy as not to be frightened. Four censers and four rich candelabra hung at the corners of the bier when the service was done. Then all crying ceased and everyone vanished. The hall that was so great and wide remained empty and frightful, and a stream of blood ran from a vase where the lance stood, through a rich silver tube. [98]

There is much here that would require another book to unpack, but it is worth noting that the island of the Grail in *Sone* and the Island of Plenty in *Perlesvaus* are clearly related, and that the Square Island and the Island of Need are almost certainly the same place. It is probable, given the extremely religious tone of *Perlesvaus*, that the author is making a fairly direct symbolic comparison between the two islands and heaven and purgatory, but the details are so similar that we are once again forced to the conclusion that the authors of *Sone* and *Perlesvaus* were very likely drawing on the same source. There is a sense that the details in *Perlesvaus* complement and even add to our understanding of the mystery in *Sone*; to read both is to better understand either text.

Another possible link is found in the medieval Latin romance *Historia Meriadoci*. [99] Though an exact dating of this work remains uncertain, it was almost certainly composed in the first

---

97. Bryant, *The High Book of the Grail*, 251.
98. We may notice the presence of the rich silver tube, not unlike the copper tube described in *Sone*. The translation is from lines 261–76 of the *Elucidation* by Matthews et. al. from *The Lost Book of the Grail*.
99. Day, *Meriadoc, King of Cambria*.

half of the twelfth century, making it possibly earlier than Chrétien's *Conte del Graal*. Essentially, it is a dynastic story in which the hero fights to recover his lands, which had been usurped by another man. The important parts of the story relate to two buildings, described in vivid detail, which include the setting of the Grail castle.

The first of these is a splendid palace built of marble and porphyry, with "carved and painted pillars. Lofty paneled ceilings, and inlaid flooring—a deep moat and high wall encircling it all." This beautiful building appears as if from nowhere in a plain where Meriadoc himself had been hunting only a few days earlier. Within it, at the top of a great porphyry staircase, is a hall ruled over by a mysterious lady who calls Meriadoc by name. She is surrounded by a rich court, including men who play chess and call upon her for blessings at all times. She is thus revealed as the goddess Fortuna, whose interest in Meriadoc charts the course of his subsequent life. It is notable that Fortuna watches over three kingdoms: Cambria (Wales), Albany (Scotland), and Logres (Britain), whose rulers she chooses by lot. This may remind us of the choosing of the Grail families, either by the sacred vessel itself or those who watch over it. There are also clear analogies to the Joy of the Court episode from Chrétien's *Erec and Enide*. In a passage that can only recall the scene in *Le Conte del Graal* where Perceval first finds his way to the castle of the Fisher King, Meriadoc and his companions are invited to a splendid banquet where everyone maintains utter silence. In the end Meriadoc breaks the silence by asking the name of the lady.

As a result of this reversal of the normal Grail question, all hell breaks loose and Meriadoc and his friends must flee into a dark forest where they encounter a second castle every bit as splendid as the one belonging to Fortuna but in this instance owned by the villain of the piece, the magician Gundebald, who lives in a wasteland of mud, tar, and bitumen, known as The-Land-From-Which-No-One-Returns. There, within a fortress that is exactly square, divided in four by specially built roads, Gundebald has his palace—an elaborate affair watered by streams diverted from the surrounding hills and planted with splendid fruit trees. The description here perhaps resembles more the setting for the Throne of Solomon, which we shall examine in depth in chapter 7, while the division of the castle into four parts resembles the design imposed on the forts and cities of the Roman Empire. The existence of two buildings, one bright, the other dark, recalls the two islands in *Sone*, while the resemblance of the story to the Grail myth shows that traditions predating the Grail romances were still active in the memories of the writers who compiled them.[100]

---

100. See M. L. Day, "The Goddess Fortuna as Mistress of Destiny in *Historia Meriadoci*" (unpublished paper).

✦ ✦ ✦

As noted earlier, the story of Sone de Nansay rather peters out here, at least in terms of the Grail story. There is, in fact, a huge tract of story still to go, narrating Sone's further adventures, his growing family, and his battles against the Saracens. Finally, in section 30 of the poem, Sone begins to feel his death approaching. Journeying to Rome, where one of his sons, Milon, is now pope, he crowns his other sons and divides his goods (along with his personal qualities as a knight and king) between the surviving members of his family.

> To Houdiant he gave the sacred vessel, the sword of Joseph of Arimathea, and his reason; to Henri his valor and the sword of Brudon; Margon received his oliphant, his carbuncle, his charm and his courtesy, and Flori, his warhorse. Finally, to Milon the favour that was always his own, to be ever regarded with affection.

We must assume that the Cup is the Grail, and that, for this time, Houdiant becomes its new guardian. Sone now prepares for death. He is absolved of his sins by his son, the pope, and all things are made straight. He dies holding the wood of the True Cross in his arms, followed almost immediately by his faithful Odée. They are buried side by side in a copper coffin in front of the high altar of St. Peter's in Rome. Sone's son Henri becomes emperor, and the romance ends on a note of quiet resolve.

In all of the texts examined here, we find again and again descriptions of the home of the Grail following a broadly similar form. In each case there are details drawn from descriptions of the earthy paradise, while the establishment and maintenance of a lineage of Grail guardians, beginning with Joseph of Arimathea, is strikingly similar. *Sone de Nansay* is the first to place many of these themes together, drawing upon the writings of Chrétien and Robert de Boron and upon possibly older documents known to all three authors.

We now turn to the second major romance that, like *Sone*, has been largely neglected but that adds significantly to our understanding not only of the Grail itself but of its ever-blossoming temple.

✦ ✦ ✦

4

THE GREAT TEMPLE

When I received the Grail, by the authority of a holy angel,
splendid in his power, I found instructions written upon it.
This gift was never held by human hands before mine.

✦ ✦ ✦

Wolfram von Eschenbach, *Titurel 1:6*

The second of our two neglected (and for the most part untranslated) texts is *Der Jüngere Titurel* ("The Later Titurel"[101]) attributed to Albrecht von Scharfenberg.[102] Composed in the late thirteenth century, circa 1270—and thus at almost exactly the same time as *Sone de Nansay*—it adds a number of important details both to the creation of an earthly home for the sacred relic and to the growing family of Grail guardians.

The poet seems to have written two other romances, *Seifrid de Ardemont* and *Merlin*, which are no longer extant. Linguistic evidence suggests he may have been from Bavaria and worked in Thuringia or elsewhere in northern Germany. *Der Jüngere Titurel* survives in eleven complete manuscripts and about fifty fragments.

The exact identity of Albrecht remains in question, despite the fact that he is routinely described as "von Scharfenberg." Recent scholars have cast doubt on this. The leading expert on the text, Charles E. Passage, sums up his character as devout and "marked with an excessive

---

101. Despite the fact that *jüngere* means "younger" in German, the translation of the title as "later" refers to the context in which Albrecht's work is seen as following Wolfram's uncompleted poem.

102. Possibly another Albrecht according to recent evidence, though the author continues to be cited as von Scharfenburg, which we shall use here.

✦ ✦ ✦

concern with cult objects and religious symbolism."[103] Werner Wolf, the first editor of the poem, believes that Albrecht may have become a churchman in later life; while this is not impossible, Passage's summing up of the poem seems to suggest otherwise:

> His poem gives the effect of a very long saint's legend, where stasis and colour are primary principles and where a dreamy, if wholly sincere, religiosity is the prevailing quality. Albrecht's mournful sense of the transitoriness of all earthly things dominates the total work.[104]

The poem is in fact a patchwork, based in part on Wolfram von Eschenbach's works, including both *Parzifal* and the fragmentary poem of *Titurel*. The opening, a lengthy prayer in which Albrecht professes his faith, is based in part on the opening of Wolfram's non-Arthurian poem *Wilihalm*. Albrecht then adds some 6,300 lines to Wolfram's *Titurel*, building on the love story of Sigune and Schionatulander found in his *Parzifal*.[105]

Wolfram's original poem seems to represent his intention to write a prehistory of the Grail, but in the end he only managed approximately 170 stanzas (some of which are not definitively by him) that told the life of Schionatulander, the knight loved by Sigune, who is already dead in her arms in *Parzifal*. Possibly Wolfram intended this to be a more secular romance, balancing the spiritual intensity of his other work.

As with Chrétien's unfinished *Perceval*, the existence of an unfinished poem by the great Wolfram von Eschenbach (the fragmentary *Titurel*) generated a vastly extended completion by Albrecht, who pretended to *be* Wolfram until almost the very end of his romance. He was definitely a lesser poet, though able to handle extremely difficult verse forms, but his imagination was much less distinctive than Wolfram's.

The complexity, length, and often-impenetrable style of the work (circa 600,000 lines in length) have largely relegated *The Later Titurel* to the ranks of forgotten texts, but a careful examination shows that, like *Sone*, it includes much that is important to an understanding of the Grail myth.

The structure of the poem—or perhaps *poems* would be a better description—is in roughly three parts. The first relates the history of the titular hero and of his family and its association with the Grail (roughly verses 77–475). The second, and longest, portion tells the story of

---

103. Passage, *Titurel: Wolfram of Eschenbach, Translation and Studies*.

104. Passage, *Titurel*.

105. These are the same pair as the damsel cradling the dead body of her lover in Chrétien's poem of the Grail.

Schionatulander and Sigune (verses 476–5963), which expands on the references found in Wolfram's *Parzifal*. The third part deals with the later history of the Grail and, in fact, continues from the end of part one in such a way that if part two was removed, it could be read as a single work. Given that the story of Schionatulander and Sigune also stands alone, there is a possibility that the work was originally two poems that were combined, either by the original poet or by a later scribe. Here we shall concentrate primarily on the opening and closing sections, along with a new version of the description of the Grail Temple in English.

◆ ◆ ◆

From the outset, as noted, Albrecht does not identify himself but pretends to be Wolfram until near the end of the poem. He makes it clear that he intends to explore and extend material from *Parzifal* and indeed incorporates much from the fragmentary poem of *Titurel*, actually composed by Wolfram circa 1217. In verse 77 he says:

> *He of Provence that through Flegetanis spoke,*
> *Told much of the Grail in both Arabic and French.*
> *These I shall relate here, if God permits, in German,*
> *What Parzifal conceals will be brought forth*
> *without need of torchlight.*

According to *Parzifal*, Flegetanis was the name given to the Arabic astronomer who is described as being the first to read the mystery of the Grail in the stars, and who wrote of it in a book that was later discovered by a poet named Kyot of Provence, whose work formed the basic source of Wolfram's epic. Albrecht, writing as Wolfram, suggests that he will reveal things that were left out or concealed—bringing these to light without the need of torches!

In the verses that follow, Albrecht tells us about Titurel's origins, tracing his family back to Troy and through Aeneas to Rome. He tells us that the hero's great-grandfather who ruled over Cappadocia was called Senabor.[106] His son, Titurel's grandfather, is named Barillus, apparently from the sea-green precious stone called beryl. Together with his brothers Sabilor and Assibor, he becomes a Christian, and soon after the three brothers are summoned to Rome by the emperor Vespasian and given three princesses to marry. With this marriage comes the gift of rule over three areas. Barillus gets France, Sabilor Anjou, and Assibor Cornwall. Barillus's wife

---

106. A possible anagram of Porsenna, the Roman hero Lars Porsenna (Passage, *Titurel*, 41).

◆ ◆ ◆

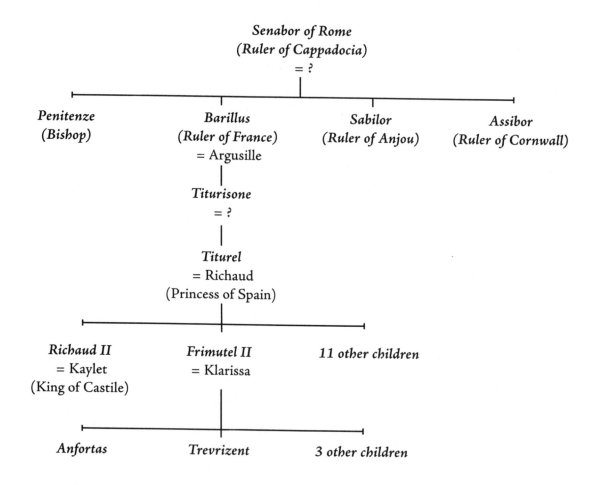

Figure 2 ◆ Titurel's Family Tree

◆ ◆ ◆

is actually the emperor's daughter, Argusille, who bears him a son whom they name Titurisone.[107] It is he who is the father of Titurel.

When the child is born, an angel announces his coming and says that his name will be a blending of his parents' names: "Titur" and "el." As he grew to manhood, he learned many skills: reading, the ways of chivalry, love for God (gifts shared, we may remember, by Sone). But his mother did her best to prevent him having any knowledge of human love, rather as Perceval's mother hides all knowledge of chivalry in Chrétien's *Conte du Graal*. At an early stage in his development, one of Titurel's tutors explains the difference between human and divine love, and Titurel chooses to follow a path of chastity. On reaching manhood, he and his father ally themselves with the Carolingians and undertake to bring war to all heathens. (This once again mirrors the later career of Sone, who wages war on the Saracens and is compared to the Carolingian king Charlemagne.) When Titurisone finally dies, Titurel takes on this task alone until the age of fifty (though he still looked no more than thirty), when his life changed forever by the appearance of another angel who instructed him to build a temple for the Grail.

Appointed as guardian of the Grail at the age of fifty, Titurel remained in office for 400 years and lived on for a further fifty after that, dying at the age of 500. It is clear that he should be identified with the old king in the side chamber who is fed by the Grail in most versions of the story.

As Wolfram had written, proximity to the Grail could preserve the life of anyone close to it. This is interesting for a particular reason: if Wolfram scholar Charles E. Passage is correct in his calculations[108] dating the birth of Titurisone to some time in the first century AD, his death would have been in the sixth century, making him a contemporary of the "historical" Arthur. Whether Albrecht was aware of this time frame we cannot say with any certainty, but the timing is remarkably close to the period when Arthur is believed to have lived.

The end of the first part of the poem, from verses 416–475, describes the building of a temple for the sacred relic, as translated below. At this point the Grail still hovered over the building. Hitherto the vessel had not been touched by human hands, but with the completion of the building, "on the Mountain of Muntsalvasche in the kingdom of Salvaterre," an angel places it in a tabernacle created for it within the temple, and fresh writing appeared upon the sacred relic, indicating that Titurel (hitherto chaste) should marry Richaud, the daughter of

---

107. It is interesting—though probably no more than a coincidence—that the last part of this name is "sone." The beginning of Titurisone's name, intriguingly, echoes that of Vespasian's actual son, Titus, whom ruled over Rome from AD 79–81.

108. Passage, *Titurel*.

✦ ✦ ✦

the recently deceased Spanish king Frimutel. The lady was brought to the site of the temple, and following their wedding the couple "knew great joy." Richaud bore Titurel twelve children before she unexpectedly died "in her youth"—making her another long-lived member of the Grail family. Of the twelve, only two are named: Richaud II, named after her mother, and Frimutel II, named after his maternal grandfather.

Continuing this fascinating family tree, Albrecht next tells us that Richaud II marries Kaylet, King of Castile, and Frimutel marries Klarissa, daughter of a converted heathen king named Granat de Grosie. Of the five children issuing from this marriage, only two are named—both familiar to the story of the Grail: Anfortas, who becomes the wounded Grail king in *Parzifal*, and Trevrizent, the huntsman-turned-hermit who also plays a leading role in Wolfram's epic as an advisor and interpreter of the Grail mysteries. As in the narrative of *Sone*, the Grail king founds a dynasty whose continuing task is to guard the Grail.

Titurel, we are told, is still alive and sees all his grandchildren, but all is not well in the kingdom of the Grail. Rivalry for possession of the sacred object has broken out amongst the company in the land of Salvaterre. Albrecht says that the West (or possibly the Western Church) has become so sinful that the Grail should no longer be housed there. Not all the company agree, however, and in the end, when fervent prayers prove fruitless, the company divides, taking the real Grail to a new home in the East, while a copy is taken to Constantinople.

At this point, Albrecht paraphrases the beginning of Wolfram's fragmentary poem of *Titurel* in which he seeks to resign from his long custodianship of the Grail in favour of his son Frimutel. We then move to the long central section concerning Schionatulander and Sigune.

The entire middle part of the work—perhaps, as suggested above, once intended to be a separate poem—takes up the next 5,487 verses. Most of this falls outside the scope of this book, so we shall move on to the third and final part, occupying verses 5964–6207. As noted, this seamlessly continues the account begun in part one, returning to a description of internecine strife within the Grail kingdom. This turns out to be another site—one that extends the history of the Grail Temple both forward and back in history.

The Vision of Titurel

Given the extreme complexity, and at times extreme confusion, of *The Later Titurel*, perhaps it is not surprising that despite references in various explorations of the Grail romances, no one has attempted a full translation of the poem nor, until recently, of its most fascinating and intriguing section, which describes the creation of a home for the Grail—a temple built as the result of a collaboration between God and man.

✦ ✦ ✦

Previously, a partial translation by John and Doris Meeks[109] chose to reorganize the structure of the text to make it read more smoothly, thus rendering it useless for students of the work. The more recent translation by Cyril Edwards[110] (renowned for his work on Wolfram's *Parzifal*) is certainly more accurate but at times equally confusing. Albrecht seemed determined to put in every detail of the building of the Grail Temple, but with a randomness that is often confusing. Lists of precious stones used to decorate the walls and detailed descriptions of carvings and high-flying angels are scattered throughout, and many are prolix and often confusingly repetitive.

The frequent complexity and the obscurity of the text is in part the result of a style of verse known as *ornatus difficilis* (ornate and difficult), which caused authors to write in language little short of nonsensical in order to show off their verbal skills and ability to use complicated internal rhyme schemes. Albrecht frequently uses words of his own devising, especially in naming the many precious stones with which the Grail Temple is decorated. Even the very able translators of the most recent edition of the Grail Temple section admit that some of their work is speculative.[111]

The same is true of this version, in which we have tried to find the inner meaning of the work rather than following its exact wording slavishly. We had access to both the previous translations, as well as to the 1995 edition by Werner Wolf, and whilst we resisted the temptation to reorganize the text to make more sense of it, we opted to clarify the meaning wherever necessary. Thus, for example, where Albrecht used the word "choir" we have opted for "chapel," since this is evidently the intended meaning. Elsewhere, we have smoothed out the occasional awkwardness in the text while retaining the meaning as close to the original as possible. The text featured here, prepared by John Matthews, is better classed as a version rather than an exact translation, though it is hoped that it accurately preserves the original.

109. Meeks, "The Temple of the Grail."
110. Barber and Edwards, "The Grail Temple in Der Jüngere Titurel."
111. Ibid.

✦ ✦ ✦

DER JÜNGERE TITUREL
by Albrecht [von Scharfenburg];
text prepared by John Matthews

The Temple of the Grail
(VERSES 329–439)

When he was fifty years of age, an angel emerged from the Grail and spoke to Titurel. It made known to him that all of his life from this point should be devoted to its service. With celestial music the angel guided him through a deep and seemingly impenetrable wilderness—the Forest Salvasch in the land of Salvaterre—which contained many exotic plants and trees. Amongst these were cypress, cedar, almond, myrrh, and aspind—the very tree from which Noah built the Ark.[112]

Many strange birds inhabited the forest, filling it with song, and many precious stones were buried in the earth of that place. At the heart of the forest rose a mountain named Muntsalvasche, concealed from fallen man—both Christian, Jew, and Pagan—for all time. The mountain and all that were upon it were protected from all evils. There Titurel found gathered builders from all nations of the world, who had been led to this place in order that he might carry out a task.

The Grail hovered over the mountain, held by angelic hands. All could see it who were worthy. First a wall was built around the mountain, then Titurel built a fair castle, so mighty that not even all the armies of the world could make it yield even so much as a loaf of bread, though they laid siege to it for as long as thirty years. From here he emerged to do battle with the pagans, driving them back beyond the borders of Salvaterre.

Here Titurel resolved to build a temple to house the Grail, which still hovered above the mountain. No wood was to be used except for the seating, where aloe wood alone was used; all else was constructed of pure gold and precious stones that brought warmth in winter and coolness in summer. Titurel sought counsel from those learned in the virtues of such stones, as they had once been taught by Pythagoras and Hercules. Thus he learned of the firestone known as abestus,[113]

---

112. Though aspind may possibly be a reference to aspen, this is in any case different to the wood traditionally used to build the Ark—gopher wood, which itself remains of uncertain meaning.

113. Asbestos.

which sends forth constant fire; also the water-stone elitropia,[114] which has healing properties and is good against lies, deception, and poison. These he chose to be the basic materials of the temple. Dishonor and poverty were not permitted to enter there, for the Virgin and her Son were worshipped and adored to such a high degree as king and queen over all creation. To them Titurel was most grateful.

To begin with, Titurel cleared the plants and grass that covered the top of the mountain. Underneath was a block of pure onyx, projecting thirty feet around the temple. Titurel ordered the onyx to be polished until it shone like the moon. Then, as he was contemplating the best design for the temple, he received guidance from the Grail. There, on the polished stone, he found a ground plan drawn that told him the exact dimensions the building should take. The dimensions were such that the building should resemble the palace of Prester John.[115]

The temple was based upon a rotunda, wide and high, around which were twenty-two chapels[116] of octagonal shape. The vaulting of the building rested upon pillars of bronze,[117] while the interior, lined with precious stones, shone forth in a multitude of colours.

Arches rose to meet sweeping buttresses, intricately carved with elaborate designs, decorated with pearl and coral. High above the pillars were seen the forms of angels, so beautifully carved and cast that anyone who saw them would have believed them to be real. Amongst them were many statues of our Lady, and beside them crucifixes crafted to the finest degree, with no thought for cost.

Though I have not the knowledge to judge such things, I am obliged to continue my description. The altars were richly adorned in God's honour, and they were true masterpieces. Richly decorated reliquaries rested upon them, along with many precious images, and above all a great ciborium[118] ornate with images of the saints.

114. Heliotrope.

115. This reference to Prester John, a famous guardian of the Grail, appears only in one MS: "H." As we shall see, this is developed still further at the end of poem and provides an important link to the sighting of the possible model for the Grail Temple (see chapter 7).

116. Or seventy-two in certain manuscripts. Twenty-two seems more likely within this context, as seventy-two would have been impossible to realise at the time. See plate 1 for a full projection of the Grail Temple based on the description in Der Jüngerer Titurel (after Sulpiz Boisserée).

117. As in the description contained in the Conte del Graal.

118. An ornate canopy suspended from four pillars and used to house the sacred bread of the Eucharist. As we shall see, this is mirrored in a later depiction of the Grail Temple (see chapter 7).

◆ ◆ ◆

Rich sapphires adorned every altar. They were chosen because they possess the ability to drive out sins. There are three kinds of this jewel, and only the best was used in the temple.

Curtains of green velvet hung above the altar, and when the priest sang the Mass, a cord could be pulled that caused a dove and an angel to fly down from the arch above. When they met it was as if the angel flew forth from paradise and met with the Holy Ghost, to the great honour and solace of all Christians.

The windows were not of conventional glass but from transparent crystal, which focused the light so brightly that it could have blinded a casual viewer. Inlay there was in plenty, designed to diffuse the brightness so that the lavishness of the temple and the Grail could be best appreciated.

Master carvers decorated everything with rich stones of many colours. Sapphire gave the colour of azure, emerald a clear green, while other stones gave yellow, red, brown, and white. The amethyst gave three shades of colour: purple, violet (which offers a cure for sickness), and rose, bright and clear. Topaz was there also, giving two shades—yellow and golden. Anyone who saw it felt strengthened.

The garnet hyacinth gave forth the colour of fire, while sardonyx shone white; an equivalent stone was found for all the colours of the paintbox. The mighty jasper gave forth no less than seventeen different shades and was much prized therefore. Amongst others it gave forth black, which offered great contrast to the other stones. Radiance came also from chrysolite.

Other stones—chalcophanus, ruby, cornelian, chrophrase, diparasme—were dizzyingly bright, while as many as sixty shades were attributed to exakovasien, octalamus, karisian, ardisen—all beyond my ability to praise.[119]

Pearls and coral were inlaid all over the windows also, and the sun picked out each colour of these and of all the stones, creating a dazzling display throughout the temple.

As for the roof, that was of red-gold overlaid with niello work. This stopped the brilliantly reflected light from blinding those who entered there. The work was carried out with masterly skill.

God was so pleased with Titurel that he gave him guidance and aid equal to that of Solomon when he built the Templum Domini in Jerusalem. There the stones themselves came directly from God. They were already cut so that the people of Jerusalem did not have to be disturbed by the sound of hammering and chisels. Thus were Solomon's labours graced by God.

---

119. Many of these jewels remain unidentified. Their names may have been invented by Albrecht.

+ + +

From heaven itself God feeds the world. Whoever follows him shall find his way to paradise. Any man who keeps his soul pure and does not give in to the desires of the flesh, God will reward.

The work [on the temple] was so great that it could never be finished [by human hands alone]. Therefore the Grail sent the king a message in writing: Whatever he needed would come to him from the Grail—including every requirement of the master builder.

The company of the Grail gave thanks and praise to God for the help thus proffered; no wonder the work proceeded apace!

The brilliance of the windows was not truly needed, so great were the lights of the many stones. Their light was reflected from the gold a hundred times, making their brightness almost too much to bear.

The chapels within the temple had sheltered seating. The cost of this was never considered, so great was God's help. For this reason the building was the finest in the entire world, having no equal anywhere.

The great vaults of the building were covered with sapphires, amongst which the light of carbuncles shone like stars. Their brilliance was indeed as bright as the heavenly bodies themselves and gladdened the hearts of anyone who was troubled by sorrow.

The brilliance did not end there. Both the sun and the moon were modeled in silver and gold. In addition, clocks were made with subtle and extraordinary mechanisms that showed the passage of time. Golden bells announced the seven canonical hours.

Four mighty winged statues of the evangelists were cast in gold, their wings stretched wide. They were designed with one purpose—to make all that saw them think of the Throne of Heaven and to forget all earthly pursuits.

There were no paintings, as these were considered trivial compared to the likenesses carved in stone and decorated with precious stones.

The altars in the chapels were oriented towards the Orient. The chapel which faced the Orient was the largest of all, twice as big as the others, and dedicated to the Holy Ghost, who was the patron of the whole temple. Next to this was a chapel dedicated to the Virgin, the mother, and the Child, who hold both Heaven and Earth in their hands. The third chapel was named for St. John, while the remainder of the disciples had their own chapels close by.

In the middle of the temple was a magnificent edifice, a miniature copy of the temple. This edifice was completed in thirty years, and there was a single altar in this smaller temple. It was reserved for the Grail. Here the Grail was kept every day, and when it was raised on high a sacristy was revealed beneath it.

◆ ◆ ◆

There were three entrances [to the temple]. One faced towards the Meridian,[120] the second to the Occident,[121] the third to Aquilon,[122] from which an ill wind blew.

The great hall faced the Meridian. It had many entrances with graceful steps leading within. The portals were made of red-gold, decorated with precious stones, and bolted by elaborate locks. In front of each portal were examples of the precious stones that decorated it, each having a description that described its name and nature.

Such great work was carried out on the portals that it is beyond my skill to describe. So many wonders were accomplished, how might I describe them?

Above the gates facing the Occident was placed on organ with such a clear tone that all wished to hear it. It was played on every feast day, as is the custom in Christendom.

A tree of red-gold, covered in elegant foliage, branches, and twigs, was also created. Birds were set upon this, and a bellows sent breath through them, causing them to make sounds in close imitation of their natural songs, some higher, others lower, depending on which keys the operator pressed. On the ends of four of the branches were angels, each one holding a trumpet that they blew loudly, while with their other hand they appeared to beckon all who saw them, as if to say: "Arise, those who are dead!"

In this same place was a carving of the Last Judgment, intended to remind everyone that after sweetness may come bitterness, so that no matter how happy one may be, one should ever think also that sorrow may come after.

Two great doors led into each chapel. Within each stood an altar, above which were vaulted chantries supported upon thin columns forming a circle of almost six feet. All the doors giving admittance to the chapels had railings of gold fastened with clasps, so that all who attended might have the best view.

The walls of each chapel were richly ornamented, with great newels and arches rising above them. Here there were golden trees on whose branches sat [more] birds. Even those who were normally at odds with each other were seen to have settled their differences.

Whatever the human mind could imagine was created. Carved vines curled up around the arches, bending over the seats on either side, each six feet tall. Below them a wood was created, and roses bloomed amid the leaves, bushes, and boughs,

120. The South.
121. The West.
122. The North. Winds from this quarter traditionally brought bad luck and danger.

✦ ✦ ✦

bearing red and white blossoms on green stems. Other flowers of many colours, of every conceivable plant, were there also, seeming as real as possible.

These vines were made of pure gold, painted green and decorated with emeralds. They offered shade to those who were seated beneath. The leaves hung thickly and could be heard rustling as if in a real wood, accompanied by the sound of bells as if a great flock of falcons rose into the air with their bells chiming.

The vines were full of angels, as though brought thither from paradise. They moved with the rustling of the leaves as if they were alive. The lights of the sacred chapels were ornamented with great beauty, again in the likeness of vines, with angels above them. A bellows caused wind to circulate there.

Music there was aplenty, whenever was required. A wise master had but to give direction and the clergy would sing sweetly, sounding like angels—wordless melodies filled with beauty. So much joy was felt by all, that all gave thanks to God and beat their breasts, crying: "God, our Father, what must heaven be like since you have given us such glory here below?"

Were there crypts in the temple? No. For pure ones should have no truck with those false beings that live under the earth or gather in crypts! Christian faith and love should only be proclaimed in light.

There were crystals small and large, gold and black, which hung next to two vessels of balsam that seemed to burn as if with bright fire. Six of these hung in every chapel. Higher still, angels hung on golden wires, so thin as to seem invisible. The angels appeared to be holding the lights that shone down into the temple. This was costly work.

According to custom, many of the carved angels around the walls held candles. Though there was plenty of balsam, the company did not wish to dispense with candles. Thus there were numerous golden candelabra hanging there. One angel, more than six feet high in the air, held a candle in each hand, so that it seemed as if the light would be carried right up into the sky itself. None knew these were hung from golden wires.

Whatever voice was heard in the temple, the effect of the gems were such that an echo filled the space, giving it a sweet tone, as that made by young birds in Maytime. The altars were lit at all times by two vessels of balsam. Only during the divine office were the candles lit.

I cannot begin to do justice to such richness of adornment as was to be seen there. Nowhere was there as much as six feet, inside and out, that was not decorated with mouldings, engravings, and painted to the greatest artistic quality.

Though it cost them nothing (being the gift of God), it was greatly to be praised. Even as the company took council as to how they might give thanks to

+ + +

God and the Grail, they were once again relieved of such concerns [as all was provided].

The pulpits [within the temple] were intricately carved with newels and turrets, and in every niche there were renderings of apostles, confessors, virgins, patriarchs, martyrs, and prophets. Powerful quotations were carved upon their pedestals. Alongside these were carved people of great sanctity and those who received the charity of he who wears the crown in heaven. Beautiful maidens with garlands of gold were just as wondrous to behold.

The arches, both small and large, supported by flying buttresses, met in the centre, converging from four directions, and wherever their shape left angled corners, there were angels and evangelists carved in plenty.

At the very centre was an emerald, cylindrical in shape, with the Lamb of God carved above it, holding a cross in one paw and a banner of red in the other. This was the sign of the eternal defeat of Lucifer and of our salvation.

On the outer walls were many carvings of the dangers encountered by the Templars in their everyday journeys into the world, showing how they fought in the name of the Grail, protecting it against evil.

[Also outside, where] the shape of the chapels rose up in great curves, all was decorated with vines, leaves, and curious creatures such as dwarves and sea monsters. Such things caused many who saw them to smile.

Between these, all along the walls, were even more wonderful carvings. My neighbour would run out of food before he could walk around the building and see all there was to see.

When the chapels had reached their full height, Titurel had six-storey-high belfries constructed on every second chapel. These were as strong as the enormous temple, forming a garland in stone in honour of the Grail. More costly than even ten kings could afford, nothing was omitted in the cause of splendour.

Eight sides there were to the temple, as to every chapel, with as many corners, all richly carved. There were no low mouldings and the work was perfect. If anyone does not believe me, they can have never felt the power of great artistry—endued expense.

Each storey had three windows carved with spindles of bradem.[123] If one raised one's eyes to the heavens, one could only marvel at the craftsmanship. At the crown of every window was a ball carved from ruby that seemed to burn with fierce fire. Above these were mighty crosses carved from crystal white as snow.

123. Possibly *brasime*, which is used elsewhere to describe a green mineral. Barber and Edwards, "The Grail Temple in Der Jüngere Titurel."

◆ ◆ ◆

They warded off all attacks of the Devil, checkmating his wiles. All of the court was thus protected from sin.

Soldered onto every one of these crosses was a golden eagle. From a distance, due to the transparency of the cross, it seemed that the eagles were hovering over the temple.

A single great tower rose from the centre of the temple, crafted in pure gold inlaid with thousands of bright stones. These decorated the whole tower, which was twice as tall as the rest.

At the very summit of this tower was a huge carbuncle, its radiance bright enough to lighten the darkness. If the Templars found themselves still outside when night fell, they could always find their way back to the temple by seeking this light.

All around the carbuncle were many more precious stones. Let no one speak of seven stars—here there were thousands: red, yellow, green dark and light, white, brown, and blue. All who sought the temple were cheered by their radiance—and by the light of the Grail itself. If any knight was vanquished, it could only be because of sin.

Above all other sounds in beauty is the plangent note of the harp string. Yet even this paled beside the sweet tone of two bells cast from arzibiere[124] with clappers of gold.

One of these served the temple only, and the other called the company to meetings or to be acknowledged for their battles. They desired nothing more than this but followed the monastic law in honour of the Grail.

Beneath the surface of the onyx floor, fish and other wonders of the ocean were carved in exact likeness. Pipes brought air to them from outside, causing them to move beneath the crystals that covered the floor. From some distance outside, windmills provided the power for this illusion of movement.

The floor thus had the appearance of a lake of rippling water covered in ice. Within it one could see fish, animals, and sea monsters that seemed to fight amongst themselves. Here the Bishop Penitenze, one of the brothers of Barilus,[125] greatly honoured by the French and those of many other kingdoms, consecrated the temple and its many altars.

124. Another unknown substance, presumably metallic.

125. Titurel's grandfather, related to both Pelleas and Parzifal. One thinks the bishop is clearly a penitent!

❖ ❖ ❖

The Home of the Grail

There is much here which adds to an understanding of the Grail Temple. The narrative reads as if Albrecht is describing an actual building, as he may well have been. He is breathless with excitement and continually tells us he does not have the words to describe the wonder of what he sees. The apparent repetitions within the poem also suggest someone walking around the great building exclaiming over everything he sees. There are great human touches, such as the reference to the neighbour who would run out of food before he had seen all there was to see. As we shall see, it may well be the case that Albrecht either visited the site of such an extraordinary temple or had talked to someone who had.

The description of the temple itself reads as an elaborate allegory for the struggles (and rewards) of the spiritual journey through life. Symbolism is rife, mostly taken from scriptural and theological readings destined to sound a familiar note in the poem's listeners or readers. Once again, as did the author of *Sone*, Albrecht provides an elaborate genealogy for his Grail family.

Albrecht says that he will not describe the Great Hall of the building because "we" have heard about it in *Parzifal*; but this was perhaps merely part of the continuing plan to keep his listeners thinking this is actually Wolfram speaking. He follows Wolfram also in sighting the temple on the mountain of Muntsalvasche, usually translated as Mountain of Salvation. Albrecht himself used a curious archaic word to gloss the meaning of the site as he saw it: *bhaltenunge*. This is not an easy word to translate, but according to Passage, in English it would have the sense of "preservation," "maintenance," "protection," and even "the keeping of a secret."[126]

Albrecht's statement, with which we began this book, makes it clear that his intention was to show how the mysteries of the temple could be experienced through his writing:

> I have made the temple worthy of Christians, so that they may learn by studying its shape and design (v. 516.2).

The same is true of the statement that all who follow the Grail shall reach paradise. This phrase may be seen as a common enough idea at the time, but in the context of *The Later Titurel* it is much more than that, adding to the idea that the land of Salvaterre is itself a kind of earthly paradise.

---

126. Passage, *Titurel*, 53–54.

This is entirely in line with the purpose of all the Grail Temples, chapels, and castles discussed here, going back to Solomon's Temple and its Holy of Holies. By studying the shape and form of the buildings, we learn the secrets of the Grail.

The Templum Dominum

Almost the first thing we come across in the description is a comparison with Solomon's Temple, still the first point of reference for medieval travellers—or, indeed, for a writer who may never have left his birthplace.

> God was so pleased with Titurel that he gave him guidance and aid equal to that of Solomon when he built the Templum Domini in Jerusalem. There the stones themselves came directly from God. They were already cut so that the people of Jerusalem did not have to be disturbed by the sound of hammering and chisels. Thus were Solomon's labours graced by God.

Solomon, of course, had the mysterious *shamir*, insects that were able to cut and shape stones, gems, and ivory; in this instance the Grail itself is proactive. It directs the building of its own temple via written messages, plans sketched out on the mountaintop, and it supplies workers and building materials from which the temple itself can be constructed. It even organizes the marriage of Titurel and Richaud, thus setting up a new lineage of guardians for the future.

The description of the mountain of Muntsalvasche bears a striking resemblance to the mountain described in later alchemical writings, in particular those of Thomas Vaughn (1621–1666). Although these were not written until long after *The Later Titurel*, the information, which in many instances derives from more antique sources, gives us a glimpse into the symbolic reality of the Mountain of Salvation as it continued to be understood throughout the ages.

In Vaughn's highly allegorical work *The Holy Mountain*, we find the following description:

> There is a mountain situated in the midst of the earth or centre of the world, which is both small and great. It is soft, yet also above measure hard and stony. It is far off and near at hand, but by the providence of God, invisible. In it are hidden the most ample treasures, which the world is not able to value. This mountain—by envy of the devil, who always opposes the glory of God and the happiness of man—is compassed about with very cruel beasts and ravening birds—which make the way thither both difficult and dangerous.[127]

127. Allen, *A Christian Rosecreutz Anthology*.

Vaughn makes it clear that if one succeeds in facing these perils, in recognising that the mountain is not just a mountain and the treasure not just a treasure, the result will be of lasting effect:

> The most important thing [on the Mountain] and the most powerful, is a certain exalted Tincture, with which the world—if it served God and were worthy of such gifts—might be touched and turned into most pure gold. This Tincture...will make you young when you are old, and you will perceive no disease in any part of your bodies. [128]

Here Vaughn is clearly referring to the philosopher's stone, or elixir of life, which alchemists sought from the start of the Middle Ages and well into the Age of Enlightenment, believing that it could both extend life and turn base metals into gold. Here it replaces the Grail but is reverenced in the same way.

The reality behind this was the transformation of flesh into spiritual matter, and it is this that brings the philosopher's stone into the realm of the Grail. Vaughn was influenced by the mystical writings that flowed out of Germany in the seventeenth century. The imagination of the German Protestant mind kept the seeds of devotion to the Grail alive without referring to it directly. The ideas expressed in Vaughn's writings are at times so like those of medieval mystics that it is hard not to believe that its author was directly influenced by the medieval romances—perhaps even by *Titurel* itself, where we see the guardian of the Grail living to the age of 500 because he is in the presence of the Grail. Looking again at *Parzival*, we can see just how close the two texts are.

To begin with, we find the following passage in Wolfram which, when set alongside the above extract from *The Holy Mountain*, displays remarkable similarities. The passage in question is where Wolfram describes the Grail and its effects:

> There never can be human so ill but that if he one day sees the stone [that is, the Grail] he cannot die within the week that follows...and though he should see the stone for two hundred years [his appearance] will never change, save that his hair might perhaps turn gray. [129]

At the end of *Titurel*, when the old king wishes to pass the guardianship of the temple to his children, he has to be taken from the sight of the Grail; after which, no longer affected by its miraculous powers, he can die peacefully.

Wolfram himself described the Grail as "a stone of the purest kind...called *lapsit exillas*." This phrase has long been taken to be a reference to the philosopher's stone, the *lapis philoso-*

---

128. Ibid.
129. Wolfram von Eschenbach, *Parzival*.

phorum, and while the wording has been dismissed as Wolfram's bad Latin, a variant found within *Der Jungëre Titurel* offers another suggestion. Albrecht agrees with Wolfram that the Grail is a stone but diverges from this by telling us that it was carved into a dish. He also tells us that the stone was made of jasper and flint—or, as he writes it, *jaspis et silix.*

This is most interesting, as it may offer a solution to Wolfram's much-debated term. If, as seems possible, *lapsit exillas* is a scribal error for *jaspis et silix,* this would mean that both Albrecht and Wolfram believed the Grail to be made from these elements. Charles W. Passage, whose work is invaluable on this point, notes that in the Bible the stone designated as *jasper* (Latin) is said to be green[130] and to be one of the twelve jewels on the breastplate of the high priest of Solomon's Temple. It is also, in each instance, associated with a visionary experience. Significantly also we may note that amongst the healing stones placed around the bed of the wounded King Anfortas in *Parzifal* is jasper.[131]

The secondary element, *silix* (Latin *silex*), is a type of flint and is sometimes described as being used to kindle the fire in which the phoenix immolates itself. How the stone can partake of both elements is unexplained; neither are we told who exactly carved them into the form of a dish—specifically said to contain the elements of the Eucharist.

This is an important aspect of Albrecht's definition of the Grail, for where Wolfram names it simply "the Grail" (as Chrétien names it "a grail"), Albrecht terms it "the Holy Grail." As Passage rightly notes, this probably came from Albrecht's knowledge of Robert de Boron's poem *Joseph d'Arimathea* (circa 1201), which, as we saw earlier, was the first text to associate the Grail with the passion of Christ. Robert is also the first of the medieval Grail authors to include the story of Joseph of Arimathea acquiring the cup used at the Last Supper and subsequently to catch some of Jesus's blood during the preparation of his body for burial. This of course makes the Grail a relic not only of the Last Supper but also the Crucifixion, which it generally remained from this time onward—with the exception of *Parzifal,* in which Wolfram follows his own path in making the Grail a stone brought to earth by angels.

Albrecht marries these two streams of thought by making his Grail a stone but having it carved into a dish used to celebrate the Eucharist, though as Passage notes, "with no hint of the Crucifixion relic containing Christ's blood."[132]

130. See Exodus 28:20, 39:13; Ezekiel 28:13, and Revelation 4:3, 21:11, 18 and 19.

131. Passage, *Titurel.*

132. Ibid, 53.

◆ ◆ ◆

There are other parallels between the story told by Wolfram and the alchemical mystery described by Thomas Vaughn. In *Parzival* we read:

> As to those who are appointed to the Grail [that is, to be its guardians]—hear how they are made known. Under the top edge of the Stone an inscription announces the name and lineage of the one summoned to make the glad journey…Those who are now full-grown all came here as children. Happy the mother of any child destined to serve there! Rich and poor alike rejoice if a child of theirs is summoned and they are bidden to send it to that Company! Such children are fetched from many countries and forever are immune from the shame of sin and have a rich reward in Heaven.[133]

This is very much in the spirit of a document that would have been well known to Vaughn. Called the *Fama Fraternitatis*, it launched a new philosophical and mystical movement known as Rosicrucianism, after its supposed founder Christian Rosencreutz.[134] Here we learn of the existence of a brotherhood called by God to bear witness to the great mystery of Brother C. R., whose task is to remain hidden until the time when the world is ready for their message. A description of the Rosicrucian mysteries by one of its disciples, Robert Fludd (1574–1637), makes the connection clear:

> Here then you have that House or Palace of Wisdom erected on the Mount of Reason. It remains, however, to learn who are those…to whom this House is open. These most fortunate of men and their spiritual house are described by the Apostle in the following manner: "To whom come, as unto a living stone…[the] chosen of God…[to whom] are built up a spiritual house, a holy priesthood, to offer up spiritual sacrifices, acceptable to God…A chosen generation, a royal priesthood, an holy community, a ransomed people, that you should practice the virtues of him who has called you out of darkness into his royal light. For previously you were not a people, but now you are the people of God."[135]

This is certainly an echo of the "Christian progeny bred to a pure life [who] have the duty of keeping [the Grail]" in Wolfram's poem. The followers of Christian Rosencreutz are summoned to their task in the same way as those who follow the Grail to Muntsalvasche.

The story that Titurel's cousins of Anjou and Cornwall give him lands on which to build seems no more than an attempt to place the temple in actual territory, but since it is evidently in neither place and since the land of the Grail is called Salvaterre (Wolfram's *Terre de Sal-*

---

133. Wolfram von Eschenbach, *Parzival.*

134. The best selection of Rosicrucian texts are to be found in *A Christian Rosenkreutz Anthology*, edited by Paul M. Allen (Rudolf Steiner Publications, 1981).

135. Ibid. Fludd is quoting Peter 2:4.

◆ ◆ ◆

vaesche), the suggestion seems redundant. We may also notice that Salvaterre is still occupied with pagans until Titurel drives them out. This suggests that the setting of the temple may be in the East rather than the West—a notion born out by the later part of the poem. Added to this we have the detail that tells us the largest of the altars in the temple is oriented towards the Orient. Was the Grail Temple situated in the East? As we shall see, the answer is almost certainly yes.

It seems likely that Albrecht was hinting at further symbolic references when he listed the various gems that decorated the temple. The majority of these names seem to be invented and no reference to them has so far been discovered, but some are familiar and add to the significance of the symbolic language with which the temple is described.

For example, according to the hagiography of St. David, we are told that he went on a pilgrimage to Jerusalem and brought back with him a piece of the floor from the Holy of Holies called sapphire, which features in the vision of Ezekiel. There is still a piece of this stone in the Cathedral of St. David's in Western Wales.[136] It is also said, according to Hebrew myth, to be the stone upon which Moses wrote the Ten Commandments.

Albrecht's reference to a huge emerald at the heart of the temple "… cylindrical in shape, with the Lamb of God carved above it, holding a cross in one foot and a banner of red in the other" which "was the sign of the eternal defeat of Lucifer" is a direct reference to Wolfram's statement that the Grail itself was an emerald that had fallen from the angel's crown as it fell to earth.

He makes clear the importance of the temple as a sacred enclosure. Within, everything—every detail, from the angelic carvings to the very furniture—is sacred and perfect; only outside is there room for the secular and the magical, with images of sea monsters and their like carved on the walls. These decorations were never intended simply to impress; they were symbolic waymarkers to all who came in search of divine inspiration.

Sacred Land

The central part of Albrecht's work can be seen almost as an interpolation into the story of the Grail. It was perhaps his intention to join his own work (hitherto separate) with Wolfram's via the latter's fragmentary *Titurel* poems. It takes us off on a wild range of adventures with Schionatulander and Sigune, many of them at Arthur's court. In the end Schionatulander is killed by his nemesis Orilus, and after a long period of mourning, the stories briefly merge when Percival meets Sigune with the body of Schionatulander in a linden tree. The only part of the story that

---

136. We are grateful to David Elkington for drawing our attention to this detail.

✦ ✦ ✦

is of interest to us here is that in which Sigune has a hermitage built for her on Muntsalvasche. Albrecht tells us that it is next to the *Font Salvasch* (Fountain of Salvation) and is covered in gold and jewels such as those used to adorn the temple of Solomon.

In the same section we learn of the death of Perceval's father, Gahmuret, while serving in the East. On the return of Sigune, who had accompanied him to the war against the infidels, Herzeloyde, as Gahmuret's queen, gives the care of her kingdoms to Schionatulander. A few days later she gives birth to Perceval, who will one day inherit the guardianship of the Grail.

The third and final section of the poem, as noted, continues the story of the Grail as if the middle section had never existed. This has led more than one scholar to wonder if the poem was not originally intended to be two, which were later put together either by Albrecht himself or by an anonymous scribe. In any case, it has a number of variations to the more familiar description of the Grail story, which have been largely ignored due to the tendency of most scholars to concentrate on the description of the temple of the Grail. The following summary, which extends beyond previous references, leads us to some interesting areas and suggests an important link with another early account of a sacred temple.

As noted above, dissension breaks out amongst the company of the Grail, and it is decided to take it to another place. Led by Titurel, the true followers of the Grail set out, crossing many countries until they arrived at the port of Marseille. From here they take a ship, guided and fed by the Grail itself and accompanied by the scent of lilies brought on a breeze from paradise. They reached an island called Pitimont, which is five hundred miles from the nearest place. There they remained for four days. The people who lived on the island accepted food and wine from the Grail and asked Titurel to stay and rule over them. But he refused and on the fifth day the travellers resumed their journey. The people of the island renamed their city Grals and built a new temple with 22 (or 72) galleries.

This is, of course, strikingly similar to the description of the Island of the Grail in *Sone*, while the building of the temple with 22 galleries (as in the text translated above there is a variant version which numbers this as 72) shows them creating their own version of the Grail Temple.

The voyage is perilous due to the fact that they sail too close to the Lodestone, a naturally magnetized rock at this time believed to lie somewhere beneath the ocean and to cause ships to veer off course. But despite this they reach the land of India, ruled over at this time by Prester John. His realm is said to include much of Asia, extending close to the walls of the earthly paradise, separated only by a gleaming mountain from which a river of jewels flows. A description of the whole area follows. The herb assidôse, famed for its healing properties, grows on the banks of the river, and crops of pepper grow close by. There is mention of a second mountain

✦ ✦ ✦

called Olimpius, and of a sea of sand (presumably a desert) on the edge of which live the Jews. A third mountain, Agremonte, is full of fire, where salamanders live and weave a mysterious substance called *pfelle*.

Prester John is described as a great hunter, a warrior who is known to have slain 200,000 heathens in a single day. His palace is unbelievably rich, and at its heart is a vast courtyard in which one hundred and twenty-five steps, built in concentric circles, lead up to a pillar, on top of which is a vast ciborium.[137] Above this, floating apparently without support, is a mirror that allows those in the palace to observe the activities of their enemies.

The richness and splendour of the kingdom is only equaled by that of Prester John himself, who comes out to meet the travellers. When he sees the Grail he wishes to know what it is. Titurel replies at some length (see below), differing at several points from Wolfram's description in *Parzifal*. At the end of the disquisition, Titurel begs to be released from his service to the Grail. The only way this can happen is to be prevented from seeing the vessel, since anyone who cannot will not pass into the afterlife. Granted his wish, Titurel dies soon after and is given an impressive funeral. Prester John then becomes the new guardian of the Grail, and on this triumphal note the poem ends.

The bringing of the Grail to the country of Prester John is significant for a number of reasons, not the least of which, as we shall see, are the links it forms between Western and Eastern settings of the temple. The account of Prester John's kingdom in Albrecht's poem clearly shows that he had seen an actual document believed to have been written by the Priest-King himself and addressed to the crowned heads of Europe, which can be seen to connect both with other extant descriptions of the earthly paradise (as mentioned by Albrecht himself) and with the description of the Grail castle and temple in *Sone de Nansay* and elsewhere. These descriptions will, in due course, help us to identify a site that in all probability influenced the description of the sacred enclave in all of these sources and that, in turn, connects to a period long before the time of the Grail romances.

The presence of the mysterious herb assidôse, with its healing properties; large areas of pepper growing wild; and the even more curious substance called *pfelle*, woven by salamanders, can all be seen to derive from older descriptions of the earthly paradise. *Pfelle* is, in fact, simply a variant of *felle*, skin, so that we can see that the salamanders are weaving a kind of covering just as they wove the cloaks embroidered with doves worn by the Grail knights in *Parzifal*. Assidôse was a herb said to drive off unclean spirits. The hovering mirror that allows Prester John to

---

137. See note 118. As we shall see, the importance of the presence of this device in the temple is considerable.

❖ ❖ ❖

observe the actions of his enemies is clearly borrowed from Wolfram's description of the mirrored pillar in the castle of the anti-grail king Clinshor, which also allows him to spy on anyone who comes near to his home. Another such mirror is found in the description of a church at Ettal in Southern Germany, which bears a striking similarity to the Grail Temple (see chapter 7).

The pillar—brought, it is said, from "Araby"—seems to serve as a kind of *camera obscura*: just one of the many shadowy imitations created by Clinshor. Wolfram describes the pillar in some detail:

> From the lands of Feirefiz the wise Clinshor had brought (it)...It had been wrought by sorcery...a shining pillar...of diamond and amethyst—the adventure tells it all—of topaz and garnet, of chrysolite, ruby, emerald...The adventure tells us what wondrous properties it had...(Gawain) found a marvel so great that he could not take his eyes from it. It seemed to him he could see in the great pillar all the lands around about, and it seemed the lands were circling the column and the mighty mountains collided with a clash. In the pillar he saw people riding and walking, others running standing still.[138]

Wolfram himself, towards the end of *Parzifal*, tells us that Feirefiz, Parzival's half brother, marries the Grail maiden Repanse de Schoye and the two journey to India, where Repanse gives birth to a son, whom they name Prester John—adding "*And ever since, they call their kings by no other name*"[139] and that while in the West the country where they settle is called India, to the people of that land itself, it is known as *Trabalibot*. The fact that the mirror is brought "from the lands of Feirefiz," who is the father of Prester John, will be seen to be of singular importance later in our study.

The timings do not match up here. Titurel's visit to Prester John's kingdom takes place long after the building of the Grail Temple and even longer before the events described in *Parzifal*, yet here we have Prester John ruling over an established kingdom and knowing nothing of the Grail. Thus *The Later Titurel* should not be seen as a sequel to Wolfram but perhaps as a parallel text.

However, Albrecht's description of the Grail, as given by Titurel in response to Prester John's question, is interesting in that it differs in several significant details, not only from *Parzifal* but also from other extant Grail texts. We give it here in our own version, based upon that of Charles E. Passage.[140]

138. Wolfram von Eschenbach, *Parzival*.

139. Ibid., 408.

140. Passage, *Titurel*, 48–49.

♦ ♦ ♦

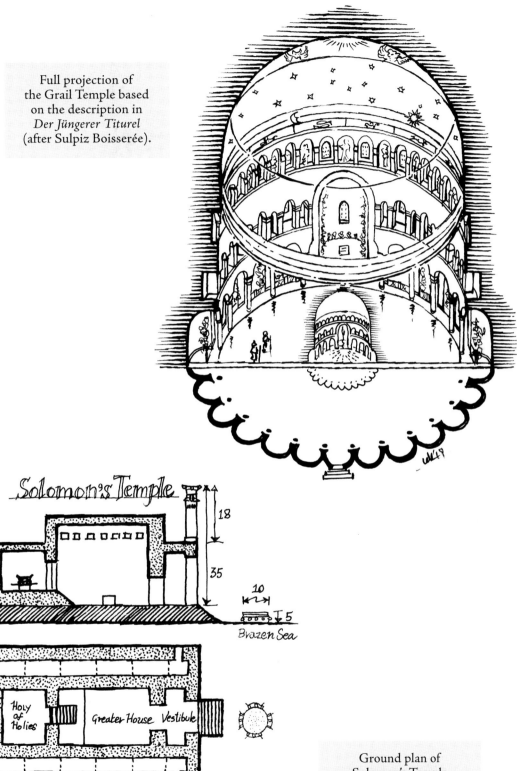

Full projection of
the Grail Temple based
on the description in
Der Jüngerer Titurel
(after Sulpiz Boisserée).

Solomon's Temple

18

30

35

10

5

Brazen Sea

Holy
of
Holies

Greater House   Vestibule

20

60

distances in Cubits

wk '19

Ground plan of
Solomon's Temple
showing the position
of the Holy of Holies.

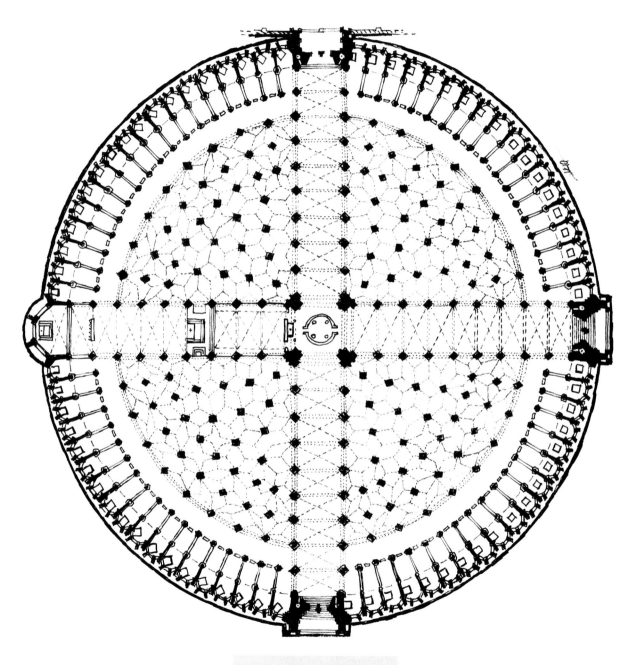

Projection of the Grail
Temple ground plan
(after Sulpiz Boisserée).

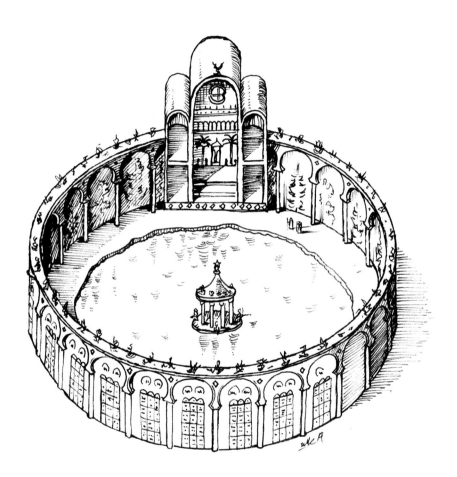

Projection of the Takht-e Soleyman
based on a bronze salver from the
time of Khosrow II (after Ringbom).

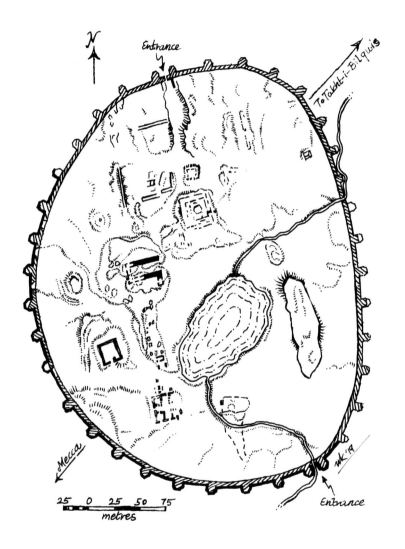

Map of the Takht-e Soleyman site
(after D. Wilber, who helped survey and
record the site during Pope's expedition).

Long ago a heavenly host brought the Grail to earth.
It was a stone of great splendour.
From this was fashioned a dish.
Jasper and flint it was named.
From it the Phoenix rises renewed
After it has immolated itself in the fire.
This same dish was deemed worthy of Jesus Christ,
For whatever is most precious
Could serve as a vessel for the Divine Eucharist
Of which He partook with his disciples.
From this Holiness the Grail transmits its qualities,
Preserved since the day the angel
Brought the Grail to me on the Mountain.
Here it remains forever unchanging.

A second dish, costly and precious,
Was fashioned in the likeness of this one.
It is flawless and holy.
The people of Constantinople took it to their land
Where, finding it beyond compare, they deemed it the true Grail.
But Joseph of Arimathea knew which one was the real Grail
And since he loved Jesus Christ purely
He preserved the true dish
Until the angel brought it to me
Naming it the Grail with an angelic voice
Since when I have known it for five hundred years.

(THE LATER TITUREL, VERSES 6172–6177)

Here Albrecht develops his history of the Grail significantly and in an unusual way. He shares the idea, presented in Wolfram's text, that the Grail was brought from heaven by angels (Wolfram is specific in naming these as the neutral angels who sided neither with God nor Lucifer in the great heavenly war, and agrees with Dante in making them "fallen"). Passage, in his analysis of this part of the poem, suggests that while Wolfram gives the impression that the bringing of the Grail to earth takes place "soon after the creation of the world,"[141] he believes that Albrecht places the event "at the beginning of the Christian era and ... probably [in] Palestine."

---

141. Passage, *Titurel*, 49.

♦ ♦ ♦

After this the Grail "hovers" overhead until the temple described in the first part of *The Later Titurel* is complete, at which point it is placed within the tabernacle built for it in the form of a miniaturized copy of the temple itself. Passage also suggests that Albrecht may have been thinking of the star of the Magi from Matthew 2:9 that also "hovered over the earth" in the East and led to the birthplace of Jesus.[142] This seems very much in keeping with the eventual reorientation of the Grail to India, Prester John's kingdom, while the Priest-King himself claims descent from the Magi. The significance of this, as we shall see, is not inconsiderable.

Both Robert de Boron and Albrecht connect the Grail with the family of the emperor Vespasian and his son Titus. As we saw earlier, in his poem of *Joseph*, Robert tells the story of the Arimathean's imprisonment in a deep pit, where he is visited by Jesus and entrusted with the sacred vessel and its secret teachings. It is Vespasian who reopens the case against Joseph after either he or his son Titus is healed of leprosy by the Veil of Veronica—a story originally told of the emperor Tiberius.[143] Having learned the fate of Joseph, Vespasian makes his way to the place of his interment and lets himself down into the pit. There he finds Joseph well and happy to instruct the emperor in the story of the fallen angels. Here we may also remember the details included in the abbot's outline of Joseph's life in *Sone de Nansay*.

Significantly, in the year AD 67 Vespasian himself, not yet emperor, had the Jewish general and future historian Josephus brought out of "a deep pit communicating on one side with a wide cave," where he was hiding. Later, on becoming emperor, Vespasian made Josephus his advisor.[144]

Could it be that Robert de Boron had learned of this story and transferred it from Josephus to Joseph of Arimathea, adding the mystical elements of the Grail history to these historical events? Let us not forget that in Albrecht's account of the family of Titurel, he has Barillus marry the emperor's daughter Argusille and names their son Titurisone, a name which, as already noted, contains the element of Titus.

The reference to the copy of the original vessel that is taken to Constantinople appears in no other text. It may perhaps refer to the relic known as the Edessa Icon, believed by some to be the shroud of Jesus, on which an image of his face appeared. This relic, now held in Turin Cathedral, was reported to have been brought to Constantinople in 944. Robert de Clari, writ-

---

142. "They went on their way, and the star they had seen when it rose went ahead of them until it stopped over the place where the child was."

143. This was described in an apocryphal text known as *Cura Sanitas Tiberii*. The transfer to Vespasian is first noted in an eleventh-century chanson de geste known as *La Destruction de Jerusalem*.

144. Flavius Josephus, *The Jewish War* (Penguin Classics, 1959), 207–212.

ing an account of his participation in the Fourth Crusade, describes a chapel in the Pharos, the treasury of imperial relics in the Bucoleon Palace:

> Within this chapel were found many precious relics; for therein were found two pieces of the True Cross, as thick as a man's leg and a fathom in length. And there was found the lance wherewith Our Lord had His side pierced, and the two nails that were driven through the midst of His hands and through the midst of His feet. And there was also found, in a crystal phial, a great part of His blood. And there was found the tunic that he wore, which was stripped from Him when He had been led to the Mount of Calvary. And there, too, was found the blessed crown wherewith He was crowned, which was wrought of sea rushes, sharp as dagger blades. There also was found the raiment of Our Lady, and the head of my Lord Saint John Baptist, and so many other precious relics that I could never describe them to you or tell you the truth concerning them.[145]

While this is clearly not a Grail as such, the crystal phial containing Christ's blood could certainly have suggested the sacred vessel to the medieval writers. It is interesting that in the same text de Clari also refers to Arnoul, the future builder of the copy of the Holy of Holies in his own version of the Grail chapel at his home in France.[146]

Albrecht is clear that Joseph of Arimathea recognizes the true Grail—the implication being that this is *not* the copy taken to Constantinople—and he proceeds to tell the story that he had almost certainly found in Robert de Boron's work, which has Joseph surviving his imprisonment, learning the secret teachings of Jesus, and leading a group of followers in search of a proper home for the Grail. Crucially, Robert and Albrecht diverge at this point, with Robert sending his company to the Vale of Avaron in the West (generally identified with Avalon, and in turn with the small town of Glastonbury in Somerset), while Albrecht has Titurel journey to the East and to the country of Prester John. As we shall see in the next chapter, this plays a highly significant role in the history of the Grail Temple.

The closing words of the poem declare that "the souls of all who read it or copy it cannot miss entering paradise." While this is a type of ending used by other authors writing at the time, in this instance the reference is literal: to follow this story of the Grail is indeed to reach paradise. As we shall see, there are many visions of such a place, some based on the same, or similar, sources.

145. Hopf, *Chroniques Greco-romaines inedites ou peo connues.*
146. See chapter 1.

◆ ◆ ◆

5

THE KINGDOM OF THE GRAIL

… there is a land far, far away, mysterious, inaccessible—
an earthly paradise that lies at the true center of the
world. There, crowning a great mountain, is a castle or
temple of fabulous splendour containing the most
precious of all objects, the Grail itself.

◆ ◆ ◆

A. U. Pope, *Persia and the Holy Grail*

From the castle of the Grail, the temple evolved; from the temple grew something greater still—a kingdom, ruled over by a figure as famous in the Middle Ages as the Grail itself: Prester John. It was perhaps inevitable that the *Letter of Prester John*, one of the most copied and most discussed documents of the Middle Ages, should influence the literature of the times. Paraphrases or direct quotes from the original letter, along with many interpolations and re-editing, can be traced from the twelfth to the nineteenth centuries, yet one of the most important borrowings remains largely ignored: the one to be found in the last third of *The Later Titurel*. Here we have not only a radically different version of the priest-king's legend, but the most specific connection yet between that legend and the story of the Grail.

Albrecht borrowed heavily from the text of the letter for his description of the Grail Temple, but he went further when he spoke of the quarrel that split the Grail family and caused a copy of the original cup to be taken to Constantinople, while the true Grail went East, to the land of Prester John. In this he far extended the brief mention in Wolfram's *Parzifal* to the parentage of the priest-king. Though this was, of itself, important, as it connected Prester John to the family of the Grail, Albrecht chose to ignore it; instead, he extended the story to encompass both a

◆ ◆ ◆

detailed description of John's kingdom and the fact that the Grail was to be kept there for an indefinite future.

In doing so he opened up the world of the Grail hugely, making it part of the vast realm of the priest-king, which was itself only a small corner of the infinitely greater earthly paradise.

The Mysterious Kingdom

To understand how this came about, we must look further at the legend of the priestly lord ruling over a vast and mysterious land. It first became widely known when, in 1165, a letter was delivered to the Byzantine emperor Emanuel Commemnos, the Holy Roman emperor, Frederic Barbarossa, and the king of France. It claimed to be from a monarch who was also a priest—hence *prester*, priest-king—ruling over an impossibly rich land situated somewhere in India. The exact origins of this letter, along with the identity of its author, remain a mystery, though we can point to a number of older documents that contributed to it. The letter itself caused a sensation; the idea of a Christian monarch ruling over a kingdom in the East was extraordinary. It became an overnight talking point amongst the courts of the West, and everywhere debates took place as to the reality of Prester John and the impact his existence, if true, would have on the continuing wars between Christian and Moslem. The letter offered proof that a powerful Christian ally existed behind the Islamic kingdoms—an ally with a vast army at his disposal and a willingness to come to the aid of the Christian West.

There are innumerable versions of the *Letter of Prester John* and a good number of translations. We chose the one made by Robert Williams, taken from the fourteenth-century Welsh Hengwrt Manuscript collection in 1892. This is, in many ways, the most poetic rendering of the text, and with a few corrections from more recent editions and some modernization of the language, it reads well and gives a good feeling of the original document.

We were also intrigued to note that the same collection of manuscripts includes a fifteenth-century Welsh amalgamation of the *Quest del Saint Graal* and *Perlesvaus*, known today as *Y Seint Greal*, as well as extracts from the Gospel of Nicodemus, which includes some of the earliest references to Joseph of Arimathea and a version of Seth's quest for the Oil of Mercy. As we shall see, this is yet another parallel to the Grail quest, and while almost certainly no more than a coincidence, it suggests that all three texts were in circulation at the same time. The manuscripts in question are Peniarth MS 5 and Jesus MS 111, now in the collection of the National Library of Wales. The opening paragraph seems to be unique to this version, and since the letter is clearly not a book suggests that at one time there might have been a longer account of the kingdom of Prester John. The divisions were made by Robert Williams and are retained here for convenience.

◆ ◆ ◆

THE LETTER OF PRESTER JOHN
edited and translated by Robert Williams

This is a Book that the King of India sent to the Emperor of Constantinople, in which many diverse strange things are understood, and in it there are new things that have never been found in other books, and never shall be found. And this is the force of that book.

I. John the Priest, by the might and strength of God, our Lord Jesus Christ, King of earthly kings, and Lord of Lords, sends to him that stands in the place of God, namely the Ruler of Rome, joy and greeting by the grace of poetry, and thereby rising to things that are above. It was told to us that you love our excellence and the plenitude of our greatness, and we have learnt through our messenger that you wish to send us things that are amusing and pleasant; and that is good in my sight. Of the things we possess we send by our messengers to you, and we desire to know whether you share our faith and believe wholly in our Lord Jesus Christ.

II. Where we ourselves know ourselves to be mortal, the Greeks think that you are a God. Yet, since we know you are mortal, and that you are subject to human corruption, if you desire any of the things that bring joy, notify us through your messenger, and by the munificence of our bounty, you shall have it. Therefore take this gift of Hawkweed,[147] in my name, and make use of it, and we will joyfully use your gifts, so that we may strengthen ourselves mutually in our power. If you wish to visit the nation from which we are sprung, we will place you amid the greatest things in our palace, so that you may make use of our abundance, and the many things that are in our midst; and if you would return, you shalt go home rich. Remember, however, the last thing, which is the end of your life, and you will sin no more.

III. Now, if you would know our majesty, and the excellence of our highness, and in what lands our power holds sway, understand and believe without doubt that I am John the Priest, Lord of Lords, excelling all the Kings of the earth in

---

147. Hawkweed is a common name for *Hierakion pisosella*, a genus of the sunflower family related to dandelion, chicory, prickly lettuce, and sow thistle, which are part of the tribe Cichorieae. *Culpeper's Herbal* says it is a singular herb for wounds both inner and outer. Given the wounded nature of the Grail king, this gives one pause for thought.

strength and power, in all kinds of riches that are under heaven. Seventy-two kings pay tribute to me. I vow that I am a devout Christian; and that everywhere we give succour to poor Christians. We have also undertaken a vow to visit the Sepulchre of Our Lord with a great host, as it befits the glory of our mightiness to subject and subdue the enemies of the Cross of Christ, and to exalt His Blessed Name. Our land stretches from the extremities of India, where the body of Thomas the Apostle rests, and extends through the wilderness to the setting sun, to the Babylonian desert, near the tower of Babel.

IV. Seventy-two kings serve us in bondage, and of those but few are Christian; and each of them has a king of its own, and these all pay tribute to us. In our country are born animals—elephants, dromedaries, camels, hippopotami, crocodiles, methagalinarii,[148] camelopards, pantheræ, curanthers, white and red lions, white bears, white merlins, silent grasshoppers, gryphons, tigers, lamias, hyenas, wild buffaloes, archers, wild men, men with horns, fauns, satyrs, and women of the same race, pigmies, giants forty cubits in height, one-eyed men, cyclopes, the bird that is called the phœnix, and almost all the kinds of animals under heaven. In our country there is abundance of milk and honey; in another quarter in our land no poison hurts, no frog croaks, no snakes hiss in the herbage. No venomous animals can abide there, or do harm to anyone. In the midst of some races called pagans, through one of our provinces, a river called Ydonis runs, and this river, coming from Paradise, goes noiselessly through our entire kingdom by a series of mazes. Here are found natural stones—these are their names: emerald, sapphire, carbuncle, topaz, chrysolite, onyx, beryl, amethyst, sardonex, and many others.

V. Here springs the herb called Assidôse.[149] Whoever bears the root of that plant, it will drive evil spirits from him, and will constrain such spirits to say what they are, and what their name; therefore the evil spirits dare not corrupt any man here. In another kingdom of ours there grow all kinds of pepper, which are collected and exchanged for wheat, skins, cloth, and bread; and those regions are wooded, as if thickly planted with willows, and all full of serpents. And when the pepper ripens, the people come from the nearest kingdoms and bring with them chaff, and dry branches; and they kindle the wood round about; and when a mighty wind blows, they set fire throughout the forest, so that not one of the

---

148. Possibly a combination of *metagon* (hunting dog) and *gallinarii* (poultry) to mean something like "attack chickens." Other suggestions include guinea fowl.

149. As we saw in *The Later Titurel*, this is also present in the Grail Temple. Again, since it is related to *Stellaria media* (starwort) and chickweed, both of which are excellent treatment for wounds, we begin to see a certain consistency in the presence of these herbs.

✦ ✦ ✦

serpents may escape. And so within the fire, after it has been thoroughly kindled, all the serpents perish, save those that reach their caves; and when all the fire has died out, all come, men and women, small and big, with forks in their hands, and fling all the serpents out of the forest, and make great heaps of them. And when they have finished shaking the chaff, the grain that is gathered from among the fagots is dried, and the pepper is boiled, but how it is boiled no one from another country is allowed to know.

VI. That forest is situated under Mount Olympus, and from there an excellent spring flows; and the water has every kind of taste, and the taste changes each hour, day and night. And from there, it is but three days' journey to Paradise, from which Adam was driven out. Whoever drinks of the water of that spring during his fast, no disease will come upon him from that day forth, and he will ever be thirty years of age. There, too, there are stones called Midriosi. Eagles bring these to us, and through them they revive and recover their sight if they lose it. Whoever bears this stone on his hand, his sight never fails, and if he would hide himself, it will make him invisible. It drives hatred from all, and induces unity, and repels jealousy. This, too, is a strange thing that our country has, among other things: there is a sea of sand there, which moves without water, and it surges in waves like other seas, and never rests; but one cannot go on it by ship or in any other way, nor can it be in any way known what kind of land there is beyond; but on the side towards us there are found many kinds of fish, so sweet and so good that man never saw their like.

VII. There are likewise three days' journey from this sea, mountains from which flow a river of stones like water, and it runs through our land to the sea of sand. And when the river reaches the sea, the stones disappear, so that they are not seen again. Three days in the week the stones move and slide, both small and great, and take with them some trees, as far as the sea of sand, and so long as they move, no one can ever cross it. On the other four days a passage is obtained. This is another marvel that is there; hard by the desert near the mountains where no one dwells, there is a river beneath the earth, and no one can find a road to it, except by chance; sometimes the earth trembles, and whoever then happens to be passing by can find a road to the river, and he must travel in haste, lest perchance the earth close upon him; and whatever sand he brings with him will become precious stones and jewels. This rivulet runs into another river larger than itself, and therein is none of the gravel or sand, but only precious stones. Into this river the men of that country go, and seize and bring with them a multitude of precious stones and jewels. But they dare not sell them until they first show them to us. And if we would fain have them in our treasure, we take them, and give the men

♦ ♦ ♦

half their value. If we do not want them, they are free to sell them where they will. Children are raised in water in that land to enable them to seek the stones, so that they can live under water for as long as three or four months.

VIII. Beyond this stony river there are ten tribes of the Jews. Though they possess kings, yet they are subject to us, and are tributaries to our majesty. In another kingdom of ours, beyond the place where the island lies, there are worms, called in our tongue Salamanders, and those worms can live only in fire. They have around them skins like the skins of worms that make silk; and to spin this is the work of our ladies in our palace, whereof is made all kinds of apparel for the use of our majesty. These clothes cannot be washed save in a large and strong fire. In gold, silver, precious stones, in elephants, dromedaries, camels and dogs, is the abundance of our greatness. No one is poor among us; no adulterer is found there; all men of strange lands, to wit, guests and pilgrims, we receive. No thieves, no oppressors, no misers are found in our midst; there is no envy here.

IX. Our men have abundance of all kinds of riches; there are not many horses among us, though they are poor. We liken none on the face of the earth to us in riches. When we go to war in force against our enemies, we let carry before us fifteen magnificent crosses made of gold and silver, with precious stones therein, one in each van, instead of standards, and behind each one of them twelve thousand men of arms, and a hundred thousand foot soldiers, without counting the five thousand who carry our food and drink. But when we walk abroad in peace, a wooden cross precedes us, without any legend whatever, either of gold or silver, so that the suffering of our Lord Jesus Christ may be brought back to our remembrance constantly. And we take also a vessel full of earth, so that we may remember that our flesh returns to its source—that is, to earth. Another vessel, full of gold, is borne before us, that all may understand that we are the Lord of Lords.

X. In all the kinds of riches that are in the world our greatness abounds and excels. No one tells a lie among us, nor is anyone able to tell one; and whoever tells a lie willingly, straightway he dies, and no ill will is borne of him. All of us follow after truth, and all love one another mutually; no kind of sin reigns here. Every year we go on a pilgrimage to the place where lies the body of Daniel the Prophet, taking great hosts with us, to the Babylonian desert, and those under arms because of wild animals and serpents which are deemed frightful. In our country some fish are caught, and from the blood of these the most precious purple dye is found.

XI. We have many places of power and are the bravest people in the world. We lord it over the races called Amazons and Brahmans. The palace wherein we dwell was made in the form and likeness of that which the Apostle Thomas ordained

✦ ✦ ✦

for Gondoforus, king of India; and its wings and structures are exactly like it. The columns of the hall, its pillars, and its fretwork, come from a tree called acacia. The roofing of the hall is made of ebony, since no one in the world can burn it. On the topmost part of the roof of the hall are two apples of gold, and in each of them there is the precious stone called carbuncle, so that the gold may give light during the day, and the stones by night. The largest parts of the hall are made of stones called sardonex, inlaid with serpent's horn, so that no one may secretly bring in poison. Other parts of the hall are made of ebony, and the windows are of crystal; the tables we eat on in our palace are some of gold, and others of the precious stone amethyst. The pillars that support the tables are of whalebone. Before our palace there is a street, wherein our justice is wont to look on those triumphant in battle. The top of the hall and its walls are made of onyx, the purpose being that energy may arise in our combatants by the virtue of the stones. In that hall light is not kindled at night, save that which the precious oil called balsam feeds.

XII. The chamber wherein our majesty rests is fitted with wonderous work, and that of gold, and every king of precious stone in the world, because of the excellence of onyx, which gives us light. Around this is made a foursquare work so that the purity of the onyx may be judged. Precious ointment is at all times burned in this chamber; our bed is made of sapphire because of the stone's virtue of chastity. We have the fairest wives in the world, but they come in to us only four times in the year, that we may have heirs; and thereafter each one returns to her own place, blessed by us as Beersheba was by David.

XIII. In our palace we eat once a day; each day thirty thousand men eat at our board, besides the guests that come and go. And these all receive their charges from our palace, both in horses and other supplies. That table is made of the precious stone called emerald, and is supported by two pillars of amethyst. The virtue of this stone is that it suffers no one to get drunk so long as he sits thereon. Before the doorposts of our hall, near where our warriors sit, there is a watch-tower of great height, to which one climbs by one hundred and twenty-five steps; and of these steps, some are made of porphyry, blended with the blood of serpents and alabaster ointment. The lower parts of these are made of crystal, jasper, and sardonex, and those at the top of amethyst, amber, jasper, sardonex, and panthera. This watch-tower is supported by one pillar, and on this there is a base, and on this base two columns; and on these there is a base, and on this four columns, and again a base, and on this sixteen columns; and so the work proceeds, until the number thirty-four is reached, and then the number of the bases lessens, and the columns, as they increased before, descend to thirty-four.

❖ ❖ ❖

XIV. The columns and bases are of the same kind of precious stone as the steps by which men ascend. On the summit of the highest there is a mirror placed by graceful skill, so that no one in the various kinds of land subject to us can work any fraud, or treachery, or dissension against us, nor those among us, without it being clearly seen from that watchtower without it being known who they are or what they do. There are three thousand men of arms ever guarding this mirror night and day, lest by chance it be broken or overthrown to the ground.

XV. Each month in the year seven kings serve me, each one of them in his order, and forty-two princes, and three hundred and fifty-six earls. That number is always at our board, without those placed in the various duties in our palace. At our board there eat each day, on the right, twelve archbishops, and on the left twenty bishops, and the patriarch of St. Thomas and he that is Pope.

The Welsh text ends here, but there is more still. This is from our own translation of the original Latin text of the *Letter*:

XVI. "…the Bishop of Samarkand, and the Archbishop of Sousa. Every month each one of these prelates returns home, but others stay always at our side. Abbots serve us every day of the year in our chapel, taking turns to be with us and in their own homes—but there are always as many as there are days in the year that remain with us.

XVII. We posses another palace which, though of no greater length or breadth than the other, was built by my father according to a vision that he had. So great was his holiness and justness that he was named Quasidus.[150] To him it was told in a dream: "Build a palace for your son who, when he is born to you, will be king over all the kings and lords of the earth.

"The palace will have so much grace conferred upon it by God, that no one who enters there will leave unsatisfied; and even if one desperate with hunger enters there and is sick to the point of death, even though he stays there for a long while, he will be satisfied—as though he had eaten a hundred courses of food—and as healthy as if he had never suffered any infirmities in his life." Next morning Quasidus, my father, fearful of this vision, got up. Greatly disturbed, he heard a sublime voice, which all who were with him heard also. It pronounced: "Quasidus—do what you have been told, do not hesitate, all will be well as it was predicted."

XVIII. This voice comforted my father greatly, and immediately he ordered the palace to be built, using only precious stones, and the best gold as cement.

150. Godlike or semi-divine.

✦ ✦ ✦

Its heavenly roof is of sapphire, and brilliant topazes were set in between them, so that the sapphires were like the purest heaven and the topazes were stars that illuminated the whole palace. The floor itself is covered with large crystal flagstones, and there are no chambers or compartments there, merely fifty columns of the purest gold, slender as needles, set in the palace near its walls. In each corner is one greater than the rest, which are set between them. The height of one column is sixty cubits, its breadth such that two men are able to encompass it with their arms. Each one has at its top a carbuncle as great in size as an amphora, and from this the palace is eliminated as the world is illuminated by the sun. If you ask why the columns are sharpened to needlepoints, it is because if they were as wide at the top as at the bottom, the floor and the palace would not be sufficiently illuminated from the brightness of the carbuncles. Likewise if you ask which of the two jewels is the brightest, the truth is that the brightness is so great that nothing, however small, even if it lies upon the floor, cannot fail to be seen. There are no windows or openings there, so the brightness of the carbuncles and other stones cannot be eclipsed by the brightness of the sun. On our birthday, when we wear the crown, we enter the palace and remain there for as long as it takes to eat a meal, and we leave satisfied as if with all kinds of food.

XIX. If you ask also why, since the Creator of All has made us the most powerful and glorious of mortals, our sublime nature does not allow us to be called by any title more honorable than that of Presbyter, you should not be surprised. For we have in our court many officials more deserving of such ecclesiastical titles. They are provided with a divine service even greater than ours. Indeed our steward is a primate and king, our cupbearer an archbishop and king, our marshal a king and archimandrite, and our chief cook a king and an abbot. On this account I have not allowed myself to be distinguished by the same rank with which our court is full. Therefore we choose to be called by a lesser name and inferior rank, on account of our humility.

XX. We cannot presently tell you all about our power and glory, but when you come to us you will see that we are truly a Lord of Lords over the whole earth. In the meantime you should know that our country extends in breadth for four months in one direction, and that in the other no one knows how far our kingdom stretches. If you can count the stars in heaven and the sands of the sea, you may calculate the extent of the kingdom and our power.

＋ ＋ ＋

CHAPTER 5

The Meaning of the Letter

The letter itself is clearly a fantasy, created almost certainly from a desire to have an ally in the East who would help win the Holy Land back for the Christians. But it was not the first such account, and the earlier ones, from which the writer clearly borrowed, are in themselves every bit as intriguing today as they were in the twelfth century. They also cast a new and surprising light on the Grail myth.

The oldest of these documents, the *De Adventu Patriarchae Indorum* ("On the Coming of the Patriarch of the Indians") is dated circa 1122 and describes the visit of a mysterious man to Rome. Calling himself John, Patriarch of the Indians, he is very clearly a forerunner of the priest-king. Arriving at the court of Pope Calixtus II, who reigned from 1119–1124, he regaled the astonished pontiff and his court with an account of a land of marvels and miracles, including an apparent revivification of the preserved body of the apostle Thomas—widely believed at this time to have converted the people of India to Christianity.

The description that follows is startling to say the least; not only for the way in which it sets the tone of the later Prester John material, but for the number of ways that it foreshadows the Grail romances. Because the document itself, discovered in the 1870s by Friedrich Zarncke, the premier scholar of the *Letter of Prester John*, remains of uncertain origin (though it does seem to date reasonably to within a year of 1122, from interior references), we cannot be certain whether any of the Grail authors would have seen it. However, the striking parallels to the earliest Grail myth, as ascribed to Chrétien de Troyes, as well as later retellings, make it hard to dismiss as an important source for the developing legend.

John the Patriarch begins with a description of the chief city of his country, which he calls Hulna. It takes four days to travel from one side to the other, and its walls are very tall and thick enough to allow two Roman chariots to drive side by side along them.[151] Though the midst of the city runs the River Physon, which flows out of paradise.[152] It washes out much gold and many precious jewels, which have made the people of the land very wealthy.

Only devout Christians live there, and if any wicked unbeliever enters the city, he or she is likely to fall dead. Nearby is a mountain surrounded on all sides by the waters of a deep lake that rise almost to the mountaintop for most of the year, only receding when it is time to celebrate the sacred mysteries of Christ in the church that was founded by the apostle Thomas.

---

151. As described in both the description of the Island of the Grail in *Sone* and the castle of Gundebald in *Meriadoc*.
152. Genesis 2.10–12

◆ ◆ ◆

This makes the church inaccessible throughout most of the year, and even the patriarch, elected as a high priest, only visits it once a year, when it is time to celebrate the sacred mysteries.

The description that follows is astonishing, especially in the context of the Grail story and the texts we have been exploring:

> ... within the Holy of Holies of the church is a ciborium of magnificent workmanship, its cover woven with gold and silver, decorated with precious stones of the kind which the river of paradise deposits there. Within this ciborium is the most precious silver shell hanging from silver chains ... but although it is placed in valuable metal, a greater treasure lies within. For there is the body of the apostle, preserved to this day whole and unharmed. The body stands erect above the shell as though still living, and a golden lamp filled with the sacred balsam hangs by ropes of silver before him. From the previous year, when this lamp was first lit, until the current moment, it is found with neither the Balsam diminished nor the lamp extinguished. And by the will of God and the intervention of the apostle, these things are still there until the year passes over ...
>
> As has been said before, according to the custom of the place, when the patriarch returns every year to the church, a great gathering of people follow him, men and women standing before the platform of the glowing apostle, shouting out as one for a portion of the sacred balm. [153]

In another echo of the Grail story, those who stand before the "glowing" body of the apostle, and who are touched by ointment from the lamp that hangs before him, are healed. The presence of a ciborium, as we have seen, is a distinctive factor both in the description of the Grail Temple in *The Later Titurel* and in the account of the building of the temple of the apostle Thomas in the *De Adventu*.

What follows is even more striking. With trembling hands, the patriarch and his priests lift the body of Thomas and place it in a golden chair next to the altar. The description of the apostle is detailed:

> The shape and integrity of the body endures still, through the will of God. He seems as he was when he moved though the world in life, and his face glows with the light of a star. He is most handsome, with red hair to his shoulders and a short, curly red beard. Even his clothes are as fresh as on the day when he first donned them. [154]

153. Our translation, from the Latin text included in Keagan Brewer's *Prester John: The Legend and Its Sources*.

154. Ibid.

❖ ❖ ❖

This is followed by a description full of echoes of the Grail story:

> Once the body is placed upon its throne [… and …] when the time comes to administer the Eucharist, the patriarch gathers offerings, which are placed in a golden dish on the altar. These are then offered on bended knee to the Apostle, who, according to the will of God, takes them in his right hand, prophetically outstretched, so that he seems to be not dead but alive. Keeping the offerings in his outstretched hand he allows one to be taken by each person, approaching in turn and receiving the offering in their mouths with great awe.[155]

These miraculous events continue for a week, with each member of the faithful community receiving the offering, which we can assume to be the sacred wafer. Only those who are pagan or of doubtful belief are turned away, the apostle closing his hand to deny them.

The reference to the tomb of the prophet Daniel is also intriguing. There are actually a number of supposed resting places for the prophet, but the most usually cited is at Susa, where it is still revered today and which is mentioned in the *Letter of Prester John*. Discovered in AD 640, the prophet's remains were said to bring good fortune. A bitter dispute broke out over this between the two tribes who were guardians of the relics. They lived on opposite sides of the River Choasps, and those on one side were perpetually poor while those on the other were rich. This good and bad fortune was tied to the presence of Daniel's body, and fighting broke out between the two tribes for their possession. Eventually this was stopped by the Persian shah Sanjar on the grounds that it was disrespectful to the prophet. He ordered the bier on which the body was laid to be chained at the exact center of a bridge across the river and had a chapel built there which was open to all. The shah also forbade all fishing near the bridge, declaring that it was dangerous due to the presence of goldfish in the water at this point.

This is curiously reminiscent of the division that occurs in *The Later Titurel* between the guardians of the Grail, while the reference to the ban on fishing, though not an exact correlation, reminds us of the daily activity of the Fisher King. The setting of the prophet's grave in Iran may have its own significance due to its proximity to another important site with major connections to the Grail, while the fact that the body is kept on a bier, or bed, is more than slightly reminiscent of the wounded king on his bed in the castle of the Grail.

A total of eighteen manuscript copies of this document have so far come to light, dating from the middle of the twelfth century to the end of the fifteenth. This means that it could have been seen by any one of the major Grail authors, including Chrétien, Robert de Boron, Albrecht, and the author of *Sone*. Though not a Grail text as such, it nonetheless contains

---

155. Ibid.

several essential elements that became central to the evolving myth. The apparently undead Thomas in his chair is very much like the description of the Wounded King in the side chamber of the Grail castle; the presence of a sacred reliquary containing an even more sacred relic (in this instance the uncorrupted body of Thomas); and the fact that this was kept within a ciborium—a canopy resting on four pillars—reminds us of the setting of the hall in Chrétien. The fact that, as we have seen, this is also included in the description of the Holy of Holies in the Solomonic temple and that a ciborium is mentioned significantly in *The Later Titurel*, adds to the importance of its presence—especially as it is a term used by the anonymous author of the *De Adventu*. Nor should we forget that the apostle Thomas (known as Doubting Thomas) is the only one of the disciples to touch the sacred blood of the risen Christ when he doubts the evidence of his eyes and is invited to put his fingers into the wounds. Again, the link with the Grail and its sacred contents is significant.

Reports of the Patriarch John

We might be inclined to dismiss the appearance of the patriarch John as a piece of fiction were it not for another document that describes the visitor from the East in such a way as to leave little doubt that he really existed.

The document in question is a letter from Odo, abbot of the monastery of Saint-Remi in Rheims. Odo's tenure was from 1118 to 1151, which gives us a period in which the letter was written—probably within a year or so of the *De Adventu*. Odo claims to have been present during the visit of the mysterious John (here called Archbishop of the Indians rather than Patriarch). While the letter bears a close similarity to the account of the *De Adventu*, there are also a number of small details that differ, implying that Odo probably wrote from memory and was not simply copying from the existing report.

> On his arrival at the Roman court he reported to officials that he was the head of the church where the body of the Blessed Thomas was laid. Truly, amongst other details he described concerning the location of the aforesaid church, its vast wealth and mighty treasures, he mentioned something that can only amaze those who hear it. [156]

Odo then repeats the description of the church, enclosed on all sides by water, which only receded shortly before the date of the apostle's feast day. Finally he repeats the description of the saint's body being brought forth and how his arm was raised and his hand extended. Into this was placed offerings of one sort or another, which were all received by the saint—excluding

---

156. Our translation from the text in Keagan Brewer's *Prester John: The Legend and Its Sources*.

◆ ◆ ◆

any offered by pagans or unbelievers, at which the fingers closed. This is slightly different from the *De Adventu*, where the saint appears to dispense the host to the congregation.

An interesting coda to Odo's letter is that the pope was apparently suspicious of the visitor and required him to swear to the truth of his account on a gospel. When he did so, the prelate relented and everyone praised the miracles of Thomas.

This depiction of the visitor rings true, though it does not enable us to identify him. One recent authority describes him as an "imposter," but there is actually no reason to see him in this light. He may well have been a visitor from one of the Nestorian churches traditionally founded by St. Thomas or perhaps the long-lost sect of the Nasoreans, whose teachings are reflected so deeply in the earliest Christian writings.[157] Perhaps the writer was making up an account of the wonders of his homeland; we cannot know this. What we can be certain of is that when we hear an account of a mysterious personage called John from a semi-paradisal realm to the East, the description echoes that of both the *De Adventu* and Odo's letter.

The next account appeared in 1143, in a chronicle entitled *De Duabus Civitatibus* ("On the Two Cities") written by Bishop Otto of Freising. This work, which recorded events from the mid-twelfth century, includes an account of a story related by a certain Bishop Hugh of Jabala, in Syria, who had reported to Pope Eugenius III (reigned 1145–1153) concerning the fall of Edessa and a great battle in which

> …a certain John, king and priest, who lives beyond Persia and Armenia in the furthest east, and who with his people, is a Christian, though Nestorian, made war on the brother kings of the Persians and Medes, called the Samiards, and stormed Ecbatana, the seat of their kingdom.[158]

This fatal battle, which ended in a victory for Prester John, has been identified with an actual battle that took place on 9 September 1141 between the armies of the Seljuk sultan Sanjar and Yelu Dashi, leader of the Kara-Khitai, a nomadic tribe from China. This may seem a long way from the battles of the priestly king and the Persia Samiards, but it has been reasonably argued that this encounter, which ended in the destruction of the Moslem army of Sanjar, left behind such echoes that when news of it reached the West, it had become transformed into a Christian victory over the forces of Islam. From this, it is suggested, grew the legend of the Christian monarch ruling over a kingdom in the East who promised to come to the aid of his fellow believers in their time of greatest need.

157. We are grateful to David Elkington for this suggestion.
158. Translated by Keagan Brewer, *Prester John*.

❖ ❖ ❖

It is also perhaps worth noting that Otto's relation of Bishop Hugh's account includes the intriguing statement that the priest-king was descended from "the ancient race of the Magi" and that he ruled over his people with a scepter of emerald. Such details had the effect of making Prester John even more imposing, implying as it did both an ancient and mystical heritage and a great and richly endowed power.

The Mysteries of Thomas

The focus of the *De Adventu* and other documents relating to the origins of Prester John are of great interest, as they suggest several further connections to the works we have been examining. Thomas, one of the original apostles of Christ, was also named *Didymus*, "the twin," which has led to some speculation that he was a twin brother of Jesus. He was also known as "Doubting Thomas" because of his reluctance to acknowledge Jesus's resurrection until he had actually touched the wounds—which, as noted, made him the only one to actually touch the holy blood of the Messiah, which was later to be caught in the Grail.

Early Christian tradition relates that Thomas travelled far to the East, taking word of Christianity as far as India. To this day he is regarded as a patron saint of India, and there is a surviving group in that country that call themselves Saint Thomas Christians.

At some point, possibly around the beginning of the sixth century, the followers of St. Thomas became associated with a Christian splinter group known as the Nestorians. These were followers of Nestorius (AD 386–450), a patriarch of Constantinople from AD 421–431, who pronounced a belief separating the human and divine aspects of Jesus, while the more orthodox fathers of Christianity taught that these were one and the same. Nestorius's teachings brought him into conflict with other theologians and churchmen of the time, and his writings were eventually declared heretical. When this occurred, a number of Nestorius's followers moved to join a breakaway sect known as the Church of the East, located in and around parts of the Persian-Sasanian Empire and modern-day Iran.

The connections between the followers of Thomas and Nestor are best seen as a matter of location rather than of specific belief. But the presence of both groups in the Eastern kingdoms, especially the area once ruled over by the Sasanians, is important, as we shall see, since it connects the story of Thomas, the extraordinary building in which his uncorrupt body was said to be kept, and the later legend of Prester John and the Grail. As we shall see in chapter 7, a collection of buildings, the foundations of which are still extant, are situated within the area once part of the Sasanian kingdom; that they influenced descriptions of the temples of the Grail in the works we have been examining here is almost certain.

+ + +

Vsevolod Slessarev, one of the foremost experts on the Prester John legend, believes that the story of Patriarch John originated in Edessa, a city that has connections both with the Nestorian church and St. Thomas, and was, at one time, said to have possessed the greatest relic of Christendom—the Holy Grail! He believes that the city of Hulna, otherwise unknown, could well be either Edessa itself or a nearby town, as claimed by another medieval traveller.[159] Edessa was itself the site of the tomb of St. Thomas, and at this period it possessed two outer walls with a raised street between them—very like the description of the city contained in *De Adventu*. In addition, the early historian Gregory of Tours (circa 539–594) in his book *De Gloria Martyrum* ("On Glorious Martyrdom") mentions a pilgrimage made by a certain Theodore to the lands of the East, who described a church in India where relics of Thomas were to be seen, and where a lamp burned constantly before the altar without ever needing to be refilled. This, of course, is remarkably like the descriptions in both *The Later Titurel* and the *De Adventu* and again points to a historical aspect in the evolving legend of Prester John.

Slessarev believed that the Thomas legend sprang from a relic—perhaps a hand—belonging to the apostle, which had originally been kept at Edessa and was subsequently taken to a church further east. This is certainly in keeping with the story of Patriarch John's visit and the information he gave to the pope. Whatever the truth, the most important factors remain the description of the relics and their veneration within the temple built to house them. These, together with the connection with the Nestorian church and the followers of St. Thomas, are essential pointers for our developing argument.

The New Grail King

The *Letter of Prester John* itself arrived in Europe less than a decade later than these writings, but in these few years something had happened to the visitor from afar—he had become a far more mythical figure. He had become the priest-king John.

We can see immediately how many borrowings there are, both from the letter itself and from the older source of the *De Adventu*, in Albrecht's description of the Grail Temple. Its construction is done at the bidding of angels, and many of the components used are the same, with lists of precious stones extremely close. Even the lists of curious beasts are close to those in Albrecht's account, as are other details, such as the fact that no one who enters the building goes away hungry and the sick are restored to health within a day of being there. There is no

---

159. Slessarev, *Prester John*, 18–21.

mention of a sacred object such as the Grail or the Ark, but the building is a place of power and the priest-king himself an imposing and perhaps semi-divine figure.

An interesting variation is the name of Prester John's father, who in Wolfram's *Parzifal* is called Feirefiz but is here given as Quasidus. This is a name that might tentatively be translated as "semi-god" or perhaps semi-divine; other suggestions are "god-like" or even "face-of-God."[160] The important factor is that, like Titurel, he is instructed by a heavenly voice to build the palace—though he does not appear to have the divine help provided by the Grail. That the palace is described more in terms of a temple is significant, as is the fact that it is created for the future king of kings. We can see how Albrecht and others could have seen this as a highly appropriate home for the most sacred of relics.

We also learn that this not the first such heavenly inspired building connected with this story. Earlier, the apostle Thomas, whose history inspired the figure of Prester John, had been commanded to build a palace for a King Gondoforus. The mention of this monarch is interesting, as it leads us to an account in the great medieval book of Christian mythology known as *The Golden Legend*, attributed to the twelfth-century author Jacobus de Voragine. There, we learn:

> When St. Thomas was at Cesarea, our Lord appeared to him and said, "The king of the Indies, Gondoforus, hath sent his provost Abanes to seek out workmen well versed in the science of architecture, who shall build for him a palace finer than that of the emperor of Rome. Behold, now I will send thee to him." And Thomas went and Gondoforus commanded to build for him a magnificent palace, and gave him much gold and silver for the purpose.
>
> The king went into a distant country, and was absent for two years; and St. Thomas meanwhile, instead of building a palace, distributed all the treasures entrusted to him among the poor and sick; and when the king returned, he was full of wrath, and he commanded that St. Thomas should be seized and cast into prison, and he meditated for him a horrible death.
>
> Meantime the brother of the king died; and the king resolved to erect for him a most magnificent tomb; but the dead man, after that he had been dead four days, suddenly arose and sat upright and said to the king "The man whom thou wouldst torture is a servant of God: behold I have been in Paradise, and the angels showed to me a wondrous palace of gold and silver and precious stones, and they said, "This is the palace that Thomas the architect hath built for thy brother King Gondoforus."

160. M. Uebel, *Ecstatic Transformation: On the Uses of Alterity in the Middle Ages* (New York, 2005).

◆ ◆ ◆

And when the king heard these words, he ran to the prison, and delivered the apostle and Thomas said to him, "Knowest thou not that those who would possess heavenly things, have little care for the things of this earth? There are in heaven rich palaces without number, which were prepared from the beginning of the world for those who purchase the possession through faith and charity. Thy riches, O King, may prepare the way for thee to such a palace, but they cannot follow thee thither." [161]

From this we see that not only was there an earlier temple, based upon one seen by the king's resurrected brother, but that the palace is perceived as a metaphor for the heavenly city or temple in the paradisal realm. If we are right in our belief that the underlying purpose of the accounts of such buildings, and even more of their physical manifestations, is the creation of places where the individual may encounter the Divine directly, just as those who go in search of the Grail are allowed to do, this fits exactly.

The legend of St. Thomas and King Gondoforus was well known throughout France during the Middle Ages; it is depicted in one of the windows of the cathedral in the ancient city of Bourges and is also the subject of one of the medieval French mystery plays, once acted with great popularity in Paris during the fourteenth century.

The mention of mysterious salamanders can also be seen as the source of both Albrecht and Wolfram's vision. The weaving of the material called *pfelle*, which simply means "skin," probably refers to the confusion of the lizard-like creatures and the cocoons spun by silkworms, who were widely believed to spin the threadlike material asbestos and until as recently as the eighteenth century were still believed to live in fire. According to Wolfram, Gawain's surcoat was woven by salamander worms in the hottest fires close to the mountain of Muntsalvasche. The fact that Prester John also owned a mirror that enabled him to see what his enemies were doing recalls that owned by the anti-Grail king Clingchor in Wolfram's *Parzifal* and a replica of this described in the creation of a church in Southern Germany, which partially replicated the Grail Temple in *The Later Titurel* (see chapter 7).

There is no question that the *Letter of Prester John* had an enormous effect on the romance literature of the Middle Ages. Descriptions that perfectly mirror those contained in the letter are found not only in the context of the Grail myth, but in the medieval romances of Alexander the Great and the travel writings of Sir John Mandeville. Albrecht would have been familiar with at least some of these and with one of the many copies of the letter itself.

---

161. Text from *Sacred and Legendary Art* by Anna Jameson (London, 1911), 245–50.

As we have seen, Albrecht altered the focus of the Grail castle to that of a temple. He refers to a "hall," which seems to echo both Wolfram and Chrétien's description of the castle of the Grail, but now the castle is a sacred temple. How this change occurred may be traced back to the simple fact that Albrecht's borrowing from the *Letter of Prester John* meant that the country of the Grail had became synonymous with the earthly paradise, making a temple more appropriate as a building created to house the Grail than a secular building that represented the chivalry and warfare of knightly endeavor.

The Beautiful Garden

India became the home of Prester John because it was considered to be where the entrance to the earthly paradise lay. *The Later Titurel* is not the only Arthurian romance to associate one of its heroes with a paradisal setting with close similarities to the priest-king's realm. In the long Dutch poem *Roman van Walewein* (Gawain) by Penninc and Pieter Vostaert,[162] Gawain makes his way to a castle that echoes not only the description from the *Letter of Prester John* but also Albrecht and others, who each sought to place the earthly paradise in a specific spot. The English poet John Gower, in his *Confessio Amantis*,[163] made it clear that India was where Prester John dwelled. Where else, indeed, should one situate the Grail but there?

In *Walewein* Gawain's chief adversary is a king named Assentijn, who seeks to prevent Gawain from wooing his daughter Ysabel. In order to win the girl, Gawain has to make his way to Assentjin's castle, which lies somewhere in "distant India." Within this castle is a kind of paradisal garden in which Ysabel holds court. In it is a type of Fountain of Youth, which, like the Grail, sustains the life of anyone who drinks from it.

> It is right for me to praise this well, for from the Earthly Paradise itself flows a stream which wells up at this splendid and sparkling clear fountain … Though a man were 500 years old, if he were to taste but a drop from the fountain, he would surely and without a doubt become as strong and as young as if, at that very moment, he had become as he was when he was 30 years old.[164]

Above the fountain grows a splendid olive tree on which sits a golden eagle that protects the spot from any evil. Also present are rose bushes, bay trees, and many sweet-scented herbs, not to mention a golden tree with hollow branches through which air is pumped by eight men with

162. Penninc and Vostaert, *Roman van Walewein*.

163. Gower, *Confessio Amantis*.

164. Lines 3550–57, 3686–92 in Putter, "Walewein in the Otherworld and the Land of Prester John," 79–99.

✦ ✦ ✦

bellows hidden in a chamber beneath. On every branch sit little golden birds that sing sweetly when the air is pushed though them. These also have healing properties:

> The man who hears that sweet music,
> Though he were wounded to the quick
> If he were there but a short space of time
> And heard those little birds sing
> He would be healed of all his pain. [165]

The castle itself echoes the descriptions of the Grail castle in the works we have explored. It is surrounded by twelve walls, each one with four score towers, while between every second wall runs a moat. Gates of copper and bronze, bound with steel and iron, are the only way in, and these are each guarded by at least eighty armed men.

Aside from the striking similarity to the descriptions of the Grail Temple in *Titurel*, there are other echoes. In the description of Quasidus's temple in the *Letter of Prester John* we find again twelve gates, which may be modeled on the twelve gates of the heavenly Jerusalem (Revelation 21:12). It has also been suggested[166] that these references may derive from another apocryphal medieval text, *The Vision of St. Paul*, where we read:

> I entered the city of Christ. It was all gold and twelve walls encircled it, and there were twelve towers inside it…[An] angel…said to me: "The second is better than the first, and likewise the third is better than the second; for one excels the other right up to the twelfth wall." [167]

The descriptions are consistent throughout, and though there are inevitable variations, the general indication is that the vision of the earthly paradise followed a distinctive pattern that can be traced from biblical sources (and earlier) through the romance literature of the Middle Ages. It is very clearly present in both the *Letter of Prester John*, the description of the Grail Temple and its setting in *Titurel*, and the description of the Grail Island in *Sone*.

To the medieval mind, the otherworld was an absolute reality. Entrances to faeryland hid behind bushes and rocks, while the rivers of paradise flowed into the Euphrates and the Tiber. In *Walewein* the hero finds himself on the banks of the River of Purgatory, while a stream out of paradise rises in the garden of his beloved. Thus, when the medieval audience heard or read tales of quests and adventures leading to strange lands full of curious beasts and splendid build-

---

165. Lines 3344–48, trans. Johnson in Penninc and Vostaert's *Roman van Walewein*.

166. Ibid.

167. *St. Paul's Apocalypse*, 30–33.

ings, these were as real to them as accounts of heaven, hell, and Eden. These could all be located on earthly maps, and often were, and the realm of Prester John was believed to be reachable—provided one had the strength of will and the courage to get there. So, too, the castle of the Grail and the various shrines, temples, and chapels that held the holy relic were just as likely to be real, and when described in the kind of detail lavished upon them by the authors of *The Later Titurel* and *Sone*, this became even more deeply embedded in the imaginal world of the medieval poets and storytellers.

That the character of John mostly vanished from the later texts can be ascribed to two things—the recognition of the important part played by Joseph of Arimathea in the stories that drew upon the Passion narratives of the four canonical Gospels, and the gradual loss of belief in the existence of the king of the far distant, paradisal realm of the Indies. Perhaps also we may see it as a more simple triumph of nearer and prevailing myths of the West.

In short, Prester John was written out of the Grail narrative, with the exception of the brief reference in Wolfram's *Parzifal* and the much longer and more detailed account found in *The Later Titurel*. Yet even the briefest reading of the *Letter of Prester John*, with the addition of the information found in the *De Adventu*, one at least of which was almost certainly available to our authors, shows that the story could not be completely excised.

The detailed descriptions of the Grail kingdom, as well as of the temple and the Fisher King's castle and the island in *Sone de Nansay*, all point significantly to a common thread, which was very much in the forefront of the imaginal world of the medieval poets and storytellers, who established Prester John as the latest in a line of Grail kings and guardians.

With such remarkable figures keeping watch over the Grail, it is small wonder, then, if the actual buildings where they dwelled were seen as magical and powerful. Before we look more closely at some actual sites that had an enormous influence on the way the Grail Temples were presented, we must examine the nature of those who dwelled within these temples and castles.

◆ ◆ ◆

6

GUARDIANS OF THE GRAIL

As to those who are appointed to the Gral, hear how
they are made known. Under the top edge of the
Stone an inscription announces the name and lineage
of the one summoned to make the glad journey.

◆ ◆ ◆

Wolfram von Eschenbach, *Parzival*

If the Grail had a home, where it was preserved for those who would come in search of it, that home needed guardians. This seems to have been a given from the very earliest Grail stories, and when we look at the work of Chrétien de Troyes and Robert de Boron, Wolfram von Eschenbach or the author of *Sone*, we can see that all are very clear on this matter. Though Chrétien failed to make this specific, the implication is that the Grail is associated not only with a place, but a family. Robert expanded this in his *Joseph* and Wolfram opened the way still further in his *Parzifal* by making it clear that the family was extensive and that a larger group of guardians were involved. That he chose to call this group *Templiesen* (Templars) has caused an association that may or may not have existed between the Grail and the Knights Templar. This is not the place to argue the rights and wrongs of the theory one way or the other; what is clear, from Wolfram's text onwards, is the growing circle of Grail guardians, families whose lineage are linked to the sacred relic. In both *Sone* and *The Later Titurel* a lineage is established whose members and their decedents become kings, emperors, and popes ruling over much of Europe. We have also seen how, in *Titurel*, the Grail itself is proactive in arranging a marriage between the previously celibate Titurel and the Spanish princess Richaud, and how one of the latest

◆ ◆ ◆

guardians to be mentioned, the priest-king John, was written out of the story by the increasing emphasis given by the Grail writers to Joseph of Arimathea.

Before we can proceed further with our account of the temples of the Grail, we need to look at the evolving story of these guardians, beginning with Robert de Boron.

The earliest sources for the Grail family are the *Joseph d'Arimathie* and the *Didot Perceval*, the first definitely by Robert and the second attributed to him. As we have seen, it is to Robert that we owe the first melding of the Grail story with apocryphal Christian sources in the shape of the Gospel of Nicodemus and the Acts of Pilate, both documents omitted from the final canon of the New Testament.

In Robert's poem, Joseph of Arimathea is the first guardian (not yet a king) of the sacred vessel, followed by his son Josephus. Robert names Alain le Gros, twelfth son of Bron, Joseph of Arimathea's brother-in-law, as the third keeper of the Grail. Alain's son is identified as Perceval in the *Didot Perceval*—making him the fourth keeper—though elsewhere his father is either named Gamuret or Bliocadran.[168]

One of the four continuations of Chrétien's *Conte del Graal*, attributed to Gerbert de Montreuil, tells us more of the history of the Grail family. At the Castle of Maidens, the wounded Perceval is given a fuller account than that offered by Chrétien. After treating Perceval's wounds, Ysabel, the mistress of the castle, tells how her cousin, Philosofine, who is here named as Perceval's mother, came with the Grail from across the sea and, because the land was waste and full of sinful people, angels bore the sacred vessel away to the house of the Fisher King. The implication here is that it was intended to be lodged in the Castle of Maidens but was taken, for safekeeping, to the Grail castle.[169] The name of Perceval's mother as Philosofine suggests a connection with a long lineage of female Grail bearers stretching back to Wisdom, the Shekinah, who dwelled with exiled humanity in the Holy of Holies within the first temple of Solomon.

From this we may see a possible reference to a convent of nuns, perhaps a more appropriate home for the Grail, though in Gerbert it has more of an otherworldly feel. In several Arthurian romances nuns are regarded as practitioners of magic, as in Malory's *Le Morte d'Arthur*, where the king's half sister Morgan le Fay is "put to school in a nunnery, where she became a great clerk of necromancy."[170]

---

168. Bryant, *The Complete Story of the Grail*.

169. Ibid.

170. Malory, *Le Morte d'Arthur*.

From Chrétien we learn that the Fisher King is over three hundred years old and that his name is Mordrain. While staying at an abbey, Perceval is told how, forty years after Christ's death, the lands of a heathen king named Evalac of Sarras had been ravaged by a king of Syria. Joseph of Arimathea tells Evalac that he could vanquish his adversary if he became a Christian. This fell out as Joseph had predicted and Evalac, taking the name Mordrain, became a devout Christian. When Joseph later came to Britain, Philosofine accompanied him. She brought with her "a trencher brighter than the moon and a lance that bled constantly," while Joseph brought "the most beautiful vessel ever seen." This offers a slightly different lineup to the usual Grail hallows and tells us more about the burgeoning family.

A wicked king named Crudel now imprisons Joseph and his followers, and when Mordrain hears of this, he sails to ravage Crudel's lands. However, in the process, Mordrain is badly wounded; when Joseph shows him the Grail, in the hope of healing him, Mordrain tried to peer into it, at which an angel with a fiery sword appeared and told him he had done wrong, his wounds would never heal, and he would not die until a true knight without sin relieved him of this burden.

The collapsing of the time-scale in this retelling, and the family relationships implied by it, give us pause. According to this account, Joseph of Arimathea and Perceval's mother are contemporaries, while the connection between the apocryphal accounts of the aftermath of Christ's Passion and the time of Arthur is made even stronger.

Robert's *Joseph* was created out of a blending of the canonical Passion narratives and the non-canonical fourth-century accounts found in the Acts of Pilate and the Gospel of Nicodemus. It retells the story of the vessel as both the cup in which Christ celebrated the Last Supper and the vessel in which his blood is caught after the Crucifixion. The cup passes into the hands of Pilate and is given by him to Joseph, who, as a soldier in the Roman army, comes to ask for a gift in return for his long service. Pilate also permits Joseph and Nicodemus to take the body of Jesus, and Joseph catches some blood in the vessel as the body is prepared for burial.

However, while Christ is descending into hell to free Adam and Eve and their faithful descendants, the tomb is broken open by the Jews, who, fearful of the retribution that might fall on them for not guarding the now-vanished body, arrest Joseph and put him in prison, sealing it up. Here the story deviates in detail from the account given by the Abbot of Gwales in *Sone*. Joseph survives his long incarceration and is visited by Christ, who brings the light-filled vessel of the most precious blood to him. Joseph is bidden to keep the vessel, which he is told has three powers that he may call upon for help when in need. Robert dares not tell us about these: "I couldn't even if I wanted to, if I did not have the high book in which they are written, and that is the creed of the great mystery of the Grail."

Once released by Vespasian, Joseph goes to the household of his sister Enigeus and her husband, Bron. They and their people are suffering from severe famine, and so Joseph prays before the vessel and asks for guidance. He is instructed to set a table, like that of the Last Supper, with an empty place between Bron and himself to signify the seat of Judas. This place, he is told, cannot be filled until a son of Bron sits in it. Bron is then told to go fishing and to bring the first of his catch, while Joseph lays the table, putting the vessel on it and covering it with the edge of the tablecloth. When everyone is seated, the company senses "a sweetness and fulfilment of their hearts." Those who feel nothing are sent away, for it is their sins that have brought the famine upon all. Everyone asks about the vessel and what it should be called; they are told:

> Those who wish to name it rightly will call it the Grail, which gives such joy and delight
> to those who can stay in its presence that they feel as elated as a fish escaping from a man's
> hands into the wide water.[171]

All those who have eaten, including a man named Petrus, remain a long while in a state of grace. Bron and Enigeus have twelve children and ask Joseph's advice about them. They are told that they should all be married off but that if one does not wish to do so, he should be sent to Joseph. The twelfth son, Alain li Gros, elects to remain celibate and is taught about the Grail's history. Another of Bron's company, the same Petrus who had been so deeply affected by the Grail, is sent ahead into the West to await Alain's coming. He will not be able to pass from life into death until this happened, but instead he will go to the vales of Avaron (Avalon). Joseph is instructed to prepare Bron as the keeper and guardian of the vessel after him. He then adds, "All who hear tell of him will call him the rich Fisher King because of the fish he caught."[172]

At this point Robert breaks off, taking up the story in his next work, *Merlin*, where we hear of the birth of the great enchanter, the coming of the Pendragon dynasty (including Arthur), and the establishment of a third table, the Round Table. (The first two are the table of the Last Supper and the table of Joseph.) Uther Pendragon wonders greatly about the empty place at the Round Table and is told that it will not be filled in his time, but that someone will come during his son's lifetime. When Arthur comes of age, Merlin tells him how Alain and Bron came to the isles of Ireland, but that Bron (now called the Fisher King) is woefully ill. When a renowned knight comes and asks the question about the Grail's service, the Fisher King will be

171. Bryant, *Merlin and the Grail*, 36.
172. Ibid., 42.

healed and impart the secret words of Christ, told to Joseph of Arimathea, to the new keeper of the vessel. With that the enchantments of the land of Britain will vanish, and the prophecy will be fulfilled. The implication is also that the Grail family will continue its guardianship of the sacred vessel, which will remain in the world for the time being.

The next stage of the story is found in the text known as the *Didot Perceval*, after its first editor and owner, which it has been suggested is a prose version of a poem by Robert, now lost. In this version of the story we learn that Alain le Gros's son, Perceval, wishes to come to Arthur's court. The story of the young knight's adventure is then told, substantially as we know it from Chrétien, only now, following the account found in *Joseph* and *Merlin*, we are aware that he is of the lineage of a family associated with the Grail. We hear about his seven-year quest and are told that

> Chrétien de Troyes says nothing of this—nor do the other trouvères who have turned these stories into jolly rhymes … Merlin saw and knew exactly what befell Perceval each day.[173]

Perceval comes to the Grail castle following a path shown to him by Merlin, entering into his grandfather's presence and finally asking the purpose of the Grail procession. As soon as he asks this question, Bron, the Fisher King, is healed. Knowing that he will now die within three days, Bron tells Perceval about his ancestors and places the sacred vessel into his hands. From it arises a melody and perfume so sweet that all present feel as if they were in paradise. At the same time the enchantments upon the world are broken. Merlin comes to the house of the new Fisher King, Perceval, and the rest of the Arthurian story speeds to its end with the breaking of the Round Table through the treachery of Mordred and the death of Arthur.

Robert de Boron's skill in seamlessly attaching the apocryphal Gospel of Nicodemus to the Arthurian legends by means of the Grail is unsurpassed. It has a shapeliness and symmetry that only a good storyteller can bring to it. By making the story of Christ's Passion and its major relic into a vessel that "delights the heart of all worthy men," Robert makes it a means of healing for all ills. By making Perceval the great-nephew of Joseph of Arimathea, he ensured that the knight would forever be seen as one of a lineage of Grail guardians.

The Secret Families

From the first romances concerning the Grail, the lineage of guardians began to be consciously woven into a pattern of secrecy. In *Parzival* we are told that those born into the Grail lineage are subject to an extraordinary dynastic regulation. The children of noble families, who are called

---

173. Ibid., 147.

✦ ✦ ✦

to the Grail when they are small, attain paradise when they live and die chastely, with only the Grail king marrying. But there are exceptions; if a particular country needs a ruler, girls may be sent openly and boys in secret to become wives or husbands as required. They are, however, forbidden to tell anyone from whence they come.

Apart from the covert secrecy and chastity, this is not much different from the usual arrangement of dynastic marriage in medieval times. In *Parzival* Wolfram also binds together the Grail legends and the Crusader ethic of his time by making the soldiers of the Grail *templeisen* who defend the Grail and its places. These are men who do not marry but who are wholly in the service of the Grail.

The Grail family and its interconnections provide the legends with a means of ancestral destiny. The Fisher King, who starts out as an almost otherworldly figure in his undying, unageing court, soon becomes an ancient king ruling over a wasted land, but with the promise of healing from the hands of a descendent.

The lineage of the Grail kings varies according to different storytellers, each of whom seeks to establish a different family, giving the Fisher King a host of relatives, forebears, and descendants, and giving the Grail legends a sense of consistency through time.

In the Lancelot-Grail cycle, the *Estoire del Saint Graal* lists the following lineage: Josue (the first Grail king), Aminadap, Carcelois, Manaal, Lambor, Pellehan, and Pelles/Pellam, who rules over the Grail lands in Arthur's time and whose daughter Elaine is the mother of Galahad (fathered upon her by Lancelot). Thus the Christian and Arthurian stories become forever linked.[174]

Wolfram, writing less than twelve years after Robert, named Titurel as the first of the Grail kings, followed by Frimutel, Anfortas (his name for the Wounded King), and Perceval and his son Lohengrin, the Swan Knight whose story we shall explore further in chapter 7. As we have seen, this was a lead followed by Albrecht in *The Later Titurel*. Here the Grail lineage is extended vastly, including many generations of Titurel's family, so that when his time comes to die, aged 500, his descendants are already set up to continue the family connection with the Grail—though it is Prester John, who stands apart from the family, who eventually assumes this mantle.

Another German writer, Heinrich von dem Türlin, writing in his epic *Diü Crône* ("The Crown") around the time of Wolfram's death in 1220, emphasizes the curse laid upon the Grail family and has his hero, the great Arthurian knight Gawain, save them from a living death. In

174. *The Lancelot-Grail: The Old French Arthurian Vulgate and Post-Vulgate in Translation.*

♦ ♦ ♦

the process Heinrich gives us one of the most detailed versions of the Grail procession. But it is to Gawain alone that the Grail king himself explains its true meaning, and thus the story changes direction by making Gawain a successful Grail winner.

> Sir Gawain, this marvel which is of God may not be known unto all, but shall be held secret, yet since ye have asked thereof, sweet kinsman and dear guest, I may not withhold the truth … Of the Grail may I say no more save that ye have seen it, and that great gladness hath come of this your question. For now are many set free from the sorrow they long have borne, and small hope had they of deliverance. Great confidence and trust had we all in Perceval, that he would learn the secret things of the Grail, yet hence did he depart even as a coward who ventured naught, and asked naught. Thus did his quest miscarry, and he learned not that which of surety he should have learned, [and thus] freed many a mother's son from sore travail, who live, and yet are dead. Through the strife of kinsmen did this woe befall, when one brother smote the other for his land: and for that treason was the wrath of God shown on him and on all his kin, that all were alike lost.
>
> That was a woeful chance, for the living they were driven out, but the dead must abide in the semblance of life, and suffer bitter woe withal. That must you know—yet had they hope and comfort in God and His grace, that they should come even to the goal of their grief in such fashion, as I shall tell you.
>
> Should there be a man of their race who should end this their sorrow, in that he should demand the truth of these marvels, that were the goal of their desire; so would their penance be fulfilled, and they should again enter into joy: alike they who lay dead and they who live, and now give thanks to God and to ye, for by ye are they now released. This spear and this food, they nourish me and none other, for in that I was guiltless of the deed God condemned me not. Dead I am, though I bear not the semblance of death, and this my folk is dead with me. However this may be, yet though all knowledge be not yours, yet have we riches in plenty, and know no lack … And know of a truth that the adventures ye have seen came of the Grail, and now is the penance perfected, and forever done away, and your quest hath found its ending.[175]

Already we are informed that a knight of the linage is the one who should bring healing. In this instance, Gawain, who is nowhere else connected to the Grail family, does so.

As the day begins to dawn, the company slowly fade from sight, except for Gawain's two companions and the maidens who carried the Grail and the other wondrous objects.

> And Sir Gawain was somewhat sorry, when he saw his host no more, yet was he glad when the maiden spake, saying that his labour was now at an end, and he had in sooth done all that pertained unto the Quest of the Grail, for never else in any land, save in that Burg alone,

175. Weston, *Gawain at the Grail Castle*, 42–45.

might the Grail have been beheld. Yet had that land been waste, but God had hearkened to their prayer, and by his coming had folk and land alike been delivered, and for that were they joyful."[176]

Here not only the Grail king, but also his entire family, along with their followers, appears to suffer. Instead of the Grail king alone being kept alive by the Grail, the whole community has been dead for a very long while, and only Gawain's asking of the fateful question sets them free. We cannot help remembering the pit from which issues the sound of lamenting in *Perlesvaus* and the sorrowful people on the Island of Gwales in *Sone*. In the *Crown* Gawain is the one who relieves the great lamentation that afflicts all at the Grail castle and beyond, just as Sone, Perceval, and Galahad, amongst others, are destined to do in the later romances.

The Coming of Joseph of Arimathea

Before the long lineage of Grail knights and maidens, one figure stood out as the first and most important guardian of the Grail. Though Albrecht is alone in making Joseph of Arimathea the first wounded Grail king, the fact that he does so points to the importance of Joseph as central to the history of the sacred vessel. As the one responsible for obtaining the Cup of the Last Supper and some of Christ's blood, and later of receiving the secret teachings of the saviour, it was inevitable that he should take centre stage. In tracing the story of Joseph back from the medieval period, the story of the Grail is also shifted back in time to several hundred years before Chrétien and Robert de Boron created their own visions.

It is a general assumption among Arthurian scholars that Chrétien invented the story of the Grail as we know it today, and that Robert de Boron was the first to connect the story with the Passion of Christ. There are, however, a number of problems with this, based as it is on standard assumptions dating back to the earlier studies of the Grail in the nineteenth century. While the word *grail* or its variants had apparently not been used in this context at the time, the basic constituents of the stories had been written about by early theologians and even possibly sung by jongleurs and told by storytellers as early as AD 500. The evidence also suggests that the story was not a simple romance, written for entertainment, but a far more serious polemical text that sought to explain the deeper significance of the Eucharist as something more than a spiritual reality, but also as a means of transmitting a far older theological tradition, dating back to an even earlier period. It is only when we begin to look at these early sources, including those

---

176. Weston, *Gawain at the Grail Castle*, 45–46.

we have been exploring, that we begin to see both why and how Joseph's role became so crucial and how this connected to the place where the Grail was kept.

The question has frequently been asked, with a variety of answers, where Chrétien found his story. Various suggestions have been advanced, including Hermetic texts,[177] Hebrew traditions, and medieval folklore.[178] But a particular set of sources, which have been largely ignored, include the writings of a number of early theological exegetes who sought to explore the mysteries of the Eucharist in symbolic terms; this at a time long before these topics were finally ratified at the Lateran Council of 1215. In the history of Eucharistic devotion, the Real Presence of Christ in the species of blood and wine was first defined in AD 1079 by Pope Gregory VII, while the Corpus Christi (Body of God) was not instituted until AD 1264 by Pope Urban IV. But from this we can see that the liturgical and devotional impulse, where the host was first processed publically in the streets, neatly frames the major period of the Grail romances.

Everything points to the probability that these writings contain the origin of the Grail myth in a form that both Chrétien and Robert would have recognized, and with which they were clearly familiar. It is also a firm basis for considering that the texts of *Sone de Nansay* and *The Later Titurel* preserved an older Grail tradition, despite being written chronologically after the works of Chrétien and Robert de Boron.

It is more than likely that both the earlier poets (who were well-educated men) were familiar with the continuing traditions that associated Joseph of Arimathea with certain objects of the Passion and understood by the word *grail* (in its many forms, as *greal, graal, gradalis*) something specific and far from the somewhat "vague" assumptions usually attributed to Chrétien.[179]

One of the most often-quoted early accounts of the Grail material comes from the writings of the early thirteenth-century poet and chronicler Hélinand of Froidmont (circa 1150–1229 to 1237). Hélinand proffers an etymology of sorts:

> A marvelous vision was revealed at that time to a certain hermit in Britain. It was about St. Joseph the counselor who took the Lord's body down from the cross and about that bowl or dish in which the Lord ate with his disciples. A story entitled "Concerning the Grail" was related about it by the same hermit. *Gradalis*, or in French *gradale*, is said to be a dish somewhat deep, in which costly delicacies in their proper succession are usually served step by step [*gradatim*] by rich people, one morsel after another in different orders. In the vernacular

---

177. Henry Kahane and Renee Kahane, *The Krater and the Grail: Hermetic Sources of the Parzival* (Illinois Studies in Language and Literature, University of Illinois Press, 1965).

178. Barber, *The Holy Grail, Imagination and Belief*, and Wood, *Eternal Chalice*.

179. See particularly Neitze, *Perceval and the Holy Grail*, and Bruce, *The Evolution of Arthurian Romance*.

✦ ✦ ✦

language it is called *graalz* because it is pleasing [*grata*] and delightful to the one eating from it. This may be either because of the container, since it was perhaps of silver or some other precious metal; or because of its contents, that is, the manifold order of costly delicacies…"[180]

It is easy to see here the suggestion of ritual process invoking the word *gradus*, "steps." The Grail quest is itself a kind of initiatic road, and we will not be far wrong in considering that the ways into and through the various Grail Temples (as in the case of the one created by Arnoul the Elder, which we explored in chapter 1) as similarly offering a ritual passage.

Neither Chrétien nor Robert invented the word *graal*. According to Professor Bogdanow, it appears in a Venetian manuscript of the *Roman d'Alexandre* composed some ten years before Chrétien wrote the first part of his *Conte du Graal*. In line 618 is a reference to a dish or platter: *Ersoir mangai o toi a ton graal* ("this night eat from your grail").[181] Nor is this the only such reference.

One of the most important of these early references is found in the *Libre de Gamaliel* ("Book of Gamaliel")[182] written by Pere Pasqual, bishop of Jaen, sometime before his death in 1300. This is a late version of the fragmentary Coptic Gospel of Gamaliel (dating from the fifth century or earlier), which brought together parts of the Acts of Pilate and the Gospel of Nicodemus.[183] These last named, as we saw earlier, were a central platform for Robert de Boron when composing his *Joseph*. The *Libre de Gamaliel*, composed in Catalan at the end of the thirteenth century, derived from an earlier—now lost—text in Occitan, which claimed to have been written by Joseph of Arimathea himself, helped by Nicodemus, with the addition of a narrative by the less familiar Gamaliel. Later, in the fifteenth century, Gamaliel was identified with a Rabbi Gamaliel the Elder, mentioned in Acts 5:34 and 22:3 and in the Jewish *Mishna*.[184] This text, written within five hundred years of Christ's lifetime, brought together the narrative of the Passion and the life of Joseph of Arimathea in a form that was to be repeated, with variants, throughout the Middle Ages, particularly within the sphere of the Grail romances. It is certainly possible that Robert had seen one of the earlier copies of the original Gospel.

180. Cabaniss, "Joseph of Arimathea and a Chalice," 61–67.

181. Bogdanow, "Robert de Boron's Vision of Arthurian History," 19–52.

182. Izquerdo, "The Gospel of Nicodemus in Medieval Catalan and Occitan Literature."

183. *The Apocryphal New Testament*, translated by M. R. James (The Clarendon Press, 1975), 96–145. Mingana, *Woodbrook Studies*.

184. Scavone, "Gospel of Gamaliel."

+ + +

The single most significant aspect of Pasqual's translation is the use of the word *gresal*, which can clearly be seen to share its origins with *gredale*. Having described the events of the Crucifixion and the healing of Longinus by the blood running down the lance, Pasqual adds:

> Then Joseph of Arimathea took a *gresal* in which he put the blood of Jesus Christ, and he kept the lance; and they all returned to the city, save for the relatives of the mother of Jesus Christ and the others who were with her, St. John the Evangelist and Joseph of Arimathea. [185]

This is the only known instance so far discovered of a word which clearly shares its origin and meaning with the word *grail* being used by an ecclesiastical writer, nor can we be certain that the anonymous author of the original Gospel of Gamaliel used it; however, we can see that in using this word, Pasqual demonstrated an understanding of the connection between the vessel used to collect the blood of Christ and the story of the Grail.[186] It bears witness to the fact that, as noted by the medievalist Alan Cabaniss, Grail literature was in its turn beginning to affect the interpretation of the liturgy.[187]

Cabaniss also noted that "the words translated above as bowl (*catinus*) and dish (*paropsis*) are the words employed respectively in the *Vulgate* Mark 14:20 and Matthew 26:23 to render the Greek *trublion* (bowl or dish)."[188] He believes that the reference here is to "the Passover dish of *charoseth* (crushed fruits and bitter herbs), as appears by the mention of delicacies in it, not to the content of the *matzoth* or the one with the Paschal lamb."[189]

As noted previously, Chrétien may well have been a convert from Judaism, in which case he would have been familiar with the Passover celebrations and rituals, but even if this is not the case, he could still have encountered Hebraic rituals amongst the educated Jews who attended the rabbinical and Kabalistic schools in Troyes.

Meanwhile, if we look again at Robert de Boron's writing, we find there much to suggest that the symbolic representation of the Grail and the mysteries of the Passion became connected through a number of theological tracts written between the sixth and eleventh centuries.[190]

185. Izquerdo, 68–9. Our italics.

186. Barber, *The Holy Grail, Imagination and Belief*, 170–1.

187. Cabaniss, "Joseph of Arimathea and a Chalice."

188. Ibid., 67.

189. Ibid., 67.

190. O'Gorman, "Ecclesiastical Tradition and the Holy Grail."

❖ ❖ ❖

Both Chrétien and Robert would have been familiar with these writings, most of which copied each other and all of which seem to have followed the important text *Ecclesiastical History and Mystical Contemplation* written by St. Germanus of Constantinople in the eighth century, some 400 years before Chrétien began his final work.[191] Here we find two distinct themes that show how both Chrétien and Robert came to make the connection between the vessel of the Last Supper and the more elaborate symbolism of the Grail. That this work was itself based on a possibly earlier text, known as the *Book of Joseph of Arimathea*, we shall demonstrate shortly.

The Mysterious Vessel

It has been often noted that the Grail as presented in Chrétien's *Conte del Graal* is not specifically Christian, because he does not use the word "Holy" to describe the vessel; however, most commentators look no further than the procession observed by Perceval at the castle of the Fisher King. Those who do so, in particular at the description offered by Chrétien in which the Wounded King is described as being kept alive for twelve years by a single host, received daily from the Grail, must surely notice that this is an exact identification of the symbolic actions of the Eucharist. Though it has been suggested that the later passage in Chrétien was added later,[192] there is no reason to suppose this simply on the evidence of its content. Certainly, Chrétien must have been aware of what he was describing, and it is likely that he had access to a number of theological texts, both contemporary and older, since the shadowy presences of these are present throughout his work as they are, even more prominently, in that of Robert de Boron.

Amongst Robert's works, the *Joseph* in particular has been claimed to contain a variety of heretical beliefs, including Bogomil, Cathar, Gnostic, and Johanite connections. While some of these may well be true—Robert was an extremely well-read man—he is also properly described as "a clerical author imbued with perfectly correct theological precepts in an age of foment and debate on all fronts."[193] The truth may well be somewhere in between, but for the moment we will concentrate on Robert and Chrétien's knowledge of theological writings, most of which they would only have known in later copies.

191. St. Germanus of Constantinople, *On the Divine Liturgy.*
192. O'Gorman, "Ecclesiastical Tradition and the Holy Grail."
193. O'Gorman, "Robert de Boron's Angelology and Elements of Heretical Doctrine."

✦ ✦ ✦

Two of the most controversial modern interpreters of the Grail story, Henry and Renee Kahane,[194] describe Robert's work as "re-creating the esoteric climate of Christian speculation." Elsewhere, in their essay "On the Sources of Chrétien's Grail Story,"[195] they suggest that the vessel known as the Krater, in which the gods mixed the elements of creation and which is mentioned at length in the collection of early pre-Christian writings known under the general title of the *Hermetica*, could be a possible source for Chrétien's work. In particular they note that the treatise *On the Krater*, translated from Greek into Syriac in the ninth century, has a number of parallels to the way in which the Grail is described in the medieval texts. It is possible that Count Philip d'Alcase (Chrétien's patron) may have brought back a copy from the Holy Land, where he was between AD 1177 and 1178, perhaps in a Latin translation that either Chrétien or Robert could have used in their accounts of the Grail.

As the Kahanes rightly observed,[196] secrecy is the watchword of Robert de Boron's narrative: Joseph's secret love for Christ; the secret safekeeping of the vessel; the concealment of the Grail community; Veronica's hiding of the cloth bearing the face of Jesus; the concealment of Christ's body; Joseph's imprisonment and the nature of the Grail secrets provided to him while incarcerated—all share this notion. Yet the secret was actually there in plain sight in the daily celebration of the Eucharist within every church in Christendom. That the romance writers, and to a certain degree the exegetes, were aware of this becomes increasingly tenable once we begin to examine the earliest documents relating to the symbolism of early Christianity.

One text in particular has been identified as the source for much of the symbolism of the Grail.[197] This is the influential work known as the *Gemma Animae* of Honorius Augustodunesis (Honorius of Autun) who was born circa 1080 and was still active in 1154.[198] It is quoted almost verbatim in Robert's poem of *Joseph*. In his exposition of the various symbolic elements of church architectures and the Mass, Honorius writes:

194. Kahane, "The Secrets of the Grail," 108.

195. Kahane, "On the Sources of Chrétien's Grail Story," 230.

196. Kahane, "The Secrets of the Grail," 108–114.

197. O'Gorman, "Ecclesiastical Tradition and the Holy Grail," 3–8; Kahane, "The Secrets of the Grail"; Adolf, "Oriental Sources for Grail Romances"; Cabaniss, "Joseph of Arimathea."

198. Honorius may also have been implemental in another aspect of the Grail story. In a work dated between 1154 and 1159, *De Imagine Mundi*, he includes a detailed account of Sheba's prophecy to Solomon, which later became part of the *Estoire del Saint Graal* (see Quinn, *The Quest of Seth for the Oil of Life*, 73).

◆ ◆ ◆

While the priest is saying "Per omnia saecula saeculorum," the deacon comes, lifts up the chalice before him, and covers it with a napkin, replaces it on the altar, and covers it with the corporal, representing Joseph of Arimathea, who took Christ's body down, covered his face with a napkin, placed it in a tomb, covered it with a stone. Here the sacrifice and the chalice are covered with the corporal, which signifies the clean shroud with which Joseph wrapped the body of Christ. The chalice signifies the sepulchre; the paten, the stone which closed the sepulchre.[199]

This almost exactly reflects Robert's *Joseph* text, where he describes Christ coming to Joseph of Arimathea, who has been shut up in the windowless room and left to die, and explaining the mystery of the sacred relics:

> When you took me down from the cross
> And put me into the sepulchre
> It became the altar on which will put
> Those who will sacrifice me.
> The cloth in which I was wrapped
> Will be called the corporal.
> This vessel into which you put my blood
> When you gathered it from my body
> Will be called the chalice.
> The paten which will lie on top of it
> Will signify the stone
> Which was sealed over me
> When you had put me into the sepulchre.[200]

Following this, Christ speaks the sacred words that Robert says he may not reveal and refers to the Trinity as "the three powers that are one being." This aspect of the symbolism of the Mass is central to Robert's retelling of the story of Joseph. The Kahanes describe Robert's "obsession" with the symbology of the trinity[201] as discussed in the *Gemma Animae*, harking back to a number of still older texts, thus demonstrating the durability of the tradition that was beginning to shape the matter of the Grail. The argument over the nature of the trinity—whether Christ shared absolutely in the divine nature of God—was to rage for many ages after and was one of the primary causes of the split between the Roman Catholic Church and the Protestant reformers.

199. Ibid., trans. Cabaniss, "Joseph of Arimathea."
200. Lines 901–913, trans. Kahane in "Robert de Boron's Joseph of Arimathea," 329.
201. Kahane, "Robert de Boron's Joseph of Arimathea," 334.

◆ ◆ ◆

We do not know the exact dates at which Robert composed his poem about Joseph. It has been suggested that the poems were not written in chronological order,[202] but this seems unlikely given that Robert declares at the end of the *Joseph* that having unwoven the strands of the story, he will "tie all [the] strands together again."[203] The prose version of *Joseph* dates to circa 1200, so the verse text must be earlier, perhaps as early as the 1170s, when Chrétien was still composing his own Grail story. Since Honorius is known to have been active in 1154, his work predates that of both poets. But there are other writers, in whose steps Honorius himself trod, which take the story back even further, possibly as far as the second century AD, when early Christian authors wrote their own accounts of what would eventually become enshrined in the medieval Grail romances.

All of this leads back to a specific aspect of the Grail story, first introduced by Robert and thereafter forming a central part of the narrative, and very much to the fore in the version given by the abbot of the Grail Island in *Sone*. We refer to the central role given to the figure of Joseph of Arimathea, who becomes the first guardian of the Grail and whose descendants retain this task up to and including the time of Arthur and the quest for the sacred vessel carried out by his knights.

The Friend of Jesus

The question—why Joseph of Arimathea?—has been asked before,[204] though few seem to understand why he should be chosen from amongst the apostles and disciples of Jesus. However, once one explores the story more deeply, it becomes clear that the growing emphasis on the importance of Joseph played a hugely important part in the dissemination of the Grail material.

In the Canonical Scriptures Joseph is simply described as a wealthy Arimathean councilor, a secret believer in Christ who requests permission of Pilate to take and bury the body of Jesus in his own tomb, aided by Nicodemus.[205] In an apocryphal Gospel of Peter he is described

---

202. Bryant, Nigel, trans., *Merlin and the Grail: Joseph of Arimathea, Merlin, Perceval: The Trilogy of Arthurian Romances Attributed to Robert de Boron* (D. S. Brewer, 2001); O'Gorman, "Robert de Boron's Angelology and Elements of Heretical Doctrine."

203. Bryant, *Merlin and the Grail*, 44.

204. Ashe, *King Arthur's Avalon.*

205. Matthew 27:57–61, Mark 15:42–46, Luke 23:50–55, John 19:38–42.

✦ ✦ ✦

as "the friend of Pilate and of the Lord"[206] (a detail repeated in the Book of Joseph which we shall examine below), while several hundred years later in his important *Vita Christi*, written in 1350, Ludolph of Saxony describes Joseph as closely acquainted with Pilate, proving his prominence by risking all in asking for the body of the renegade messiah.[207]

But the most familiar non-canonical text to reference the events following the crucifixion and resurrection of Jesus, and the first to expand the brief mentions of Joseph of Arimathea found in the Gospels into something like a biography, is the *Evangelium Nicodemi* ("Gospel of Nicodemus"), which also includes a further apocryphal document, the *Acta Pilati*, or "Acts of Pilate." It is presented as a Hebrew gospel written by Nicodemus, who is mentioned in the Gospel of St. John as an associate of Jesus.

The title is medieval and the dating of the texts remains problematic. Most scholars agree in assigning it to the fourth century AD, though the section purporting to be based on an official report of the events of the Passion written by Pilate himself is slightly older and is found originally in the Greek Acts of Peter and Paul.[208] A note by the early theologian Justin Martyr (AD 100–165), in his *First Apology*,[209] referring to the Passion and Resurrection of Jesus, mentions that "these things did happen, you can ascertain from the Acts of Pontius Pilate."

Though the editor of the *Apocryphal New Testament*, Montague Rhodes James, believes this to be no more than a reference to the existence of some kind of archival report, it is possible to infer from this that the text, or a version of it, had been in circulation for some time. Possibly the Syriac text of the *Book of Joseph of Arimathea*, which we will examine in further detail shortly, may have influenced the *Acts of Pilate*, rather than the other way around, but until a definitive edition of the text is available, we cannot be certain.

The main body of the *Evangelium* falls into two parts, describing the trial of Jesus (based upon Luke 23) and the Resurrection, while an appendix claims to be based on a written report made by Pilate himself, commissioned by the emperor Tiberius and containing a description of the crucifixion and resurrection of Jesus. The text exists in Greek, Latin, Syriac, Aramaic, and Coptic versions, bearing witness to its widespread dissemination. Some four hundred manuscripts dating from the Middle Ages have been traced; there were probably many more that have since vanished.

206. Edgar Hennecke and W. Schneemelcher, *New Testament Apocrypha*, trans R. M. Wilson (Philadelphia, 1962), 183.

207. Logorio, "Joseph of Arimathea," 56.

208. *The Apocryphal New Testament*, translated by M. R. James (Oxford, The Clarendon Press, 1975).

209. Martyr, *The First and Second Apologies*, ch. 35.

✦ ✦ ✦

Another text, known as the *Transitus Mariae*, which dealt with the Ascension of the Virgin Mary, surfaced in the fifth century. It exists in a number of versions, dating from this time to the end of the Middle Ages in Latin, Greek, Syriac, and Armenian, and emphasizes the growing importance of Joseph of Arimathea by relating how, amongst other disciples and apostles, the dying Virgin calls for him to witness her death and assumption. A colophon, possibly dating from the ninth or tenth centuries, adds the following, attributed to Joseph's own hand:

> I am that Joseph who laid the body of the Lord in my tomb and saw him rise again, and always watched over his most holy temple, even the blessed Mary, ever virgin, before the ascension of the Lord and after it: and upon this page I have written the things that came out of the mouth of God, and how the aforesaid matters came to pass, and I have made known to all the Jews and Gentiles what I saw with my own eyes and heard with my ears, and as long as I live I shall not cease to proclaim them.[210]

This is only one of several accounts attributed directly to Joseph. As we shall see, one at least of these may well have had a profound effect on the work of the Grail writers.

Following on from the *Evangelium*, the *Acta Pilati*, and the *Transitus Mariae*, we have to look to the eighth century before we find significant reference both to Joseph of Arimathea and his guardianship of the sacred vessel. The text in question was written by St. Germanus, patriarch of Constantinople from 715–730, and became the most important commentary on the Divine Liturgy of the Eastern Orthodox Church until the fourteenth century. The *Rerum Ecclesiasticarum Contemplatio* ("Ecclesiastical History and Mystical Contemplation")[211] included the following, in a passage which some have suggested could have been interpolated in the thirteenth century:

> The altar represents the sepulchre in which Joseph buried Christ … The veil covering chalice and paten is compared to the stone with which Joseph closed the tomb; the paten is compared to the hands of Joseph and Nicodemus burying Christ, and in another passage to the bed in which the body of the Lord is laid out by the priest and the deacon, who are Joseph and Nicodemus.[212]

Germanus is possibly the first to make the connection between the symbolic reference to the tomb and chalice, and the part played by Joseph of Arimathea in the events following the Resurrection. He describes the procession of the deacons and the celebration of the mysteries as an

---

210. Logorio, "Joseph of Arimathea," 59.

211. *Patrologia Graeca* 98 (Paris, 1865), 384–453; St. Germanus of Constantinople, *On the Divine Liturgy*.

212. Kahane, "Robert de Boron's Joseph of Arimathea," 111.

❖ ❖ ❖

...imitation of the burial of Christ, when Joseph took down the body from the Cross, wrapped it in clean linen, anointed it with spices and ointment, carried it with Nicodemus, and placed it in a new tomb hewn out of a rock. The altar is an image of the holy tomb, and the divine table is the sepulchre in which, of course the undefiled and all-holy body was placed.

He then adds, in even greater detail, how

the discos represents the hands of Joseph and Nicodemus, who buried Christ. The discos on which Christ is carried is also interpreted as the sphere of Heaven, manifesting to us in miniature the spiritual sun, Christ, and containing Him visibly in the bread.

The chalice corresponds to the vessel, which received a mixture, poured out from the bloodied, undefiled side and from the hands and feet of Christ. Or again, the chalice corresponds to the bowl which the Lord depicts, that is, Wisdom; because the Son of God has made his blood for drinking instead of that wine and set it forth on his holy table...[213]

This seems to be a very close reference to the sacred vessel as container of Wisdom, the divine presence of God, in the Temple of Solomon.

The *Contemplatio* also refers to a metrical hymn sung at the end of the second antiphon in both the Byzantine and Syriac Eucharistic rites and known as a troparion.[214] Its authorship has been attributed to the Roman emperor Justinian (483–565), who may have written it in AD 535–6 when seeking rapprochement with a sect known as the Monosophysites.[215] In Syriac tradition it was attributed to Severus, the Monosophysite patriarch of Antioch, who was a radical opponent of Justinian. The text is simple but carries a burden of meaning regarding the godhead of Christ and his place within the Trinity.

Only-Begotten Son and Word of God, immortal, who didst vouchsafe for our salvation to take flesh of the Holy Mother of God, and Ever-Virgin Mary, and didst without mutation become man, and was crucified, Christ, our God, and by death didst overcome death, being one of the Holy Trinity, and glorified together with the Father and the Holy Ghost, save us.[216]

Here we learn that

---

213. St. Germanus of Constantinople, *On the Divine Liturgy*, 88–89.

214. Kahane, "The Secrets of the Grail," 111.

215. Ibid., 112.

216. Neale and Littledale, "The Divine Liturgy of St. Mark."

the Only Begotten Son of the Word of God"... is a work by Joseph and Nicodemus. For in carrying the body of the Lord in order to bury Him, they were initiated into the mysteries by the venerable and life-giving body of the Lord and the Divinity inseparable from it.[217]

This suggests a number of things. First, that Joseph and Nicodemus are initiated into the mysteries of Christ through the mere presence of the dead body, just as Joseph received the secret teachings in the Acts of Pilate and in the later Grail texts such as Robert's *Joseph* and the anonymous *Estoire de Saint Graal* directly from Christ. In addition, with the emphasis on the indwelling divinity of the body, this prefigures the central focus of Robert's fascination with the tripartite mystery of Christ and the essential belief that the physical body could not be separated from the divine presence that dwelled within it. Robert[218] specifically has Christ refer to the vessel as *l'enseigne de ma mort* ("the symbol (sign) of my death"), a reference, surely, to the scene in Gethsemane in which Christ asks, "Let this cup pass from me." The Kahanes are determined in their assertion that "the text [of the troparion] must have constituted the base and essence of Robert's *Roman du Graal* ... and that the hymn "transmitted the doctrines which he annunciated."[219] This is, of course, as we saw in chapter 5, the exact doctrinal point upon which the Nestorians, with whom the apostle Thomas became linked, divided from the established Roman Church.

Some hundred years after this, in the thirteenth century, William Durand, the bishop of Mende (1230–1296), extended the account of Joseph's actions in his *Rationale Divinorum Officiorum:*[220]

> It is fitting [that] while these words are being said that the body and blood should be lifted up and put down, representing the lifting of Christ's body from the earth and its being placed in the sepulchre, because Joseph (who took it down from the cross, lifted it up from the earth, and placed it in the sepulchre) had been "admonished" and taught by Christ's "salutary commands," as his faithful disciples had been. It is therefore said of him in Mark [15–43]: "he too was looking for the kingdom of God." The consecrated body and blood are lifted up at the same time, because Joseph himself (*as certain ones say*) placed the body with the blood together in the sepulchre...[221]

217. Kahane, "Secrets of the Grail," 111–112.

218. "Joseph" in Bryant, *Merlin and the Grail*, lines 847–8.

219. Kahane, "Secrets of the Grail," 112.

220. Durand, *Rationale Divinorum Officiorum*, IV 22, 23 ed.cit.,287f.

221. Cabaniss, "Joseph of Arimathea and a Chalice." Our italics.

◆ ◆ ◆

Alan Cabaniss, who examined many of these documents, makes an important point when he notes that the phrase "as certain ones say" (*ut quidam ferunt*) suggests that by the time of William Durand, the Grail literature was in its turn affecting the interpretation of the liturgy. If we are correct in supposing that both Chrétien and Robert drew heavily upon the writings of the older liturgists, then it would not be surprising if the latter knew of—and to some degree endorsed—the writings of the poets.

Joseph Speaks

There remains one other significant text, which has been largely overlooked in more recent commentaries on the Grail after it was first noted by A. N. Wesselofsky in 1901.[222] It survives only in a Russian copy dated with caution to the seventh or eighth centuries and currently is in the Monastery of Mt. Athos.[223] Usually referred to as the *I, Joseph…* from its opening words, or sometimes *The Book of Joseph*,[224] its full title is *A Book, written by Joseph of Arimathea, the disciple of our Lord Jesus Christ. The story of the building of the church of our Holy Queen Mary, the Mother of God, in the City of Lydda.*[225]

The text has been tentatively dated based on internal references to ecumenical debates over the doctrine of transubstantiation at the time.[226] Indeed, all of the texts examined here were written before 1215, when the Lateran Council finally agreed on the definition of transubstantiation, and we should not forget that Chrétien and Robert wrote before this date, making it even more likely that they derived their approach to the Grail via the theologians discussed above. If the earliest date for the *Book of Joseph* is correct, this would make it one of the earliest texts to deal with the growing importance of Joseph of Arimathea and, ultimately, his connection with the sacred vessel of the Last Supper and the guardians of the Grail.

The text begins with an account of the events following the Crucifixion closely following the *Evangelium Nicodemi*, but adds details that are unique to this document.

We hear almost immediately from Joseph, who tells how

> after the death of Jesus Christ and His resurrection, He appeared to me, Joseph, while I was
> imprisoned, because the high priests of the people and the scribes put me in prison because

222. Wesselofsky, "Zur Frage uber die Heimath der Legende von heiligen Gral," 321–385.

223. Athos MS no. 69, 154b–164a.

224. Kahane, "Secrets of the Grail," 112.

225. Logorio, "Joseph of Arimathea," 60.

226. Von Dobschütz, "Joseph von Arimathea," especially 4–17, and van Esbroeck, "L'Histoire de L'eglise de Lydia dans deux Textes Georgiens," 109–31.

✦ ✦ ✦

I had gone to the house of Pilate the governor and asked to the body of Jesus. The group of disciples, after the saviour had been resurrected, were hidden for several days, but I was the friend of Pilate, and I was able to go and ask for what I had previously requested, and I obtained the thing that I desired, and I took with me Nicodemus who was also, like me, a disciple of Christ. And we took Him down from the cross with our own hands…

We prepared Him without fear and embalmed Him with unguents and new garments, and we just disposed Him in the new tomb which was cut into the rock, and in which no one else had been laid. And He, having the power of resurrection… crushed death and broke the gates of Hell. And he broke the iron chains and was resurrected, and he also brought out with him those that were dead.[227]

This is followed by the startling claim that

I, Joseph, have met them and I have spoken with them, and many others, and they told us of the gates and the chains and the belly of Hell, which devours all the world.[228]

Following this, when the risen Christ appears to the imprisoned Joseph, we hear

Rejoice, Joseph, for you are stronger in faith than Peter; for Peter denied me three times in one night for fear of the Jews, but you disdained fear… and boldly went to Pilate, asking him from my body, and laid it in your new grave. Believe me, my beloved Joseph, all the choirs of angels and all heavenly powers look down from on high on your firm faith.[229]

The implication here is that Joseph may actually have encountered the risen Christ before either the women or the first amongst the apostles, and his importance is emphasised still further as Christ appears to Joseph and his companions and transports them all, first to the Holy Sepulchre and then to Arimathea. The Lord then infuses them with the power of the Holy Spirit by breathing on them and instructs Joseph and St. Phillip to go to Lydda and build a church in honour of his mother.

When Joseph and Philip arrive at Lydda, they choose a site and begin to build. Once the church is complete, it is consecrated by Joseph and Nicodemus, accompanied by the apostles Peter, Paul, John, Andrew, and Thomas. Philip then commends his disciples to Joseph and departs. The story that follows is remarkable, connecting this early text with the later medieval accounts and with the myth of the Grail.

227. Translated by Caitlín Matthews.
228. Ibid.
229. Ibid.

It is now revealed that Joseph, whose own village of Arimathea is nearby and who is therefore known to the people of Lydda, had promised to restore their synagogue and supply its liturgical furnishings. Instead he has built a Christian church. The local people are angered by this and appeal to the Roman governor of Caesarea to adjudicate. The new building is closed up for forty days, at which point the governor appears and opens it up. Despite the fact that no one has been inside the building in all this time, an image has miraculously appeared on one of the walls. It depicts the Virgin as *Theotokos* (God Bearer), and under it is an inscription that reads: "Mary, Mother of the Nazarene, King Christ." The church will thereafter be known as "second after the church of Jerusalem."[230]

Joseph is thus shown as both a priest and the leader of a Christian community in Palestine. He is also specifically called a "Keeper of the Holy Blood," thus connecting him closely to the later accounts of his family's connection with the Grail. Perhaps here we may even see the first sign of the later elision of Joseph into that of the shadowy figure of Prester John.

The mention of St. Philip in this context is also interesting. It was he who converted the Galatians, a Celtic tribe living in Asia Minor. The Kahanes[231] suggest that it was through this "Celtic" connection that Joseph became associated with Britain. Certainly, if we look for a moment at William of Malmsbury's history of Glastonbury, written in 1247, we can see the scribes, who made a copy for the abbey, already reshaping the text to further their desire to possess Joseph. In a new introduction to the text, we learn that "Philip was in Gaul … He sent twelve disciples to preach in Britain, and as it is said [*ut ferunt*] he placed at their head his favourite disciple, Joseph of Arimathea."[232]

Dr. D. D. R. Owen, in an important essay "From Grail to Holy Grail,"[233] suggests that the long section in the *First Continuation* to Chrétien dealing with Joseph's part in the Grail story was drawing upon "some legend he had heard." In fact, the legend in question was probably the *Book of Joseph*, which almost certainly existed in a Latin version.

Along with Germanus's *On the Divine Liturgy*, the *Book of Joseph* points to a Byzantine link with the story of the Grail, and it is likely that the manuscript made its way to Georgia via the Byzantine Empire. If we are correct in accepting the dating of the text to between the fifth and eighth centuries AD, then both Germanus and his followers could have been influenced by it.

230. Ibid.
231. Kahane, "Secrets of the Grail," 110.
232. Scavone, "Joseph of Arimathea," 3–31.
233. Owen, "From Grail to Holy Grail," 31–53.

✦ ✦ ✦

Considering the references to the so-called Edessa Icon, supposedly a portrait of Christ taken from life, the presence of the "copy" of the Grail sent to Constantinople, as described in *The Later Titurel*, cannot help but point to a link between the Byzantine Empire and the evolving mystery of the Grail.

Considering the references to Joseph in these early theological works, John O'Gorman makes a stunningly simple statement: that the reason why Joseph of Arimathea became associated with the Grail is because all of these tracts identified the tomb of Jesus Christ with the cup. Therefore, since Joseph owned the tomb, he also, by extension, owned the Grail![234]

This idea would lead, in time, via the writings of Chrétien and Robert, to the most complete restatement of the Joseph tradition, now welded firmly to the story of the Grail in the *Estoire de Saint Graal*, part of the vast compilation of the Lancelot-Grail.[235]

Here Joseph is a mercenary officer employed by Pontius Pilate, who asks for Christ's body as a reward for his past military service. Pilate not only grants this request, but also gives Joseph the Cup of the Last Supper, which Joseph subsequently uses to collect Christ's blood after the depositions from the Cross. When Joseph is imprisoned by the Jews for having buried Jesus, the resurrected Saviour brings the holy vessel to him and says that the Holy Spirit will sustain him until his deliverance. After forty-two years he is freed by the emperor Vespasian during the destruction of Jerusalem and is baptized by St. Philip. At Christ's command, Joseph, carrying the Grail, leads a band of Christians on a missionary journey to the lands in the West.

The Grail company finally arrives at Sarras, a pagan stronghold ruled by King Evalac, who is at war with King Tholomer (Ptolemy?) of Egypt. Joseph and his son Josephe preach the doctrines of the Trinity and Incarnation to Evalac and his mages, but their apostolic efforts are unsuccessful. Praying for divine guidance before the Ark, Joseph and Josephe are both initiated into the mysteries of the Grail, and Josephe is consecrated as the first Bishop of Christendom by Christ himself. Divine intervention secures a victory for Evalac and his brother-in-law Seraphe against their enemies, and the rulers and people of Sarras and its environs are converted to Christianity.

After establishing the church at Sarras, Joseph and his followers depart for their divinely ordained mission to Britain, where they preach the gospel throughout Britain, Ireland, Scotland, and Wales until their death. The guardianship of the Grail is given to Joseph's nephews, whose descendants fulfil their sacred trust until the days of King Arthur 400 years later.

---

234. O'Gorman, "Ecclesiastical Tradition and the Holy Grail," 3–8.

235. *Estoire de Saint Graal* in *Lancelot-Grail: The Old French Arthurian Vulgate and Post-Vulgate in Translation.*

✦ ✦ ✦

The establishment of the church at Sarras may surely be seen as an echo, if not a direct reference, to that established by Joseph and the apostle Philip at Lydda in the *Book of Joseph*. Much of the story can be seen to draw directly on the works of the apologists we have examined here.

It is safe to assume the more erudite of these theologians were aware of each other's work and frequently copied it. Indeed, as Joseph Duggan[236] has pointed out, the vast literature containing the lives of the saints was often retold over and again in the same way as the fantastic tales of romance literature, with the same errors and images carried over in a variety of versions, demonstrating a continuity of transmission over a lengthy period. The same must be seen to be true of the use of the earlier texts that gave rise to the myth of the Grail long before it was assumed into the Arthurian cycle.

As Valerie Logorio wisely commented, "The monastic authors who wrote these (i.e., the Grail texts) in Northern France during the late twelfth and early thirteenth centuries were undoubtedly conscious medieval hagiographers."[237] They were indeed seeking to make of the Grail story an essential part of the Christian mythos.

Thus, while the writings cited here are sometimes separated by several centuries, the evidence for a direct lineage from one to another is persuasive. In addition, there may well be other texts that have yet to be discovered. Chrétien and Robert were truly the inheritors of a long-standing tradition. Their originality stems not from their imaginations, but from the language they used, which was that of the romance writers, and in their linking the story of Joseph with the Arthurian matter, drawing upon the extended writings of the early Christian exegetes.

In the Byzantine imagery of the Joseph story and the Syriac liturgical patterns, they found a rich heritage of symbolism that they shaped into the story of the Grail. These influences, carried by the theologians of the early medieval church, contained, as we have seen, the basic elements of the story embroidered by Chrétien and Robert into a composite whole that took the very essence of Christian belief (particularly on the divinity of Jesus) and wove it into the fabric of the Arthurian legends, where it has remained ever since.

236. Duggan, "Performance and Transmission."
237. Logorio, "Joseph of Arimathea," 54.

❖ ❖ ❖

7

THE THRONE OF SOLOMON

O ancient temple, there hath risen for you
a light that gleams in our hearts…

◆ ◆ ◆

Ibn al Arabi, *The Tarjuman Ai-Ashwaq*

It would be easy to see the elaborate descriptions of the Grail Temples in *The Later Titurel* and elsewhere as the products of the marvelous imaginations of their authors, concocted from descriptions of the Solomonic temple and travellers' tales concerning the kingdom of Prester John in the East. But there is more to it than this.

The descriptions, as noted above, do indeed resemble the temple of Solomon, but they also resemble another place, an actual site that shares so many of the patterns and descriptions found in *Sone* and *Titurel* as to suggest that they were all based on a single building—not a temple of the Grail indeed, or even a Christian foundation, but one worthy of being the home of a sacred relic.

The ruins of Takht-e Taqdis (Throne of Arches), also known as Takht-e Soleyman (Throne of Solomon), now a World Heritage site, lies in the country of Azerbaijan (Northern Iran) midway between Urmia and Hamedan, in a valley set in a volcanic mountain region, close to the present-day town of Takab and 400 kilometers west of Tehran. The choice of this site to erect the temple and other buildings was undoubtedly dictated by its natural setting: an outcrop of limestone about 60 meters above the valley, built up by sediments of calcinating water from the heated waters of the lake which rose at the top of the hill.

Built during the reign of the Persian-Sasanian emperor Khosrow II (AD 590–628) on the site of the sacred city of Shiz, the temple site dominated the surrounding country. It was first

◆ ◆ ◆

visited by the explorer and archaeologist Sir Henry Rawlinson (1810–1895) in an expedition to the area in 1838. Rawlinson recognized at once that what he was looking at was an extensive palace containing a central area that he identified as the remains of a Zoroastrian fire temple. The Zoroastrians, an ancient religious group who followed the god Ahura Mazda and worshipped fire, are still extant in parts of modern-day India and Iran. The origins of the Zoroastrians date back at least as far as the second century BC, and many of their beliefs, including the idea of a messiah, judgment after death, a heaven and a hell, and the acknowledgement of free will, have been seen to influence many of the major religions of the world, including Judaism, Christianity, Gnosticism, and Islam. Zoroastrianism served as the state religion of the pre-Islamic Iranian empire from 600 BC to AD 650. More than one scholar has drawn attention to strands of belief deriving from the Zoroastrians, which may have filtered down into the Grail myth via the Crusades.[238] Nor should we fail to note that from the earliest times to the present, the vessel in which the sacred fire is placed in the Zoroastrian temple closely resembles the images of the Grail as chalice. This may be no more than a coincidence, but certainly the spirituality of the Zoroastrians made a fertile soil for the absorption of beliefs from other cultures, including those of the West. The influence was almost certainly a two-way street, bringing beliefs from both East and West together.

Amongst other things, Rawlinson noted the immensely thick walls, many still standing today; the multiple arches, which gave the site its name; and the central fire pit, which was square and covered by a dome mounted upon four pillars. This, of course, bears a striking resemblance to the descriptions of the central hall of the Grail castle with its square fireplace covered by a dome held up by pillars present in virtually every subsequent description of the Grail Temple.

Rawlinson was probably unaware of such parallels. These are only noted much later by the American orientalist Arthur Upham Pope in the 1930s. As a specialist in Islamic culture, he came across the description of the site and recognized at once the resemblance to the descriptions of the Grail Temple in *The Later Titurel*. Soon after, in 1937, he organized an expedition to the site on behalf of the American Institute of Iranian Art. What he found stunned him. Acknowledging that "Albrecht's description of the temple is somewhat confused by the inclusion of characteristic features of a Romanesque and perhaps Armenian church," he goes on to say:

238. In particular, Kahane, *The Krater and the Grail*; von Schroeder and Jacob, *The Grail*; and Coyajee, "The Legend of the Holy Grail."

[We saw the remains of a domed temple] built at Shiz, the most sacred spot in the land, deep in the mountainous heart of Azerbaijan … The Takht was built of precious woods; cedar and teak, overlaid with much gold. Only gold and silver nails were used. The risers of the steps were gold. The balustrades—like those of the Grail Temple—were gold; and again like the Grail Temple, the Takht was heavily encrusted with jewels. As in the Grail Temple, blue stones symbolized the sky—lapis lazuli and turquoise in the Takht, sapphires in the Grail Temple. In the Takht golden astronomical tables—which could be changed according to season—were set in the dome, and on these the stars were marked by rubies, recalling that the stars in the dome of the Grail Temple likewise were marked with red jewels … or other stones, provided they were red, for example, garnets. In both, the sun and moon were displayed, rendered in precious metal. The astronomical adjustment of the Takht went even further: the whole building was set on rollers above a [hidden] pit in which horses worked a mechanism that turned the structure round through the Four Quarters, so that at every season it would be in correct correspondence with the heavens, thus making more potent the celebration of the appropriate rituals … [239]

This last detail is important, as there are several accounts of the castle of the Grail revolving in order to make entry more difficult.

Pope also noted other aspects that recalled the descriptions of the castle of the Grail in Chrétien's work and in the medieval Welsh copy of the poem included in the collection of mythic stories known as the Mabinogion under the title "Peredur." There the hero approaches the castle via a forest, a meadow, and a lake. Later he returns and approaches from a different direction by following a river though a valley. Pope noted that the approach to the Takht from the south also passes a grove of trees leading to a lake, and that from the north one comes upon it via a meadow, and in the west by a stream and a valley. While these landscape features may be no more than coincidental, the similarities of the descriptions are intriguing. We may also recall the castle belonging to the magician Gundebald in the *Historia Meriadoci* (see chapter 3). Here is the description of an arid wasteland of tar, bitumen, and stones, which could certainly be recognized as a description of the desert regions that surrounded the Takht.

The placing of the Takht at Shiz is also significant. This is notably the sacred city of the magi, of whose lineage, we may recall, Prester John is ascribed in the *De Adventu Patriarchae Indorum*. The fact that the original foundation was Zoroastrian, which to this day has followers in India, is also not without significance. The links between Prester John and India, the Zoroastrians and India, and the history of the patriarch John, also from India, all of which are

---

239. Pope, "Persia and the Grail." See plate 4 for a map of the Takht-e Soleyman site after D. Wilber, who helped survey and record the site during Pope's expedition.

◆ ◆ ◆

mirrored in the Grail romances, suggest that the authors of the Grail romances were aware of the existence of these connections.

An early description of the temple, written by the Persian scribe Hamdallah Mustawfi of Qazwin in the early fourteenth century, adds a further stand to the similarities between the Takht and the mystical temples we have been examining. He writes:

> It [the palace] stands on the summit of the hill and it was originally founded by King Kay Khusraw the Kayanian [i.e., Chosroes II]. In this town there is a great Palace, in the court of which a spring gushes forth into a large tank that is like a small lake in size, and no boatman has been able to plumb its depths. Two main streams of water, each in power sufficient to turn a mill, continually flow away from this tank; but if they be dammed back, the water in the tank [in] no wise increases [its] level; and when the stoppage is removed the water again runs as before ... being at no season more or less in volume."[240]

This immediately recalls the description of the temple built for Prester John at the instruction of St. Thomas, which was surrounded by water for most of the year, which never varied in depths from season to season until the festival celebrating the apostle fell due (December 21). The two streams are also reminiscent of the sacred rivers that fed the area around the Grail Temple. Could it even be that the idea of the dry and dead wasteland, attributed to the wounding of the Fisher King in the later romances, was a distant memory of a desert land once fed by water that somehow drained away?

The Takht itself has a long and fascinating history. It was several times described as a mirror of paradise by Islamic writers of the medieval period, thus echoing the other places described as reflecting the original presence of heaven on earth. This in itself is enough to mark out the area as being of interest to our investigation, but the presence of a whole complex of sites around the central lake and temple buildings makes it even more extraordinary.

Archeological evidence has established the Takht-e Soleyman as the most important surviving Sassanian temple complex. Known as Athur-Gushnasp and dating from the fifth century AD, it is one of only three such temples known about, and the only one to be discovered in a state that enabled it to be studied in any depth.

In his study of the site and its relation to the Grail Temple of Albrecht, Pope cited a bronze salver, now in the Berlin Museum, which dates from either a late or early post-Sasanian period.[241] On this dish was inscribed, in minute detail, the image of a circular domed building

---

240. Mustawfi Hamdallah, *The Geographical Part of the Nuzhat al-Qulib*, translated by Guy Le Strange, 2 vols. (Brill/Luzac, 1915–19).

241. *The Art Bulletin* XV (1933), 10. Also featured in Ringbom, *Graltempel und Paradies*.

◆ ◆ ◆

surrounded by symbols of trees, elegant blossoms, and jars of water, and containing twenty-two arched panels, each framing a decorative tree. Even the elaborate system of rollers designed to make the building revolve are represented on the salver, as is the miniature replica of the building at the centre, an exact correlative to the miniature temple made to contain the Grail in Albrecht. Josef Strzygowski, an expert on Islamic and early Christian church art, offered a detailed analysis of the dish, which he concluded could only be the Takht.[242] Pope also notes that "the division of the circular area into twenty-two equal units is practically unprecedented in the decorative arts and is difficult to achieve with ordinary craft methods."

The Throne of Bilquis and the Ship of Solomon

A second site, the Takht-i-Bilquis (Throne of Bilquis), is also of great importance, both as a spiritual centre and an historical foundation. The name, of course, is that of Solomon's wife, more familiarly known as the Queen of Sheba, and its presence here is highly significant for our argument as it establishes the connection with the biblical king and his consort, both of whom are described in the medieval Grail romances as having a significant role in the mysteries of the sacred vessel.

Midway though the *Queste del Saint Grail* ("Quest of the Holy Grail," the central romance within the cycle of the Lancelot-Grail, the foremost Grail knights—Galahad, Perceval, and Bors—along with Perceval's sister, Dindrane, go aboard a mysterious ship that is to take them to the home of the sacred vessel. On board are a mélange of sacred objects: a sword which has once belonged to the biblical king David and which was intended only for the best knight in the world (Galahad), a scabbard lacking a belt that would be woven from the hair of a virgin (Dindraine), and Solomon's Crown, which lay upon a great bed made from timbers cut from the Edenic Tree of the Knowledge of Good and Evil. Three pillars held a canopy over this bed, and these were made also from pieces of wood from the tree. They were of three colours: white for the innocence of Adam and Eve, green for the fruitfulness of Eve when she and Adam conceived their first child, and red for the blood of Cain when he is slain by his brother Abel. All of these had been placed in the ship at the behest of Solomon himself, who had been told, in a vision, that one of his descendants would achieve a great thing in future times. Despite his great wisdom and knowledge of the stars, Solomon was unable to discover more of this, but he still

242. In a lecture given at the Second International Congress of Persian Art in London in 1931. See also Josef Strzygowski, *Origin of Christian Church Art: New Facts and Principles of Research* (Oxford University Press, 1917). See plate 3 for a projection of the Takht-e Soleyman based on a bronze salver from the time of Khosrow II (after Ringbom).

longed to send a message forward in time to his descendent, showing that he had knowledge of his great deed. It was Bilquis who supplied an answer, telling him to "have a ship built of the best and most durable wood that can be found, such wood as neither water nor anything else can rot."[243]

Solomon duly commissioned the ship and had the sacred objects placed aboard. That night he dreamed that a mysterious man descended from heaven, sprinkled the ship with water, and inscribed the letters that tell of the nature of the sacred objects, then, having lain briefly on the bed, vanished. When Solomon woke he launched the ship upon the waters—waters not only of space but of time also, for it would appear next on the shores of Europe to take aboard the Grail knights and carry them to the sacred city of Sarras, where the sacred vessel resided. The ship indeed links not only eras but beliefs. As Esther Quinn notes in her illuminating essay on the legend, "it spans the gap between the Old Testament and the Arthurian records. The religious allegory has played its part in transforming the romantic tradition."[244]

The idea of a miraculous ship given as a gift to a hero, often by a mysterious woman, appears in several Arthurian romances. Solomon's ship turns up again in an Arthurian lay written by Marie de France. This concerns the adventures of Guigemar,[245] whose story is scarcely relevant to our present argument except that he is sent a mysterious ship containing a bed made by Solomon that takes him to an otherworldly realm not unlike the one described in *Sone de Nansay*.

In the legend of Seth we see yet another connection to Solomon and Bilquis. Not only was the original temple intended to contain the Ark of the Covenant and the Tablets of the Law, but now comes a ship that would one day carry the Grail itself, as well as its seekers, on the final journey of their quest and that already bears his own crown, the Sword of King David, and the three cuttings from the Tree of Life. Like the temple that would be based upon his own great building, it would carry the most sacred of relics, and both his name and that of his wife would be remembered at the site that became the model for the future temple of the Grail. According to another Grail tradition, Bilquis (sometimes called Sibyl or Sebile in medieval texts) gave a vessel of gold to Solomon as a wedding gift—a cup that later became enshrined in the cathedral of Valencia as a type of Grail.[246]

---

243. Matarasso, *The Quest of the Holy Grail*, 232.

244. Quinn, *The Quest of Seth for the Oil of Life*, 198.

245. Glyn S. Burgess and Keith Busby, translators, *The Lais of Marie de France* (Penguin Books, 2003).

246. Margarita Torres Sevilla and Jose Miguel Ortega del Rio, *Kings of the Grail: Tracing the Historic Journey of the Holy Grail from Jerusalem to Spain* (Michael O'Mara, 2015).

◆ ◆ ◆

To discover the origins of this part of the story, we have to turn to the medieval idea of the history of mankind from the time of the expulsion from Eden. It has long been noted[247] that there are parallels between the Grail quest and the legend of the quest of Seth, Adam and Eve's third child, for the Oil of Mercy. The story is found in numerous versions, of which the best known is the *Cursor Mundi* ("The Circuit of the World"), a hugely influential and widely copied poem written in the north of England at the beginning of the thirteenth century.

The poem sets out to describe the history of the world based on a biblical understanding, and it includes a number of legends drawn from older and chiefly lost sources, one of which tells the following story:

> As Adam feels his death coming upon him, he bids his third son, Seth, to go to Paradise and bring some of the Oil of Mercy, which would sustain his life. The path leading to the garden will be apparent because, when Adam and Eve left Eden, their footprints were burned upon the grass, and no vegetation has grown there since. When he reaches the Gates of Paradise, Seth is at first barred from entering by a guardian angel and is refused the oil. However, he is subsequently granted three glimpses of Paradise. In the first he beholds a barren tree; in the second, an adder wound around the trunk; in the third, a newborn baby held at the top. He is then told that the dry tree and the serpent represent the sins of man and that the baby is Christ, who will become the Oil of Mercy. Seth is then given three seeds from the Tree of Life and on returning home, plants them in the mouth of his dead father. From these seeds grow three trees—a cedar, a cyprus, and a pine—which remain growing in the Vale of Hebron until the time of Moses. At this time the three trees are uprooted by Moses and become the wands with which he sweetens the waters of Marah and brings forth water from the rock. King David then inherits the wands, which are united to form a single staff. Later the staff is planted and grows into a tree. In his own time Solomon attempts to use it in the building of his temple, but however the tree is cut, it is always too long or too short. Recognising its miraculous power, Solomon has the tree placed in the Temple, where a woman named Maximller accidentally sits on it. The tree instantly bursts into flame, and the woman prophesies the coming of the Messiah and his death upon the Cross. As the time of the crucifixion approaches, the wood of the tree is made into a cross that can only be lifted by Jesus, since it was destined for him.[248]

247. Quinn, *The Quest of Seth for the Oil of Life.*
248. Ibid.

◆ ◆ ◆

This brings together a wide range of Christian legends, extending backwards in time to fill in gaps left by the biblical narrative. The references to Solomon are of particular interest here as they tie in with the idea that the Grail Temples are based upon the design of the original Temple of Jerusalem. It is possible to see, within the story of the ship that carried the Grail seekers and finally the sacred vessel itself, a shadow of the mighty temples built to house it. In a certain sense the ship is a floating temple, carrying sacred objects placed there by Solomon himself. However, the reference to Seth's three glimpses into paradise and his gift of the three seeds are also significant as they make an immediate correlative to the story told in the *Quest del Saint Greal* and with some variations in Thomas Malory's *Morte d'Arthur* concerning the three cuttings from the tree that form a canopy over the bed on which Galahad will lie.

The canopy that is suspended above the bed of Solomon by the three staves of wood from the Tree of Life recalls the ciborium covering the uncorrupted body of St. Thomas in the *De Adventu*. There is also reason to believe that the Cistercian writer of the *Quest* knew the *Song of Songs*, attributed to Solomon, in which are mentioned not only a bed made of cypress and ivory, tents of cedar, swords, and the king's crown, but references to the kingdom of Galaad, which is sometimes claimed as the origin of the name Galahad. Even the story of the woman who sits upon the wood of the tree is notable—as it bursts into flames, so does the Perilous Seat (set at the table of the Grail in memory of Judas) when a man not destined to do so tries to sit in it.

Thus the vessel dreamed by Bilquis and rendered by Solomon becomes a floating temple containing the sacred relics that were to become familiar to the world through the myths of the Grail.

The Prison and the Stable

A third site, only 2.5 km west of the Throne of Solomon, is a volcanic outcrop called Zendan-i Suleiman, or the Prison of Solomon. It has the same geological formation as the Takht and its lake, but its conical summit is considerably higher. The presence of a water source at the top of Zendan was undoubtedly the principal reason for the constructions at its summit. These constructions belong to an earlier period than those of Takht-e Soleyman and are known to have had a spiritual purpose, though the exact nature of these remains uncertain. The fact that it is described as a prison cannot help reminding us of the pit into which Joseph of Arimathea was placed in various texts such as the *Acta Pilate* and later in *Titurel*.

Finally, and most significantly, is another site that bears the name of the biblical king— Tawila-i Suleiman, or the Stable of Solomon. Much has been written over the last few years concerning the apparent fascination by the Knights Templar with the so-called Stables of Solomon in Jerusalem. This large chamber, hidden beneath the foundations of the Solomonic temple, was apparently given to the Templars to stable their horses. Subsequently, rumours began to appear of excavations carried out in this space, some claimed in search of the lost treasure of the temple, more than fifty tons of gold, silver, and scrolls which vanished in AD 70 following the Roman sacking of the temple at the behest of the emperor Vespasian. More recently it has been suggested that the treasure was, in fact, the Grail. Much of this is pure speculation, a great deal without foundation of any kind, which ignores the real purpose of the large empty space below the floor of the temple. This was, in fact, intended to act as a buffer between the deeper earth and the temple above to prevent any incursions by negative forces from the lower world. It was never intended as a stable and certainly not a treasury. However, the stories have continued to be told of something hidden in Solomon's stable.

The fact that a site known as the Stable of Solomon is within a complex of sacred buildings in Iran, linked by the name of the famous king, presents us with an intriguing possibility. If there is any truth in the persistent rumour of Templar interest in the stable, could it be that these actually refer to the complex of buildings in Iran, which also, as we saw, include a site associated with Solomon's wife Bilquis and a temple bearing an unquestionable similarity to a medieval description of the temple of the Grail? Nor can we ignore the fact that the sacking of Solomon's Temple was carried out at the command of Vespasian and his son Titus—both of whom we have seen to be associated with the Grail story.

The Temple of Vision

A detailed account of the archeological investigations at the Throne of Solomon is beyond the scope of this book; however, a very useful and accessible entry can be found in the online *Encyclopedia Iranica*.[249] Some details are pertinent to our investigation, such as an extended history of buildings on the site. Interestingly, the entry mentions that the earliest level of archeology, from as early as 550 BC, shows that the designs for the oldest complex were sketched out on the ground as a master plan that was followed by the builders. This detail is so close to the description in *Titurel* of the temple plan sketched out on the onyx slab at the top of the mountain for Titurel and his builders to work from as to be astonishing. It seems impossible that the medieval author—or a traveller to the site itself—could have known this detail, yet it stands as an exemplar of the way in which events could remain in memory for hundreds of years.

249. http://www.iranicaonline.org/articles/takt-e-solayman

❖ ❖ ❖

When Arthur Upham Pope reached the site of the Takht, he knew at once that his evidence did not rest on literary evidence alone.

> Here was the mountain, a dome-like extinct volcano, dramatically set apart from the surrounding terrain, with a plateau-like top, and it was ringed by a powerful, still-standing stone wall … There were remains of important buildings … testifying to the historic role of the site; here was a crystal lake in the center, and here also the flattened, smoothed-off area such as Albrecht described, and even more astonishing, a gleaming, crust-like deposit made by the mineral waters of the lake, which, particularly around the shores where it is more exposed, has taken on the appearance of onyx, with striations of white, buff, brown and other tints. These look sufficiently like onyx to justify Albrecht's assertions that the Grail Temple stood on a bed of onyx, which formed the substance of the mountain … [250]

Even if one accepted none of the patterns of similarity between the Takht and the Grail Temple, the fact that the name of the site is the Throne of Solomon and that nearby lie the Throne of Bilquis, the Prison of Solomon, and the Stable of Solomon, these extraordinary links cannot be seen as merely coincidental. We have seen how the first temple in Jerusalem became a model on which most of the subsequent Grail Temples are based; we have seen also that it was Bilquis who foresaw the coming of the Grail in the *Queste del Saint Graal* and who persuaded her husband to build the ship that would later carry not only the sacred relics but also the three successful Quest knights to their journey's end in the mystical city of Sarras. The stable with its curious connection to the Grail search seems almost too perfect.

Was this place the origin of the Grail Temple? It seems possible, even probable, that Albrecht, and perhaps the author of *Sone* had either visited the site or talked with someone who had. Pope believed that soldiers from the army of the Roman general Heraclitus, who virtually destroyed the Takht in AD 628, could have carried descriptions of the site back to the West. Another important point is that Chosroes II had attacked Jerusalem in 614 and carried off the cross on which Christ was said to have been crucified. Heraclitus set out to get it back in 628 and, having sacked the Takht, returned it to Rome. But during the time between its theft and recovery, this sacred relic was kept in the Takht—just as *The Later Titurel* describes! Deep links between the Byzantine Empire, the Armenian Church, and European Christians have long been recognized and offer numerous opportunities for cross-cultural overlays and shared knowledge. The mysterious temple in a far-off land, containing miraculous relics, could have easily fed into the growing awareness of the search for the Grail. One of the oldest surviving manuscripts from Germany, the *Sächsische Weltchronik* ("Saxon World Chronicle"), a history of

250. Pope, "Persia and the Grail."

✦ ✦ ✦

the world compiled between 1229 and 1277, mentions the Throne of Arches and even shows a miniature of Chosroes II seated on a mechanical throne in the heavens, holding a dove and a cross and looking very like later images of God the Father in Christian manuscript tradition. This almost certainly also inspired the creation of actual buildings, as we have seen.

The Church of the Grail

The desire to give substance and dimension to the Grail Temple was, as we have seen, very much in the mind of both Arnoul the Elder and his descendants at Guines and the emperor Rudolf II at Karlstein. A third building, which can be seen to owe something of its design to the work of Albrecht in *The Later Titurel*, is the monastic Abbey of Ettal, some 45 miles south-west of Munich in Southern Germany.[251] Founded in 1330 by the emperor Ludwig (Louis) IV of Bavaria (1282–1347), it immediately garnered several myths. In one of these the emperor's horse was seen to genuflect three times on the site of an earlier church, while in another a mysterious monk gave a statue (still extant) of the Virgin and Child to Ludwig and told him to create a home for Our Lady before vanishing. The statue was said to have been carved by angelic hands and to be made of a stone "fallen from heaven." It thus recalls the miraculous painting of the Virgin that appeared with the church founded by Joseph of Arimathea and Nicodemus at Lydda. It is also strongly reminiscent of the magical stone cited in Wolfram's *Parzifal* and again in Albrecht's work, which he had previously dedicated to Ludwig's father, Duke Ludwig II (1229–1294). Emperor Ludwig therefore must have known *The Later Titurel*, so that when he decided to create the abbey church at Ettal, he seems to have used the description of Albrecht's Grail Temple as a template. Ludwig himself chose the name for the foundation: *unser Frawen etal*. This can be translated in a number of ways, including "pledged to Our Lady," "sworn of Our Lady," "the valley under the law of Our Lady," etc.[252] If we remember that the titles ascribed to the Virgin in the sixteenth-century *Litany of Loretto* include "Mirror of justice/seat of wisdom/spiritual vessel/vessel of honor/singular vessel of devotion/mystical rose/tower of David/tower of ivory/house of gold/Ark of the Covenant/gate of heaven," we can see how appropriate the dedication of Ettal was.

What he created was certainly spectacular. Despite the fact that the original building was partially destroyed by fire in 1744 and restored in the Baroque style, it is still possible to make out the original Gothic design. This consisted of a twelve-sided rotunda with a choir or chapel

---

251. See Wilson, "The Grail Utopia in Southern Germany." I owe much to this article for the exposition of the Church of Ettal.

252. Ibid., 152–153.

to the east and a central pillar supporting a corbelled roof, which must have been spectacular in its day. It seems likely that the statue of the Virgin and Child was placed against the pillar, in much the same way as the Grail stood at the centre of the temple described by Albrecht. Both these forms featured rarely in German ecclesiastical architecture.

The Abbey of Ettal was dedicated to the Assumption of the Blessed Virgin and was the home to a Benedictine double monastery with an adjacent house for a group of Teutonic knights. This gave rise to some notable misconceptions on the behalf of one of the church's first serious explorers, Hyacinth Holland, who wrote a short book about Ettal and its founder in 1860.[253] The author drew attention to the Rule of the monastery, describing it as "of such a strange nature, and so incomparable with any previous monastic institutions, that one could perhaps suspect that the emperor had in mind to realise an ideal Munsalvach (sic) with its temple knights and servants of the Grail."[254]

In fact it appears that Holland had misunderstood the nature of a double monastery, which in Benedictine terms allowed for the presence of monks and nuns in adjacent buildings. Thus the description of the foundation as holding twenty monks, six widows, and twelve married knights—with a married master to rule over the knights and a married mistress to rule over the wives—seems to be a confused understanding of the double foundation and the adjacent house for the Teutonic knights.

The other legend of the church, concerning the miraculous statue, also appears to be a fiction, as Ludwig IV seems to have brought the statue from Pisa. How Ludwig perceived the foundation is less easy to understand. Possibly the best interpretation is suggested in Simon Wilson's perceptive essay on the subject. He sees the existence of the church as symbolically intended to "entice" the Grail back to Germany, thereby restoring his country's fortunes—a device which failed in historical terms since the Holy Roman Empire was already in the process of breaking apart.

The importance of the Abbey of Ettal, leaving aside the legends, is the way in which it gave a new dimension to the ideas underlying *The Later Titurel*, *Sone*, and the other major Grail romances—the idea that it was possible to manifest the home of the Grail and thus offer a physical destination as part of the spiritual quest. In this it was like the chapel of the Grail at Guines and the Grail chapel of Karlstein. These places were not the actual home of the Grail,

253. H. Holland, *Ludwig der Bayer und sein Stift zu Ettal* (Munchen: August Rohsold, 1860).

254. Wilson, "The Grail Utopia in Southern Germany," 144.

✦ ✦ ✦

which as we noted earlier remained as mysterious to medieval pilgrims and seekers as it does today, but it gave a shape and substance to the ideas expressed by the Grail writers.

This idea continued well into the nineteenth century and eventually came to the attention of Sulpiz Boisserée (1783–1854), an art historian and collector with a strong interest in antiquarian studies and the Gothic revival in architecture. Boisserée wrote the first study of the Grail Temples in 1835,[255] making it clear that he saw the abbey church as based firmly on Albrecht's work. Boisserée's projections, based on Albrecht's depiction of the Grail Temple, demonstrated the links between the text and its physical representation. Other German antiquarians followed in his footsteps and throughout the nineteenth century helped establish the idea that Ettal was a Grail site. The ideas first set forth by Boisserée became the foundation of a much longer and more important work, *Graltemple und Paradise*, by the Swedish historian and culturist Lars-Ivar Ringbom, who also recognized the importance of the Takht-e Taqdis as a source for Albrecht's poem.[256] This book remains to this day the most important account of the buildings designated as temples of the Grail.

The association of Ettal continued to exert a strong fascination over the German people. A later descendent of Ludwig IV, the so-called Swan King, Ludwig II of Bavaria (1845–1886), was enchanted with the abbey church, which he clearly saw as a Grail Temple. In a letter written when he was only 19 to his great hero, the composer Richard Wagner, he wrote:

> In the distance, at the end of the valley, towers the church at Ettal…Emperor Ludwig the Bavarian is said to have built this church after the plan of the Grail Temple at Mont Salvat.[257]

From this moment, the impressionable and dreamy young man wanted to build his own Grail castle, which he finally achieved in 1886, when he moved into the still-unfinished castle of Neuschwanstein (New-Swan-Stone), on the hill above the village of Hohenschwangau in southwest Bavaria. The castle was not completed until after the untimely death of Ludwig, while his idol, Wagner, never set foot there at all—though he was later to compose his ritualistic work *Parzifal*, based on Wolfram's great poem utilizing the depiction of the Grail Temple as a stage set.

---

255. "Ueber die Beschreibung des Tempels des heiligen Grales in dem Heldengedicht Titurel Kap. III" in *Abhandlungen der philosophisch-phillogischen Classe der Konglich Bayerischen Akademie der Wissenchaften*, 307–92 (translated in the appendix to this book).

256. Ringbom, *Graltempel und Paradies*. (An English translation is expected.)

257. Wilson, "The Grail Utopia in Southern Germany."

◆ ◆ ◆

We may see Ludwig II's extraordinary vision as the latest and perhaps the last attempt to replicate the temple of the Grail in the everyday world—as the same desire as that of his predecessors Ludwig IV, Albrecht, Arnoul the Elder, and even Chrétien.

When we consider any of the buildings, whether real or imaginary, we have to keep in mind that even the most ordinary churches were not as we are used to seeing them today. Instead of the mostly bare walls, they were indeed hugely decorated, the walls covered in murals showing the delights of heaven and the pains of hell, as well as scenes from the lives of biblical figures and the Passion of Jesus. They were made like this because the builders wanted to remind their congregations of the way they were supposed to live their lives, as well as what to expect afterwards. The temples of the Grail, or the various buildings created in emulation of them, were the same: the symbolism of sacred stones, patterns, carved reliefs, altars, and flying angels represented the book of life spread out before them. This is the reason that the Grail Temples existed: as guidelines for those who sought to better understand life, death, and the beyond.

The association with the stories of the Swan Knights, which we examine in appendix 1, brings the story into yet another sphere entirely, where the Goddess of Love is seen as holding court inside a hollow mountain, surrounded by heroes and beautiful women, apparently in possession of the Grail. This was a different kind of earthly paradise, one that the church frowned upon. There are several accounts in German poetry from the twelfth to fifteenth centuries that refer to the mountain as the Grail, thus allowing Perceval, King Arthur, and others to dwell *within* the vessel.[258] Such a twist in the matter of the Grail must have given many seekers pause for thought.[259]

The Divine Mirror

The contemplation of the sites near Takht-e Soleyman leads us into waters that are less frequently plumbed by Grail seekers—what we might call the Eastern Grail. Writers such as the Indian antiquarian J. C. Coyajee[260] and the French traditionalist philosopher Henry Corbin[261] have long since noted the parallels that exist between the medieval understanding of the Grail and Eastern mystical ideas such as the divine drink of Soma and the mystical Cup of Jamshid, which does indeed share much of its symbolism with that of the Grail.

258. Barto, *Tannhauser and the Mountain of Venus.*

259. *Prester John and the Mountain of Venus* by J. Matthews (forthcoming).

260. Coyajee, "The Legend of the Holy Grail."

261. Carey, "Henry Corbin and the Secret of the Grail."

♦ ♦ ♦

Corbin gave particular attention to the Sufi mystic Suhrawardi (1154–1191), who flourished at the same time as Chrétien de Troyes and Robert de Boron, thus at the time when the Grail stories first flowered in Europe. Amongst Suhrawardi's collections of parables is one that actually refers to Kay Khosrow, otherwise known as Chosroes II, the builder of the Throne of Arches. Referring to the Cup of Jamshid, Suhrawardi describes it in terms of a mirror that enables Khosrow to contemplate not only the physical world but the invisible worlds also. This reference to the Grail as mirror (on which, he adds, the imprint of the world is inscribed) reminds one both of the mirror possessed by Prester John and that of the magician Clingchor in *Parzifal*. All three allow their masters to see beyond the outer world, as does the Grail itself. Corbin also drew attention to the similarity between Suhrawardi's vision of the heavenly mirror and the moment when Galahad looks into the sacred vessel in the *Quest del Saint Graal*, and also in Malory's interpretation of the scene, quoted here:[262]

> Now at the year's end, and the self same day after Galahad had borne the crown of gold, he arose up early and his fellows, and came to the palace, and saw to-fore them the Holy Vessel, and a man kneeling on his knees in likeness of a bishop, that had about him a great fellowship of angels, as it had been Jesu Christ himself; and then he arose and began a mass of Our Lady. And when he came to the sacrament of the mass, and had done, anon he called Galahad, and said to him: Come forth the servant of Jesu Christ, and thou shalt see that thou hast much desired to see. And then he began to tremble right hard when the deadly flesh began to behold the spiritual things. Then he held up his hands toward heaven and said: Lord, I thank thee, for now I see that that hath been my desire many a day. Now, blessed Lord, would I not longer live, if it might please thee, Lord.[263]

In the mirror of the Grail, Galahad sees the truth of all things and can no longer sustain his fleshly existence.

The existence of such concepts in the culture that also produced the Takht and its familial sites is fascinating. While we would not suggest that the origin of the Grail derives from Eastern mysticism, there is no escaping the fact that there are striking parallels between the two very different and endlessly conflicted worlds. The Grail can, perhaps, be seen as a kind of beacon suggesting the possibility of reconciliation between East and West, where it came into focus for both hemispheres' art at much the same time. After all, according to Albrecht, the Grail resides with Prester John, king over Far Eastern lands, while Robert de Boron states in

---

262. Carey, "Henry Corbin and the Secret of the Grail," 175–176.

263. Malory, *Le Morte d'Arthur*, book 17, ch. xix.

❖ ❖ ❖

his *Joseph* that "even as the world goes forward, diminishing every day, it is needful that all this people should go towards the west."[264]

Certainly the imagery of the Grail Temples points to a profound awareness of the similarities that exist between all humans, rather than to the divisions and contradictions that seem to speak more loudly than any idea of polarity or union. For this reason alone we can still learn from them and their stories.

264. Translated by John Carey in "Henry Corbin and the Secret of the Grail."

✦ ✦ ✦

ENVOI

Thus we have come full circle. We began with the fact that the temple of the Grail was based, to some degree, on the Temple of Solomon and on the mystical traditions that underlie its creation. Now, at the end of our journey through the romances and theological expositions that form the background to the Grail myth, we return to the one actual site that influenced all of the descriptions of the Grail's home and find that its title is the Throne of Solomon!

Having established beyond reasonable doubt that the Takht-e Taqdis/Takht-e Soleyman is the origin of most descriptions of the Grail Temple found in the medieval accounts of the sacred vessel, we need to ask an important question: Why? Why create an elaborate home for the Grail at all? Of course we can say that it was part of the subsequent elaboration of the myth into the huge panoply of the Arthurian legends, but we believe that Albrecht, as well as the anonymous writer of *Sone*—as well as the Grail authors—were trying to do more than this.

One statement of Albrecht's makes it clear that his intention was to show how the mysteries of the temple could be experienced through his writing. It is why we placed it at the head of this book.

> I have made the temple worthy of Christians, so that they may learn by studying its shape and design. (v. 516.2)

This is entirely in line with the purpose of all the Grail Temples, chapels, and castles discussed here, going back to Solomon's Temple and its Holy of Holies. Replace the term "Christian" with "all men," and we can see that what the writers of these works meant was that by entering the buildings—whether in actuality or in the imagination—and by reading the

◆ ◆ ◆

symbolism inscribed there, it was possible to understand the secrets of the Grail. This, as the author of *Sone* stated, taught us "the way we must act to enter paradise."

It was, we believe, for this reason that Arnoul the Elder built his copy of the Holy of Holies, and why he said that

> We have recalled these things and told them to you, fathers and masters, about this house, which you see, and in which you reside, not only because of you, but more for some strangers who live here with us. It is no surprise if guests and strangers do not perceive all the winding paths of this house, when many who were reared in this house from their infancy to adult age still could not know or understand the number of gates, doors, small entrances and windows.[265]

It is also, we believe, the reason for the creation of the Abbey of Ettal and the Grail chapel at Karlstein. In addition, the writers of the extraordinary texts we have been examining seem to be saying that in the centre of the castle of the Grail there is a shrine that all should seek to know and understand. Here perhaps we should be allowed to access the fragment of the Divine contained within each one of us—like the sparks of unfallen creation that the Gnostics saw entrapped within the flesh of the human envelope. These sparks are found within each of us, and the true quest of the Grail consists in bringing those lights to the surface, nourishing and feeding them until their radiance suffuses the world.

"*Chaque homme porte a jamais l'age du son temple* (each man is the same age as his own temple)," wrote the traditionalist philosopher Henry Corbin, adding that the completion of the temple on Muntsalvasche was a kind of second birth for Titurel, whom we next see five hundred years old but perfectly preserved. The temple of the Grail is really a divine clearing house for the souls of those who go in search of it—a kind of adjunct to paradise, with glass walls that reflect the true nature of the seeker and demand that he recognize himself.

The image of man as temple—as writers as disparate as Corbin, Schwaller de Lubicz,[266] and Keith Crichlow have all noted—tells us that we must make ourselves into a temple in order to be inhabited by God. This is the object of all the tests, including the turning door and the blinding light of the Grail. The concept begins with the Egypt of the pharaohs, if not earlier, in the caves of mankind's first dwelling; and it continues through Platonic and Neoplatonic schools of thought. To them the temple was microcosmically an expression of the beauty and unity of creation. Expressed thus, it was reflected in the soul and became, indeed, "a bridge for

---

265. Holmes, "The Arthurian Tradition in Lambert d'Ardres."

266. R. A. Schwaller de Lubicz, *The Temple of Man* (Inner Traditions, 1988).

◆ ◆ ◆

the remembrance or contemplation of the wholeness of creation"[267]—words that could be as well applied to the Grail or the divine enclave of which it is a part.

This is the origin of the temple of light (the *haykat al-nur*), the macrocosmic temple that lies at the heart of Islamic mysticism, of which the Sufi mystic Ibn al-Arabi says: "O ancient temple, there hath risen for you a light that gleams in our hearts,"[268] the commentary to which states that "the gnostic's heart, which contains the reality of the truth" is the temple.

Here we are back again in the world of the Solomonic Grail Temple, the image of which, transformed and altered, together with that of the earthly paradise, was enclosed in the world of the Arthurian Grail mythos. That world becomes transformed, in turn, back into the Edenic world of primal innocence, the original home of the sacred vessel, possession of which "represents the preservation of the primordial tradition in a particular spiritual center."[269]

Ibn al-Arabi wrote that the last true man would be born of the line of Seth.[270] Do we not have in this statement a clue to the destiny of the Grail bearer who will be present at the next "sacring" of the divine vessel? All the Grail knights were followers of Seth—who was the first to go in quest of it—and their adventures are transparent glyphs of the human endeavor to experience the Divine. Most of us, if we found our way into the temple unprepared, would probably suffer the fate of Lancelot. But the Grail Temple exists to show us that the way is worth attempting, that the center can be reached, if we are only attentive enough to the message it holds for us.

But what happens when we do finally reach the center? If we look at what we have learned so far about the image of the temple on earth and in the heavens, we may begin to arrive at an answer.

Dealing with the response in mankind to the voice of God, the Word, the Gnostic text known as the *Authoritative Teaching* says, "The senseless man hears the call, but he is ignorant of the place to which he has been called. And he did not ask … where is the temple into which I should go and worship my hope …?"[271] This could hardly be clearer. In the quest of the Grail, the failure to ask an important question is the cause of the failure of many knights who arrive at the castle. It is Lancelot's failure, and it is the failure of all who do not listen to the Voice of the Light.

267. Crichlow, *Soul as Sphere and Androgine.*

268. Ibn al-Arabi, *The Tarjuman Al-Ashwaq* (Acra: Theosophical Publishing House, 1978).

269. René Guenon, "The Symbolism of the Graal," *Tomorrow* 13, no. 2 (winter 1965).

270. Ibn al-Arabi, *The Bezels of Wisdom*, translated by R. W. J. Austin (London: SPCK, 1980).

271. *The Nag Hammadi Library*, edited and translated by James M. Robinson (Leiden: E. J. Brill, 1977), 282.

✦ ✦ ✦

Kabbalistic teaching has it that "the temple has been destroyed, but not the path of purification, illumination, and union that lay concealed in it."[272] For when the perfected soul of mankind "rises like incense from the golden altar of the heart and passes through the most inward curtains of his being to the holy of holies within,"[273] then the two cherubim who stand guard over the Ark of the Covenant "are united in the presence of the One in Whom the soul recognizes its eternal life and its own union with Him. Henceforward the soul is called the eternally 'living' [hayah], the 'one and only' [yehidah]," the perfect.[274] The light comes like veritable tongues of fire upon all who reach the centre of the temple and find there the seat of God in the heart of creation.

This was the aim of the Grail knights, of the Templiesen of Wolfram von Eschenbach, of Titurel, and of the priest-kings who built the Takht-e Taqdis and its temples. Before them it was the desire of the people who erected their stone circles to echo the dance of the cosmos—awaiting that moment when God would reach down and hallow their seeking with a touch. So do all Grail questers, ancient and modern, await that touch that awakens the light within them, as must all who seek to enter the temple of the Grail.

There is no reason to doubt that for the majority of medieval authors who chose to write about the Grail—Chrétien, Robert de Boron, Wolfram, and Albrecht, as well as the anonymous author of *Sone* at least—the castle or temple of the Grail was intended to represent the earthly paradise (in the anonymous romance of *Perlesvaus*, the castle is even called Eden) and that the Grail, when installed at the centre, activated the building to become an *actual* paradisal place. In each of the examples we have explored here, the aspects of paradise are made clear; the Fisher King, Prester John, even Perceval himself are high kings and priest-kings. They echo the role of the high priest in Judaic tradition, hence the parallels between the Solomonic First Temple and the temple of the Grail as it manifests in the romances and in the Takht-e Soleyman, an actual building created as a gateway to paradise.

In his powerful work on the theme, Lars-Ivar Ringbom argued that the Throne of Arches at Shiz symbolised the centre of the cosmos, paradise on earth, the place where heaven and earth met, and that it was a center of sacred kingship.[275] He believed, as do we, that Albrecht used these symbolic associations in *The Later Titurel*.

272. Schayer, "The Meaning of the Temple," 363.

273. Ibid.

274. Ibid.

275. Ringbom, *Graltemple und Paradies*.

✦ ✦ ✦

To enter the home of the Grail is to enter into the heart of the mystery. Here it is possible to experience divinity directly, without the intervention of priest, monk, or theologian. That direct experience brought forth the Grail itself and flowed into the gnostic and esoteric strands of Christianity, which offered a more profound and transcendent realization of the human and divine connection than the everyday mystery of the Mass. The existence of a place, whether temple or castle, which would only be experienced through extreme hardship or probation, became a necessity—those who sought a divine revelation were required to go there.

As the two young knights who sought out a ruined castle said at the end of *Perlesvaus*, when they return and are asked about their experience, "Go where we went and you will see." Though we have explored the journey and visits to the Grail Temple in its most powerful aspects, there is possibly no better advice. Whatever we seek from the Grail, the temple holds it, or at least the key to its greater mystery. It is secret because we cannot look openly on these things, as Christ himself says in *Le Morte d'Arthur* where he invites Galahad to look upon the things that he longs to see but has been unable to do until that moment. Yet the Grail is hidden in plain sight, available to all, initiates or not, provided the intention is pure. It is enough to set forth on the quest itself, whether we find it in its ruined state, forgotten by most people, or in the glory of its greatest manifestation, as in the imaginative descriptions in *Titurel, Sone,* or the *Letter of Prester John* or in the physical representations such as the Takht-e Soleyman, Ettal, or the castle at Guines. By whatever means we proceed, the castle or the temple awaits, receiving all comers.

✦ ✦ ✦

APPENDIX 1

THE KNIGHTS OF THE SWAN

Lohengrin to manhood grew
And gave the Grail his service true …
Across the sea a maiden dwelt …
She a princess of Brabant.
From Munsalvach he was sent
Whom the Swan did bring …

✦ ✦ ✦

Wolfram von Eschenbach, *Parzival*[276]

Two characters dominate the short prose prologue to *Sone de Nansay* that introduces the life story of the hero, and questions have been asked as to whether they really existed. One is the indomitable old lady known as Fane, the chatelaine of Cyprus and lady of Beyrouth, the other her 105-year-old servant, a lay priest named Branque who had served her for the past forty years. Branque is certainly an invention of the anonymous poet, especially when one realises that the term in old French means "imbecile"!

Fane may also be invented, as there is no record of any such person in the historical record, and given that her name can mean "temple" or "shrine," one may suspect that the author is having a joke at his readers' expense. We are told that the chatelaine had commissioned the work as a means of recollecting her distinguished relations over several generations, with the emphasis upon Sone himself, who takes pride of place in the annals of her extended family. Her claim to be a titled lady of both Beyrouth and Cyprus may seem unlikely in the light of modern

---

276. Barto, *Tannhäuser and the Mountain of Venus.*

✦ ✦ ✦

geography and politics, but not if we have some knowledge of the history of the First and Third Crusades, which were very piecemeal affairs.

Jerusalem fell to a loose confederacy led by Godfrey de Bouillon in 1099, but Beyrouth, some distance to the north, remained unconquered for years, while Cyprus became an island kingdom under the Holy Roman Empire in 1197 after the Third Crusade. It was possible for local families to have title to various scraps of territory to which they laid more or less permanent—if only titular—claim. Of such could have been Fane, lady of Beyrouth and chatelaine of Cyprus at the time when she commissioned the writing of *Sone de Nansay*, probably some time after 1265.

The family tree certainly makes for fascinating study and speculation, with its mixture of fact, fiction, and legend. Beginning with major royal characters such as the King of Hungary and Count of Flanders among the hero's ancestors, and with the addition of the pious Aelis of Gand, capable of postmortem miracles that led to her reburial. Ancient and legendary figures such as the Knight of the Swan are, surprisingly, descendants of Sone.

Our main line of interest, however, focuses upon the fascinating variations upon the Knight of the Swan and why Fane should have found him playing so prominent, intimate, and indeed recent a role in her own life.

The Swan Knight story is present in *Sone* at least partially because Wolfram von Eschenbach connects him, under the name of Lohengrin, with the Grail family, and because it was clearly important to the author to add the Swan Knight to the already starry list of descendants of his hero, including an emperor, several kings, and a pope! Another possible reason is that by adding this story and calling the Swan Knight Helias, an alternate name for Tannhäuser, the author of *Sone* was trying to connect his story with the Venusberg legends, which included King Arthur and references to the Grail Temple.

Indeed, one of the most intriguing points in the association of the Swan Knight myth with the Grail is the connection made in a number of medieval German romances between the Venusberg (Mountain of Venus) and Muntsalvasche. On the face of it, this would seem an unlikely pairing since the one is undoubtedly pagan and the other primarily Christian, but the examples which exist suggest that "Der Gral" was used as an alternate name for the Venusberg, and thus as a place where the Goddess of Love actually lived. We may cite, for example, the fifteenth-century chronicle compiled by Caspar Able, which, referring to Helias, says that "this youth Helias came out of the mountain where *Venus is in the Grail*."[277]

---

277. Cited in Clifton-Everest, *The Tragedy of Knighthood*. Our italics.

This seems to tie in with a theme referenced in German, Spanish, and Italian romances that tell how King Arthur lives, with other heroes, beneath a hollow mountain.[278] Venus is often there, as is the goddess Juno and the daughter of the Sibyl. In some instances Arthur sleeps, as in the famous account of the Nine Christian Worthies, including Charlemagne and Frederic Barbarossa, sleeping beneath Mount Etna, awaiting a call to arms; in others Arthur and as many as a hundred of his knights are awake, enjoying an entertaining time beneath the mountain in a paradisal realm ruled over by Venus. In at least one poem, by the thirteenth-century poet Heinrich von Meissen, the implication seems to be that heroes retire "to the Grail," where they enjoy a vastly extended life.[279] Perhaps not surprisingly, this was often used as an example of the beliefs of weak-minded fools and came with threats of eternal damnation for those who wandered into such an antechamber of hell. That Albrecht was aware of these stories seems beyond doubt; in the romance of *Lohengrin*, Arthur, his warriors, and "many beautiful ladies of fair hue" dwell in a hollow mountain in "Inner India," which "encloses the Grail with all the heroes…"[280] Once again, this seems to relate to the earthly paradise of Prester John, also, as we saw, placed in India.

The first evidence of the Knight of the Swan outside the literary sphere is a letter from a certain Guy de Bazoches, written between 1175 and 1180, who remarks that Baudouin I of Jerusalem, brother of Godfrey de Bouillon, is the grandson of the *miles cygni*, or Knight of the Swan.[281] More publicly, in about 1184 William of Tyre, historian of the First Crusade, alludes to the tradition, although regarding it only as fable.[282] Nonetheless the legend quickly spread and references multiplied.

The Song of Antioch is the first literary text that relates Godfrey of Bouillon to the Knight of the Swan.[283] It was written towards the end of the twelfth century and is part of a group of poems known as the Old French Crusader cycle, comprising "Helias," "The Childhood of Godfroy," "The Song of Jerusalem," and "The Captives."[284] *The Song of Antioch* itself contains fragments of an even older poem that tells us how Godfrey's ancestor sailed down the River Rhine

278. For a full-length study of these and other related legends, see Barto, *Tannhauser and the Mountain of Venus*.

279. Cited in Clifton-Everest, *The Tragedy of Knighthood*.

280. Ibid., 10.

281. Guy de Bazoches, cited in Lecouteux, *Mélusine et le Chevalier au Cygne*.

282. Peter W. Edbury, *William of Tyre, The Conquest of Jerusalem and the Third Crusade* (Ashgate, 1998).

283. Edgington and Sweetenham, *The Chanson d'Antioche*.

284. Mickel Jr. and Nelson, *The Old French Crusade Cycle*.

◆ ◆ ◆

in a small boat drawn by a swan to land at a beach near the main keep of the imperial city of Nimégan. He was clad in white and his head shone brighter than a peacock's wing.

The emperor, who could well have been Otto I (912–973), retained him with the assurance that he could come and go freely, and even provided him with a wife from one of his own female relations. He gave him a stretch of good fertile land and invested him with the fief of Bouillon. The knight led the army, carried the colours, and served the emperor as a good vassal until unexpectedly the swan returned and sailed off with the knight, the emperor unable to keep him at any price. The people were very distressed, but he left behind a pregnant young woman at the castle of Bouillon whose line some claim subsequently bore Godfrey.

A story was soon added to the legend of the Knight of the Swan to explain the origin of the swan that pulled his boat. It was not part of the original story but fits in with the mysterious figure and comes down to us in various literary forms, of which the oldest is that of Johannes de Alta Silva (circa 1190) in a Latin text called *Dolopathos*,[285] in which he tells how a young lord became lost while hunting and arrived at a fountain where a faery was bathing, holding a golden chain in her hand. He robbed her of her chain (and/or possibly her hymen), and far from wishing to escape, she agreed to marry him. After studying the course of the stars, she also predicted that she would bring six sons and a daughter into the world in a single pregnancy. The lord took her back to his castle and married her despite the opposition of his mother.

The faery's prediction came true and she gave birth to seven children, each bearing a golden chain about its neck. However, her mother-in-law seized the children and replaced them with seven puppies, then presented her son with the dogs as his children, claiming that the faery had bewitched them. The lord condemned his wife to be buried up to the breast in the great hall of the castle, gave her dog food to eat, and instructed that all who came to the castle should wash their hands over her head and dry their hands in her hair. Thus things continued for seven years.

The mother-in-law had meanwhile given the children to one of her servants with orders to kill them, but he took pity on them and left them with a forest hermit. Seven years passed and the lord came across the children when hunting in the forest and saw their golden chains. After attempting in vain to follow them, he returned to the castle and told his adventure to his mother, who, realizing that the children of her daughter-in-law had not been put to death, ordered a servant to seek them out and at least bring back the golden chains.

---

285. Gilleland and de Alta Silva, *Dolopathos*.

✦ ✦ ✦

The men went to the forest and came to a river where the six boys were swimming in the form of swans, while on the bank their sister guarded the chains that preserved their human form when worn. Nonetheless, the men seized the boys' chains from her and took them back to their mistress, who gave them to a goldsmith to fashion into a goblet. The chains resisted all his efforts, however, and one was severely damaged. He used another piece of gold to complete the required vessel, while back in the forest the boys were obliged to continue their lives in the form of swans. They flew with their sister, who could still transform between human and swan, and gathered at a lake near their father's castle. Here the girl in her human form begged for bread, which she shared with the swans and their half-buried mother, near whom, rather surprisingly, she slept at night.

This led the lord to question the girl. She told him all she knew, at which her grandmother tried to kill her, but her father saved her on learning the whole story and made the goldsmith surrender the chains so the children could regain their human form, apart from the one whose chain had been damaged. This was the one who was destined to draw the boat in which the armed knight rode. The children's mother was freed, and their evil grandmother took her place.

This story explains the origin of the swan but contains some elements that demand explanation and reveal the great antiquity of the tale. The faery's barbarous punishment disappears from later versions. The resistance of the gold to the goldsmith's tools shows that the metal comes from the faery kingdom, and in some accounts it is described as silver. Jean de Haute-Seille preserved these elements in his reworking of the story of Dolopathos, which is why his version is of considerable importance. In circa 1210 Herbert de Paris translated the story into French and varied from his source to associate the Knight of the Swan with Godfrey de Bouillon.

A later version of the story called *Elioxe*[286] is characterised by the addition of new motifs and the fact that the protagonists have lost their anonymity. It tells how King Lothaire, whose kingdom was near Hungary, became lost while hunting a stag. Tired out, he rested near a spring and went to sleep. From a nearby mountain a courteous and friendly young lady arrived, saw the sleeping king, and shaded his face with her sleeve to protect him from the sun. Lothaire awoke and, dazzled by her beauty, offered his hand in marriage and his crown. Elioxe consented and declared she would give birth to seven children, six boys and a girl, at a single accouchement, all conceived on their wedding night; she added that she would die as a result, but one of the male children would become a king in a country overseas.

---

286. Mickel Jr. and Nelson, *The Old French Crusade Cycle*.

◆ ◆ ◆

Lothaire took Elioxe back to his castle and married her despite the misgivings of his mother, Matrosilie. She was close to giving birth when Lothaire had to leave the country to fight a pagan king who had invaded his lands. In his absence, Elioxe gave birth to seven children, each bearing a golden chain around the neck, after which she died. Matrosilie took the children, put them in two baskets, and gave them to her servant Monicier to abandon in the forest. Realizing that the newborn children were in the baskets, Monicier left them before the window of a forest hermitage. A hermit rescued the children and cared for them.

When Lothaire returned from his campaign, his mother told him that Elioxe had given birth to seven baby dragons, which had torn up the entrails and flown away.

Seven years later Rudemart, a messenger of the king, was by chance taking refuge with the hermit and saw the children with the chains at their necks. Returning to the castle, he told of this meeting to Matrosilie, who ordered him to return to the hermit's house. While the children were asleep, Rudemart managed to cut the chains of the six boys with a strong pair of shears while they slept. The girl, who slept apart, escaped, but on waking saw what he had done. In the morning the six brothers, changed into swans, guided by an instinct that enabled them to follow the trail of the chain snatcher, alighted at fish ponds near Lothaire's castle, who forbade that they be hunted. Unaware of this order, his nephew Nantoul tried to kill a swan, and returning to the palace, admitted his misadventure to the king, who lost his temper and threw a goblet at his head, breaking its base. Matrosilie gave it to a goldsmith for repair with metal from one of the chains.

However, the hermit dismissed the girl, fearing the dangers of solitude for her, and she went to Lothaire's court, where she begged for bread and shared it with the swans. The behaviour of the birds toward the little girl attracted the king's attention so that he sought out the child and questioned her. The king realised, on hearing her, that his mother had lied to him and obliged her to tell him the truth. The goldsmith brought the chains still in his possession, Lothaire passed them over the necks of the swans and they transformed back into human beings. Only the one whose chain had been melted down kept his swan form.

Matrosilie was pardoned and took on the role of a benevolent grandmother. Five brothers left to take up lives of adventure as knights; the one who took the swan, according to an angel who appeared in a dream to Lothaire, fulfilled the prediction of Elioxe and went on to found a royal line overseas.

The mythical elements of the story brought to us by *Dolopathos* have been largely rationalized. The faery died, the chains remained separate, and Lothaire pardoned Matrosilie, whose role is quite astonishing. These changes tend to show that *Elioxe* and the story of *Dolopathos*

✦ ✦ ✦

come from the same source, and the alterations are due to oral transmission. It is always the little girl who keeps her chain. An epilogue also shows that the anonymous author knew the legend of the Knight of the Swan as originally told: one of the brothers arrives, accompanied by a swan, at Nimégan on the day of Pentecost and remains a guest of the emperor.

Another form of the story, called *Isomberte*,[287] further reduces the marvelous parts. It tells how, hunting in the forest, Count Eustache de Portemise sees some dogs barking around an old oak tree. There he finds a beautiful young girl, Isomberte, daughter of King Popleo, whose kingdom is beyond the sea. She is fleeing from her father, who wants her to marry, whereas she is against all thoughts of marriage, although this hostility does not last long, for she accepts when Eustache asks her to marry him. The count's mother, Ginesa, is very much against accepting this foreign daughter-in-law. Soon after their marriage Eustache has to render service to his lord, but putting this off, he keeps her at his side.

During this time Isomberte gives birth to seven sons, at whose birth an angel passes a golden chain round the neck of each. Bandoval, Eustache's seneschal, is saddened by this event, for he believes that a woman who gives birth to more than one child at a time must have been guilty of adultery. He writes to his lord, telling him what has happened, but Ginesa substitutes his letter for another saying that Isomberte has brought seven dogs into the world. Eustache replies that they must keep them and do nothing wrong to the mother, but Ginesa intercepts the message and replaces it with another ordering that they kill the mother and her children. Bandoval cannot bring himself to do this and leaves the countess alive but takes away the children, whom he abandons in the forest, where a female deer comes and suckles them. Soon after, a hermit looks after the newly born.

The children grow, and the hermit, accompanied by six of them, arrives one day at Ginesa's castle. On seeing the chains worn by the six brothers, Ginesa questions the hermit, who tells her how he discovered the children abandoned. She realizes that they are her grandchildren and tells the hermit to leave them with her. Ginesa has the chains taken from the necks of the children and intends to kill them, but they fly away in the form of swans and reach a lake near the hermitage, where their brother has remained.

Ginesa gives the chains to a goldsmith to be made into a goblet. He begins to melt one down, but to his great astonishment the gold begins to increase, so much so that a single chain is enough to make the goblet, which weighs more than the rest of the chains put together. He gives this to Ginesa and keeps the other chains intact.

---

287. Mickel Jr. and Nelson, *"La Naissance du Chevalier au Cygne"* in *The Old French Crusade Cycle*.

❖ ❖ ❖

When Eustache returns home, the conversation he has with his wife puzzles him. After a brief enquiry he accuses his mother of theft, and Ginesa admits that she has had the children killed to protect the honour of a son deceived by an adulterous woman. Did she not have seven children at once? The court takes the side of Ginesa, and Isomberte is condemned to be burnt unless she can find a champion to defend her. An angel reveals to the hermit the identity of the child who lives with him and announces that the boy must go to the town to defend his mother; God will give him the victory.

At the moment that Isomberte is taken to her fate, her son appears, takes on Ginesa's champion, and defeats him. The old countess has to admit the truth and is condemned and imprisoned; the goldsmith returns the chains in his possession. They are passed over the necks of the swans, who recover their human form. One child, whose chain was melted down, remains a swan and lives with the brother who proved the innocence of their mother. It was he who became the Knight of the Swan.

We note that the girl has disappeared from this story and the faery's origin remains obscure; the tale has been Christianized, as shown by the intervention of an angel, whether it be to pass the chains round the children's necks or to let the hermit know what the child who lives with him must do.

The final form of the story is found in *Le Chevalier au Cygne*,[288] the first chanson de geste to tell the complete legend of an unknown knight who championed Béatrix, duchess of Bouillon. We possess two redactions in prose, four fragments, and two versified songs of the legend, with some significant divergences. It is sometimes called *Béatrix* to distinguish it from *Isomberte* and *Elioxe*.

Orians, the king of l'Ile-Fort, with his wife, Béatrix (who is a human, not a faery), were looking out of their palace windows and saw a beggar woman accompanied by a pair of twins. This led Orians to regret the sterility of his marriage, but Béatrix insists that a woman who had twins must have lain with two different men. Then, during the absence of the king, she herself gives birth to six sons and a daughter about each of whose necks a faery has fastened a silver chain.

Matabrune, Orians's mother, who is called "a devil," affirms that if Béatrix had brought seven children into the world, she must have slept not only with her husband but six other men. She orders her servant Markes to drown the children and takes seven puppies to her son, claiming them to have been delivered by her daughter-in-law. Orians throws his wife into prison to await

---

288. Hibbard, *Medieval Romance in England*, 239.

◆ ◆ ◆

her fate. Markes, overcome with pity, does not drown the children but leaves them on the bank of a river; a hermit finds them and weans them on goat's milk, an animal that he believes God has sent in answer to his prayers.

Ten years pass before another servant of Matabrune, an "evil forester," passes by the hermitage and sees the children and their chains, and on returning to the castle tells Matabrune what he has seen. She orders him to steal the chains and bring them back to her. He returns to the hermitage, finds six of the children, one being absent with the hermit, and steals their chains. The five boys and the girl, changed into swans, fly off to fishponds belonging to Orians.

The brother who has escaped the change remains with the hermit and goes regularly to Orians's castle for alms, until one day he discovers the swans. In the meantime Matabrune has taken the six chains to a goldsmith and ordered him to make a goblet from them. The artisan melts down one chain and finds that it wondrously produces enough metal to make two goblets. He locks the others away.

Fifteen years go by, Matabrune insisting that Béatrix should be burnt at the stake, until eventually Orians decrees it should be the next day if she cannot find a champion to defend her. An angel appears to the hermit and reveals that the child he has brought up is the king's son and that he is destined to defend his wrongly accused mother. The hermit tells the boy of this revelation, and he immediately goes to the town and is baptised with the name of Elyas, arriving at the field of combat just in time to become his mother's champion.

The furious Matabrune has appointed a relative, Malquarré, to defend "her right," whom Elyas, armed and dressed as a knight, decapitates in the course of the fight. He then tells Orians the message of the angel and makes himself known. The goldsmith brings the remaining chains and the swans are transformed back into handsome youths and a beautiful girl. They are baptized and receive the names of Orians, Zacaryes, Orions, Johans, and the maiden Rosete.

The king presents his crown to his son and Matabrune escapes but is trapped in her castle. Elyas besieges it and after another judicial combat Matabrune is obliged publicly to admit her crimes before mounting the pyre. In the course of the following night, an angel appears to Elyas and tells him to spend the next morning in a garden beside the river, where his brother swan appears, pulling a boat, which he boards.

Immediately after Elyas has stepped into the boat pulled by the swan, the legend proper of the Knight of the Swan begins as opposed to that of the children.

In the most popular version, rendered by the scholar C. Hippeau (which follows neither the oldest sources nor the most complete but is supplemented by the so-called Paris manuscripts and a German edition by Baron von Reiffenberg), the story runs as follows:

◆ ◆ ◆

The swan takes Elyas as far as a pagan town where he fights Agolant, Matabrune's brother, but is defeated and taken prisoner, as a consequence of which Orians mounts an expedition and arrives in time to prevent his son from being executed. Elyas then kills Agolant, gives the county and fief to one of his vassals, and leaves with the swan in search of further adventure.

Rainier, duke of Saxe, has invaded the lands of the duchess of Bouillon. In the boat pulled by the swan, Elyas sails back up the Rhine as far as Nimégan, where he hears of the misdeeds of Rainier. He offers his help to the emperor, Othon, and takes on the Saxon duke in single combat as champion for the lady of Bouillon. Elyas kills Rainier and marries Béatrice, the duchess of Bouillon's daughter, after making her swear never to ask his name or where he comes from, on pain of losing him forever.

The tale then lingers, recounting the combats of Elyas against Rainier's brother, marked by a new divine intervention. Béatrix gives birth to a daughter whom they call Ida (or Yde or Idain). Seven years later, on the day of their anniversary, Béatrice breaks her word: "Sir," says the lady, "by God the son of Mary tell me your name; do not hide it from me any longer. Tell me the place of your birth and who your parents are and what is your lineage."

Elyas did not answer her questions but announced that he was obliged to leave the next day, taking leave of his wife, his daughter, and the emperor and his vassals. The swan appears, crying strangely, and Elyas tells his lord, "Sire, let me go, I can no longer delay. If you force me to stay, you will see me die here at your feet," and asks him to take care of Ida. The swan calls a second time and Elyas hurries to the boat, climbs aboard, crosses himself three times, and departs.

He leaves Béatrice with a talisman, an ivory horn. One day, when the room in which it is kept is in flames, a swan arrives who seizes it and carries it off. From then on, texts agree in seeing Ida as the mother of Godfrey of Bouillon and tell that Ida marries Eustache II of Boulogne, by whom she has three crusading sons: Eustache III, Count of Boulogne, who returned home to rule the family estates; Godfrey, first ruler of Jerusalem; and Baudouin, first crowned king of Jerusalem.

When we come to the version of the Knight of the Swan's tale as provided in *Sone's* prologue, we find a much-modified account. The final paragraphs translate as follows:

> Then the pope ordered Sone to join him (in Rome) as emperor (of the Christian world), and he had to leave. His son Houdiant, hardly eighteen months old, was crowned king of Norway and much later married Matabrune, the worst woman ever! By her he had a son, King Oriant, who married Elouse, who bore triplets, each one of the three boys with a golden neck chain. Because she hated Elouse, Matabrune broke up the chain of one of the children, who changed into a swan, so she did not dare do this again. The swan flew off to

✦ ✦ ✦

the river that runs at the foot of the walls of Galoche, and was later the swan that pulled the boat of Elyas, his brother, the Knight of the Swan.

Elyas killed the Saxon at Nimégan and married the heiress Béatrix, by whom he conceived Yde. Despite the promise she had made him, Béatrix asked him who he was. He replied, "You will never see me again after today as you have not respected my conditions." He sounded his horn and his brother arrived with the boat. Elyas boarded it and went to Beyrouth, the port where my lady still lived with her three sons.

A great battle took place at the port of Acre. 20,000 Christians and 300,000 pagans were killed. As far as is known, no miscreant survived. The battle lasted five days and five nights, and there Elyas was cut to pieces. His brother, the swan, brought him from the sea to die in the arms of my lady. No one ever saw such grief shown by his brother, the swan. No one could console it. It threw itself into the waves and thus perished.

The family units of seven children have been modified to a standard three—mostly born singly but with the occasional pair of twins such as Houdiant and Henri to Sone and Odée, perhaps to signify that multiple births do not imply adultery. Fane, who commissioned the romance, is revealed within it to have been the daughter of Henri, who became king of Jerusalem by marriage to the royal heiress Hermine. Whilst there is no shortage of such marital arrangements in the history of the Crusader kingdom, there are only two named Henri in the course of a couple of centuries, and neither of them fit the circumstances.

It is also interesting to note that a legendary couple has been introduced, Oriant and Elouse, who are not mentioned in any family history. Whatever the reason for this, it implies that Fane is an aunt of the Knight of the Swan! By naming the Swan Knight Elyas, a later version of the character which refers back to Lohengrin and Tannhauser, the author of *Sone* ties together strands of myth that include the Venusberg.

Like a faery, whose ability to remain in human zones is dependent on a particular condition (*geis*[289]), Lohengrin arrives in the kingdom of Brabant and agrees to be the husband of Elsa, heir to the duchy, provided that she never asks his name or place of origin. When Elsa breaks this promise, he departs in the swan boat in which he had arrived, never to return. We may speculate on whether the geis is a typical stipulation in Celtic mythology—an equivalent of the situation to be found in the legends featuring Melusine of Lusignan. Professor Claude Lecouteux, who has provided much information on Knight of the Swan lore in his *Mélusine et le*

---

289. *Geis*, pl. *geasa*: an Irish term for conditions and agreements that must be performed in order to preserve one's life.

◆ ◆ ◆

Chevalier au Cygne,[290] likes to think each figure originated as a Celtic goddess or Scandinavian god; our own preference is a focus on faery lore.

These tales, taken with the story of Lohengrin as it appears in Wolfram, show a half-human, half-faery lineage resembling those found in the mysterious work called the *Elucidation*. The "patient wife" motif, applied to the swan children's mother, is a common folk tale that also appears in the Mabinogion story of "Pwyll and Rhiannon." There is a curious half-echo between the story of the families of Brabant and Bouillon—whose sons were crusading heroes who secured the safety of Jerusalem and the Holy Lands—and that of Lohengrin, who as the son of Parzifal and Condwiramurs in Wolfram's poem becomes the Grail Knight of Muntsalvasche, just as his brother, Kardeiz, inherits Parzival's secular lands.

The great battle described in the final paragraph seems likely to have been the fall of Acre in 1291, which spelt the end of Crusader occupation of the mainland of the eastern Mediterranean coast. The numbers involved are, as usual, grossly exaggerated, but it was a great national disaster and a personal one as well if we are to believe the prologue account, where it appears that Fane took in some character, possibly a nephew, who liked to pose as the legendary Knight of the Swan.

290. Lecouteux, *Mélusine et le Chevalier au Cygne*.

✦ ✦ ✦

APPENDIX 2

A DESCRIPTION OF THE TEMPLE OF THE HOLY GRAIL IN CHAPTER III OF THE HEROIC POEM TITUREL[291]

Sulpiz Boisserée

Translated by Melanie Kinghan

*A*uthors' note: Boisserée's essay was intended as an introduction to his own edition of the section of *The Later Titurel* describing the Grail Temple. As this has remained untranslated until now, we decided to include it here as a point of reference to our own work. It is at times complex and almost as impenetrable as the original poem, but Boisserée's skill and his wide reading—as well as a unique access to many of the then-existing manuscripts of the work (further copies have come to light since), make this an important document for our understanding of Albrecht's work. (The footnotes alone, in which Boisserée explores much little-known material, is alone worth a great deal to anyone seeking to understand the origins of the Grail.) The author's notes in general, however, are problematical in that he uses shorthand terminology no longer current. We have not attempted to update these, as this would alter the structure of the essay. Many of the original documents referenced are either outdated or exist in more modern editions. We offer this text here as a key document that casts light on both the original work of *The Later Titurel* and the nineteenth-century understanding of its meaning. Boisserée's

---

291. Originally published as *Ueber die Beschreibung des Tempels des heiligen Grales in dem Heldengedicht: Titurel Kap III* by Druck von G. Jaquet in 1834. See plate 2 for a projection of the Grail Temple ground plan after Sulpiz Boisserée.

♦ ♦ ♦

suggestion that the home of the Grail must be Salvaterra in Biscay, not far from Vittoria, on the grounds that Albrecht says, "If you go to Galicia, you will know Salvaterre," is somewhat far fetched, though the route to Galicia was well known because of pilgrimages to Santiago de Compostella.

Some spellings, particularly of personal names and places, may differ from those found elsewhere in the book. This is due to the older forms of German in the original text, which we preferred to leave untouched. Words in square brackets have been added by the editors for the sake of clarity.

A DESCRIPTION OF THE TEMPLE OF THE HOLY GRAIL
Sulpis Boisserée, translated by Melanie Kinghan[292]

The description of the Temple of the Holy Grail is the only significant writing about the art of architecture found in German poetry to date; it is also of great importance for the history of German architecture and even German poetry. Once I discovered this material, I set myself the task of critically analysing and editing it.

Following the description of the temple, it becomes apparent that the author must have seen selected works concerning German architecture in its golden age. However, careful researches of monuments and historical facts have proven that the golden age of German architecture did not begin until the second half of the thirteenth century. Moreover, there was no mention of the significant work composed in the second half of the thirteenth century, which would have given the author reason for his views on the Temple of the Holy Grail.[293]

By contrast, research suggests that Wolfram von Eschenbach, who was named as the author of *Titurel*, created his poetic works roughly between 1190 and 1230. Heinrich von Ofterdingen, Hartmann von der Ouwe, and others who he named as friends lived around this time. In 1207 Wolfram took part in the poetic competition held at the Wartburg, alongside many rulers from the same era with who he seemed to be in close affiliation.

292. Footnotes 293–342 are from the original Boisseree text.

293. See Buesching Museum for old German literature I 27 ff.

+ + +

The discrepancy between the author's lifetime and the era of the buildings that were the basis of his description is only possible if we assume that we do not have the original text but an adaptation of it. To gain certainty, it was necessary to look at all different handwritten texts and examine them. I obtained a first confirmation in 1810 when I commissioned a transcription of the chapter in question from one of the "Heidelberg manuscripts" (handwritten), which was still in Rome at the time. My assumption was confirmed by looking at an older *Titurel* fragment, published by Docen in the same year, and kept in His Majesty's Library in Munich, in which A. W. Schlegel recognized the original work of Wolfram von Eschenbach. Schlegel's detailed evaluation in the *Heidelberg Yearbooks* for 1811 finally gave proof for this opinion.[294] Schlegel compared the philological, metrical and poetic value of both the older and newer version [of the work] and ever since it is assumed that the younger version must be an adaptation/ new edition of the *Titurel*.

Unfortunately, the fragment that has been investigated did not contain the chapter about the Holy Grail and only six of the nine remaining handwritten manuscripts[295] contain that chapter. This means we only possess seven copies of it including the old print of 1477. Of these seven, I either took copies myself or had the kind help of people who have knowledge of our language and poetry. A comparison of all seven showed that they are all a version of the second edition of the poem. There are great differences amongst them, as already mentioned by Pueterich von Reicherzhausen in the fifteenth century; he knew of thirty different ones, which did not all show strict conformity.[296]

---

294. P. 1086 and 1099.

295. These are:

    1. The second fragment of the older *Titurel* from the Ambrasser collection in Vienna, published by Schottky in the *Vienna Yearbooks of Literature*, 8th volume 1819 (Anzeigeblatt p. 28–35, print edition.

    2. the older Heidelberger Handschrift (manuscript) no. 141, fragment, handwritten.

    3. the younger Heidelberger Handschrift (manuscript), no. 383, handwritten.

    4. the Vienna manuscript of His Majesty's Library no. 40, handwritten.

    5. the Ferstlich Dietrichsteinsche (Prince of Dietrichstein) of Vienna, fragment, handwritten.

    6. the Hannover manuscript of His Majesty's Library, fragment, handwritten.

    7. the Berlin manuscript of His Majesty's Library, formerly von der Hagen, handwritten.

    8. the Regensburg manuscript of His Majesty's Library in Munich, fragment, handwritten.

    9. the Karsruhe (Carlsruhe) manuscript of the Grand Duke's Library, formerly St. Peter monastery in the Black Forest, handwritten.

296. Adelung, Pueterich von Reicherzhausen, p. 30.

♦ ♦ ♦

The old print edition (1477) might have the least significance and with it the richly decorated and detailed manuscript from St. Peter in the Black Forest which is now in Carlsruhe (Karlsruhe). It is very similar to the print edition and was only completed in 1431.[297]

The Regensburg fragment, the Berlin manuscript, Vienna manuscript of His Majesty's Library and the younger Heidelberg manuscript follow these. All of the handwritten manuscripts are relatively identical, though none as much as the first two; the closest are the Vienna and Berlin manuscripts. On the other hand, we have the older Heidelberg handwritten manuscript, which stands alone, as it seems to have the purest second version of the poem. It is also the oldest one amongst the above-mentioned manuscripts according to language and writing, and can probably be dated in the first half of the fourteenth century.

Because of this, and the fact that it contains the chapter about the temple of the Grail in full, I took the reading of the older Heidelberg manuscript as a basis, even though it is incomplete in other respects. From that basis and the other texts, I tried to create a revised text.

This older Heidelberg manuscript also had the added value of giving me more information about the author of the second edition. In 1817, when I worked with it, I found two pages glued to the top of the manuscript. I found twenty-three verses written there, partly incomplete, written by the same hand that had written the whole codex. In these verses, the author is talking about his relationship to the original poet, the author of *Titurel*. He is also talking about the reasons why there was a need for a new edition. Today, those two pages are missing—no one knows how—but thankfully I made a detailed copy of both.

The author begins with the lament that the (first) poet didn't live long enough to complete the work. Furthermore, he says that the Venetians have built a very rich temple that came with many losses of workers such as stonemasons and sculptors. New workers followed, so that the work can go on—if you cannot have the best you will have to make do with the lesser. How would the world pay tribute to von Pleinfelden (a known pseudonym of von Eschenbach), Sir Wolfram, if he were long dead! The author then sang von Eschenbach's praises and, as much as the fragmentary text can tell us, seems to take on the task of completing the poem and writing a new version. By doing so, he then talks about the false and true arts of poetry, similar to the

---

297. It finishes with the Amen from the 75th verse, 41st chapter in the old manuscript and instead of the following 13 verses you can read:

Explicit liber Tyturelis de Eschenbach

Hermanus Petri eir Notarii

Anno Dni millesimo quadringestesimo trigesimo pmo.

In die Sancti Achacii mris. Et sociorum ejus martyrum.

◆ ◆ ◆

start of the 10th chapter (of the printed version) and then calls himself Albrecht. This name is known from other places in the print edition as well as the handwritten manuscripts, as listed below. "I, Albrecht, no weakling, I never belittle anyone" etc., he says in verse 13, and a little later in verse 15 he speaks of the fact that he does not want to take away from the praise that he (Wolfram) rightly deserves.[298] Following that, he brings in another metaphor, no less significant than the first one: If someone would only see one cheek of a beautiful Lady and she was known in all kingdoms for her worthiness, it must hurt the heart of an honest man quite a lot if he never saw her again in full.

After a gap, the author then changes to a chorus of praises for his ruler. "The Prince of Bavaria he may be named, Duc Lois et Palatinus, my praise may bring him (princely) honors tenfold." The following verses suggest that he is talking about Emperor Ludwig from Bavaria (Kaiser Ludwig der Bayer) "So many Roman roads you have!" he calls out, and finally hints at those who carry the emperor's coat of arms, the eagle. He talks about the eagles that are fed and clothed by his emperor, and who fly far, and by that he glorifies other birds of prey such as falcons, hawks, and sparrow hawks (Dukes and Lords) in Swabia, Bavaria, and Franconia. From Austria to Flanders you can see his banners, and the author gives the eagle a twofold praise so that knights and ladies alike can look up to him even more.

Presumably the poet wrote these verses at the beginning of his work as part of an introduction, since we [only] find the mention of the name Albrecht in the younger Heidelberg manuscript from the Vienna and Hanoverian Library, towards the end. The author calls himself Albrecht and bemoans the loss of his princely ruler.[299] This verse is missing in the print edition and cannot be found in the older Heidelberg manuscript, as this abruptly stops half a page short. This shows that this version was never completed. Therefore, Albrecht only finished his poem after the death of Emperor Ludwig—that is, after 1347. This also explains the last two verses of chapter 39 in the print edition, in which he bitterly bemoans the stinginess of

---

298. "Es ward nie bass gesprochen von keines Laien Munde, Das Lob ihm (dem Wolfram) nicht zerbrochen wird von mir Albrecht zu keiner Stunde."

299. *Die Aventüre habende bin ich Albrecht viel ganze,*
   Von dem Wal al trabende bin ich seit mir zerbrach der Hülfe Lanze
   An einem Fürsten, den ich wohl könnte nennen,
   In allen Reichen fern, in deutschen Landen möcht' man ihn erkennen.
   Wal, Schlachtfeld; al, ganz und gar.
   See Vienna and Hannover manuscript by Jacob Grimm. There and in the Heidelberg manuscript no. 385 this verse follows verse 115 and 116 in the 40th chapter of the print. Cf. Wilken Geschichte der Heidelberg. Büchersammlung p. 457.

◆ ◆ ◆

the lords who commissioned his work.[300] Following these thoughts it seems possible that he is talking about the three sons of Emperor Ludwig. It is known that they divided their inherited land into three parts. It cannot be decided whether it is the same three Lords he describes in the 64th verse of the introduction, or whether those are some other Lords entirely—but this is of no importance here.

Now we have removed all ambiguity about the first and the second author of the *Titurel*, the earlier contradiction regarding the history of architecture is also solved. The early fourteenth-century architecture explains the knowledge of the temple of the Grail in the *Jüngerer Titurel* perfectly. Also, with the newly discovered verses in mind, we have lifted the veil of doubt of those sequences where Albrecht talks about his relationship to Eschenbach. We now certainly know the meaning of this second last verse in the print:

> *Kyot Flegetaneise der war Herrn Wolfram gebende*
> *Die Aventüre zu Preise, die bin ich Albrecht hier nach*
> *Ihm aufhebende.*[301]

(Kyot Fleganteneise was a given name of Master Wolfram, to praise the adventures that, I, Albrecht, will continue after him.)

We can also now explain the 2nd verse of the 10th chapter in the print version, which has troubled the friends of old German literature for some time:

300. *Die Aventür ich des viel gern bitte,*
   Wie Parcifal nun werbe und Ekunat sie beide;
   Ob das allhie verderbe, daran geschaerh den edlen Fürsten leide,
   Die sich da lassen kosten diese Maehre
   Gen mir als rechte kleine, ein Esel davon trüge Distel schwere.
   Wer diese Fürsten waeren, das will ich gerne schweigen;
   Sie lass'n sich nicht vermeren, wann ich ihr Gabe nimmer darf geneigen.
   Sie sind der Mitte wohl auf teutscher Erde Terre,
   Sie sind den Bergen nahe, die Milde hat aber ihn Gehauset verre.
   Vermeren: to gossip about someone, geneigen: to admire. It doesn't seem right for me to gossip about them even though I can't admire their gift. They live in the middle of Germany, near the mountains, but generosity and charity is not known to them.

301. This verse has not been found to date in the handwritten scripts. It talks about Albrecht picking up what Master Wolfram has left and how Albrecht was commissioned by Kyot Flegetaneise.

✦ ✦ ✦

Reime[302] *die Zwiefalten dem Brakenseil hier waren*
Viel ferne dann gespalten; danach die Laenge wohl von
Fünfzig Jahren
Zwiefalter Rede war diese Mare gesümet. (gesaeumet,
versaeumet.)
Ein Meister ist aufnehmende, swenn es mit Tode ein
  anderer hier gerûmet. (geräumet, d.h. verlassen.)[303]

(Verses that had two different leaders, with a rift of fifty years. Two different authors have there been, and one master will take over from the death of another.)

It is important to know that the period of fifty years from the death of the first poet until the start of the adaption by the second poet is not to be taken literally but is only a phrase. It is assumed that it is only a shadowy figure following the description of Albrecht's life above. According to that he will have started the adaption not earlier than 1310 or 1320, 80 or 90 years after Eschenbach's death. It is doubtful that this verse (fifty years etc.) was inserted by Albrecht himself, but rather later on, when the specifics of both poets' lifetimes are no longer known. It is certainly of notice that this verse is only found in the print edition, but that the four verses that follow on from it are found in the handwritten scripts that are dated much earlier. Those verses contain the poet's defense against critics of his work.[304]

But who was this Albrecht? It seems to me that we have to recognize Albrecht von Scharfenberg here, who is named in the Manessian collection of Minnesingers and is highly praised by the Munich poet Ulrich Fürterer. He named him more than once in his cyclic poem about Titurel and the knights of the Round Table.[305] Amongst other mentions we find the following: (Munich Codex Sheet 2, verse 17):

Albrecht von Scharffenberge,
Wäre ich mit Kunst dein Genoss!
Als ein Ries gen dem Zwerge
Also ist mein Kunst gen dir eben gross.

302. I used here Reime, Rîme instead of Riemen as we find it in the print: following Docen's suggestion (missive no 6). Lachmann supports this strongly: *Wolfram von Eschenbach*, mainly page 33.

303. This refers to one author picking up the work following the death of the other, fifty years before.

304. We find these verses in the older Heidelberg script: Hiemit so sind versuchet etc., 6th chapter, after 72nd verse of the print, in the Vienna script those verses follow the verse: Mit Rimen schon zwigenge etc which ends the 4th chapter in the print.

305. See Hagen, Docen, Büsching etc., Old German Museum I, pages 135, 569 and 572.

✦ ✦ ✦

(Albrecht von Scharffenberge, if only I was your companion in art; like a dwarf facing a giant is my art next to yours.)

Later (sheet 44) he makes "Frau Aventüre" address him in the following way:

> Ulrich so fang an,
> Wie du es von Herrn Albrecht hast vernommen,
> Den man nennt den von Scharfenberg;
> Der Ding wahrlich ist er zu Ende gekommen.

(Ulrich, so start now, as you have heard from Master Albrecht, the one whom they call von Scharfenberg; who truly finished his thing.)

Ulrich Fürterer wrote his poem for Duke Albrecht IV around 1478[306] and therefore was in the position to know details about the work of our Albrecht, who also belonged to the Bavarian dynasty one hundred and thirty years before. If those details, found on the book covers of the older Heidelberg manuscript, were known to Docen and A. W. Schlegel, they surely would have recognized the Albrecht [of *der Jüngerer Titurel*] as Albrecht von Scharfenberg.

So, *Titurel* is a Bavarian creation in every respect, just as Wolfram von Eschenbach was a Bavarian. This view does not result from the many mentions of Bavaria in the *Titurel* because those could be related to Albrecht von Scharfenberg, but from a specific quote in *Parzival*, which undoubtedly is Eschenbach's own creation. He says there:[307]

> Einen Preis den wir Beyern tragen,
> Muss ich von Waleisen sagen
> Die sind thörscher denn Beyersche Herr;
> Und doch, bei mannlicher Wehr,

306. On sheet no 150 verso, first volume of the Munich Codex, you can read:
> Dem Durchl. hochb. Fürsten und Herrn
> Herrn Albrecht Pfalzgraf pey Rein
> Hertzog in Ober und Nieder—Baiern etc.
> seine fürstlichen Gnaden tzo willen
> hab ich Ulrich Fürterer tzu München
> ersamelt mit einer slechten und ainvaltigen
> stumpl Teutsch aus etlich puechern
> die histori gesta oder getat von Herrn
> Lanzelot vom Lack etc. Item von
> dem Anfang des heiligen Grales etc.
> Item von Claudas und Morderot.
> Mit stumpel Teutsch, stümperhaften deutschen Sprache.

307. Müller's edition 3599, Lachmann loc. cit. page 67. 121. 7–12.

◆ ◆ ◆

Wer in den zwein Landen wird
Gefuoge, ein Wunder an dem birt.

(Who works hard in both lands, will experience a wonder, he will be an amazing man.)

Pleinsfelden is located in the Upper Palatinate, right at the border of Eichstädt and Nuremberg; and the little town Eschenbach is roughly five hours away from it, in the region of Ansbach.[308] Püterich von Reicherzhausen still found the poet's grave in 1450 at the latter location in the graveyard of the church "Unserer Frauen Münster,"[309] showing his cote of arms with the harbour on the shield and on the helmet. It might be worth checking if this gravestone is still there.

308. Büsching in the Old German Museum I, page 4–14.

309. At the market town Eschenbach, Adelung's *Püterich* p. 26, see Old German Museum I, p. 13. There is a slightly smaller town called Eschenbach in the Upper Palatinate, now the place of the regional court. It is not far from the road from Amberg to Kemnat near Grafenwöhr. Because of its distance to Pleinfelden we can assume that this is not the place mentioned by Eschenbach in the poem.

◆ ◆ ◆

Regarding the Temple of the Holy Grail (des heiligen Grales[310]), there is an understanding that the "Holy Grail" was the very bowl from which Christ offered his disciples the last

310. Garalis can be found in the 11th century: in Aelfricus, glossary Anglo Saxon. Edition Somner, p. 80 together with with the word Acetabulum (latin): It is an explanation for the Anglo-Saxon word vinegar-vessel, 12th century in Leo Ostiens in Chronic Casin, lib. I, chapter 24 and 28, listing various vessels, plural Garales. Also, in Helinandus in Chronic. p. 92 (Tissier Bibl. Part. Cisteric T. VII). The latter said in J. 720: Hoc tempore in Britannia cuidam eremitae monstrata est mirabilis quaedam visio per angelum de sancto Joseph decurione, qui corpus Domini deposuit de cruce et de catino illo suo paropside, in quo dominus coenavit cum discipulis suis; de quo ab eodem eremita descripta est historia quae dicitur de Grandali. Grandalis autem sive Gradale gallice dicitur scutella lata,et aliquantulum profundal, in qua pretiosae dapes suo jure divitibus solent apponi gradatim unus morsellus post alium in diversis oridibus, et dicitur vulgari nominee graalz, quia grata et acceptabilis est in ea comedenti: tum propter continues, quia forte argentea est vel de alia pretiosa materia: tum propter contentum, id est ordinem mutiplicem pretiosarum dapum. Hanc historiam latine scriptam invenire non potui, sed tantum gallice scripte habetur a quibusdam proceribus, nec facile, ut ajunt, tota inveniri potest. Hanc autem nondum potui al legerdum sedulo ab aliquo impetrare. Quod mox ut potuero, verisimiliora et utiliora succincte transferam in latinum. (Helindandus was a monk at the Eisterz abby Fremont, diocese Beauvais, he died 1227.) More about the meaning of the word Garalis in latin can be found in the Ducange Glossary—the related French word can be found in the Assises de Jerusalem (12th latest 13th century) in chapter 289 when they talk about serving the seneshall (etc.) on coronation day, where Gréaux (from Gréal) together with the word "escuelles" is used for bowls. Furthermore, it is used in the "Roman du Graal" (13th century) by Robert de [Boron] Bouron, Burons or Boiron, manuscript de l'eglise de Paris no. 7, fol. 4 Vso. Here you can find that Joseph of Arimathia took the vessel (bowl: escuelle) of the last supper with him to collect the blood of the wounds of the Lord: et celle escuelle est appelée le saint Graal (and this bowl is called the Holy Grail); see Roquefort Glossary d.l.l. Romane. An older glossary by Borel: Tresor des Antiquités françaises 1655 tells us that a soup bowl (Terrine) was called un Grasal or une Grasale in Toulouse, Montauban and Castres. It is of notice that both Roquefort and Ducange did not take either the Latin word nor Helinandus' explanation of the same into consideration. Because the word "Gral" has been given various interpretations—some of them quite odd: see The Hamm treasure trove of the Orient VI, p. 488—none of which are quite satisfying, I took the liberty to address this matter in such detail. The linguists have to look at that further now. Roquefort discards the favorable but quite random connection of "Saint Graal, Saint Gréal" with "Sang real, Sang royal" which was repeated on some occasions. Amongst others it can be found in Jacobus a Voragine (1244–1298) in the Genoese Chronicles (Muratori Thesaur.rer Italiae T.9). He says there: illud vas Angli in libris suis Sangreal appellant. You can see, following the above explanations, that Sangreal here is used for San Gréal and not Sang real. Roquefort also dismisses a connection with the word grès—earthenware, crockery. Quite rightly so, since all quotes talk about valuable, precious vessels and not simple day-to-day bowls even when not related to the Holy Grail. Roquefort does not come up with a new interpretation after dismissing the above.

◆ ◆ ◆

supper—and that Joseph of Arimathea kept it hidden[311] and brought it to Europe.[312] After Joseph's death no one seemed to be worthy to posses this holy vessel. Angels held it high above the earth, hovering in the air until Titurel, the son of one of the first Christian kings of France, was selected by an angel to become the Lord and King of the Grail due to his many virtues. He therefore left his homeland with a handful of devout knights, and angels brought him to Salvaterre to the mountain Montsalvatsch (Mons salvatus), which was in the middle of a great forest. Titurel built a castle on the mountain because the Grail was hovering above it.[313] No doubt that this place must be Salvaterra in Biscay not far from Vittoria, since the author says: If you go to Galicia, you will know Salvaterre.[314] The way to Galicia was well known because of the pilgrimages to Santiago de Compostella. Titurel also wished to build a temple for the Grail—and to enable this the Grail provided all instructions and resources. To understand this, one needs to know that the Grail, other than an oracle or the sacrament of the Holy Communion,

311. Titurel chapter 41, verse 35–39.

312. The Jews pursued Joseph and put him, Magdalena, Martha, Lazarus and Maxim[us] on a ship without steering wheel or sail. With God's help he made it to Marseille with his companions. The latter evangelized in France and you can still see a very special relationship and worship for those three saints in monuments and clerical rites all over France. Joseph of Arimathea on the other hand went to England and evangelized there, which is not mentioned in either the *Titurel* or the *Parzival*. The most detailed description of his journey one can find in the Chronicles of Pseudo Dexter, which according to Fabricus (Bibl. Latini etc.) have been discovered towards the end of the 14th century, in "Beim Jahr 48" (at the year 48), see Baronius Annal. B. J. 35, in William of Malmesbury. (he lived 1143) "Antiq. Eccles. Glaston. And in the Histor. Britann. Scriptor. XV Vol. I p. 299 by Thom. Gale., as well as my comments to the below listed verses, verse 71. In the 15th century and in the beginning of the 16th century the English still believed that Joseph was the first English apostle; proof of that can be found in the records of the Concilium of Constanz, sess. 30 and the note that was sent to Emperor Max I in 1517 by Robert Wingfeld, King Henry VIII's messenger. The note was made public by the following title: Disceptatio super dignitate etc. Regnorum Britannici et Gallici in Concillio Constantiensi habita. Another tale, possibly originated in England, says that Joseph of A. and Nicodemus collected the blood of the Lord together in the same vessel that was used in the last supper. It's not clear to me if the vessel with the holy blood, that was given to King Henry III of England by the patriarch of Jerusalem in 1247, who believed that this once belonged to Joseph of Arimathea and Nicodemus was the root of this tale (Matheus Paris Histor. Maj. Rer. Anglic.). But I have to note, that to my knowledge the oldest notes about the tale of the holy blood related to the Grail derive from the 13th century. They are found in the already mentioned "Roman du St. Graal" by De Borron and Jacobus a Voraginie loc. cit.—he refers to English books: "in quibusdam liberis Anglorum reperitur etc." see also Fra Gaetano il Sacro Catino p.138.

313. Titurel chapter 3, verses 2, 9, 16, 18, 31.

314. Titurel chapter 3, verse 28.

+ + +

is not just a spiritual holy object (Heiligthum) but also holds materials and producing powers. Through this, the young king was given everything that he asked for with a pure Christian sense—meat and drink, gold, gemstones, construction materials etc.[315] There hung a Christian Enchantment on this vessel, so to say: it was made of *Jasper exillis*, and through the power of this jewel the Phoenix could burn to ashes and be reborn.[316] The Grail's greatest power however was received annually when a white dove would come down from heaven on Good Friday to put a white, round wafer on its top.[317] Görres, who writes about the Grail in his introduction to the [story of] *Lohengrin*, therefore saw the Grail as a Christianized spiritual version of

315. Titurel chapter 3, verse 16, in the following verses 3, 4, 30, 31, 34 etc., Parzifal by Müller v. 7070 and 13992, by Lachmann, p. 119, verse 238, p. 225, verse 469.

316. Titurel chapter 41, verse 35, Parzifal by Müller verse 13992 and following, Lachmann p. 225, verse 469. *Jaspis* (Jasper) *exillis* in the Titurel, *Lapsil exillis* or *Lapis* and *Jaspis* (Jasper) *exillis* in the Parzifal. In Albert magn. De Lapidibus nominat. and in the poem about the power and attributes of the gemstone (Gedicht von der Kraft und der Eigenschaft des Edelsteins), Museum for old-German literature II, p. 52 and following we find no mention of Lapis exillis, I therefore think that Jaspis (jasper) is the correct one. Even more so, since we know a strange variation of Jasper known by mineralogists as *Silex Niloticus*—therefore *exillis* could have emerged from mixing silex in. The mention of the Phoenix might indicate that it is an Egyptian Jasper. Further to the above-mentioned verse 37 in the Titurel, the poet also mentions another vessel. This one would be a replica of the true one, but it wouldn't be regarded as holy. He probably hints at a treasure that the Genoese claimed to have taken as loot in 1101 during the taking of Caesarea. The very same is known by the name *il Sacro Catino* (Bowl, vessel) and this one is too, believed to be the vessel from which Jesus Christ took the last supper. It is of hexagonal shape. Despite its dimensions (roughly 13 French inches wide and 5½ inches tall) it was believed for centuries that this vessel has been made from one single piece of emerald. In more recent times, after the vessel came to Paris, a commission of the French Institute had a close look at it and discovered that it is made from very pretty coloured glass flow, a suspicion that has been around for some time. After comparing it with other similar items from the same material in the royal collection in Paris, Millin believes that the *Sacro Catino* is made from an oriental glass flow, crafted in Constantinopel. Millin magasin encycloped. Janvier 1807 and Voyage en Savoye etc. II p. 165 ff., see also Bossi sur le vase que l'on conservait à Genes sour le nom du Sacro Catino, Turin 1807 4to. In 1726 the Genoese monk Fra Gaetano wrote a very entertaining book about the origins of this vessel, which is believed a gift from the Queen of Saba to King Solomon: Il Sacro Catino, Genova 4to.

317. Parzival, Mueller v. 14022 and Lachmann, p. 226, verse 470. This reminds us on the miracle in the Church of the Holy Sepulchre of Jerusalem. The monk Bernard reports around the year 870, that every year an angel came down to light the new candle above the holy sepulchre on Holy Saturday morning during prayer. (It's well known that the Catholics light the new Light on Holy Saturday morning in every church), Bernardi Monarch. Itinerar. in Mabillon in Act. Sanct. St. Benedict Saecl. IIIPars II p. 473.

◆ ◆ ◆

the Ethiopian Sun Table[318] the Hermes Cup, of the Dschemschids [Cup of Jamshid] and the Dionysus Cup, and of the oriental philosopher's stone etc.[319] It cannot be denied that Oriental ideas have contributed to the idea of the Holy Grail, and that they had a large influence on the *Titurel* and *Parzival*. Many legends from the Orient, and oriental names in both poems, suggest that. Further investigations would probably show that both the Kaaba in Mekka (known as the right hand of God on Earth by the Mohammedans[320]) and the Shahnameh by Fedusi influenced both poems a great deal.[321] The poet himself says that Kyot the Provençal—by whom he got inspired—was skillful in pagan language and that parts of the Legend of Toledo was taken from some work by the pagan master Flegetaneis, who had Israeli origins. Other parts were taken from British, French and Irish chronicles.[322] Since many names in both poems seem to be Arabic or have derived from the Arabic, amongst others the names of the seven planets, Görres rightly suspects that the work of Flegetaneis has been written in this language.[323] The use of Arabic was also quite common in Europe in Kyot's times (twelfth century).

Two other elements cannot be overlooked in relation to our poems: the military-religious orders, specifically the Order of the Temple, founded in 1118, and the different sects of the Oriental Christians, especially the Nestorians with their Priest-King Johann, who features towards the end in the *Titurel*.[324] [There, we read that] due to the unworthiness of the Christians in the Occident, the Grail does not want to remain there. It is therefore brought to the Indian Christians by the Templeisen, and where Parzival later succeeds the Priest-King Johann [John] to become the Master of the Grail.[325] After the Grail's arrival the devoted crowd desired that both the castle and the temple of Montsalvatsch should be reunited with the Grail. The wish was answered promptly, and the Indian sun was shining on those buildings the very next morning. This miracle should not appear strange: did not the Mussulmen believe that the Kaaba and Adam fell to Earth from Paradise? The stone [of the Kaaba] got lost during the great deluge and was brought back to Abraham by the Angel Gabriel.[326] The same way, it was assumed

---

318. Herodot III 18.

319. Görres loc. cit. p. XIV–XVI.

320. G. Sale the Koran. London. 1825 8vo Vol I Prelim. Disc. Sect. 4 p. 161.

321. Görres loc. cit. p. XXVI.

322. Titurel, chapter I, verse 1.

323. Görres loc. cit. p. XLII.

324. Chapter 40, verse 303 ff.

325. Chapter 40, verse 209 ff and chapter 41, verse 64.

326. G. Sale the Koran Prelim. Disc. loc. cit.

◆ ◆ ◆

possible to move a castle and a temple to India. The legend of a similar wondrous transfer of the holy house of Nazareth to Dalmatia does not seem to have had any influence on the author. Even if the miracle was believed to have happened in 1291, when the last Christian stronghold at Ptolomais got lost, word about it and its further transfer to Loretto hardly came to Europe before the fifteenth century.[327]

The crusades helped the poet and his predecessors to get to know the oriental Christians, since all Christians without any exception came together at the Holy Sepulchre. It is the same in our time; six oriental sects—eight even, if we count the Greek and the Latin in as well—eight nations own the Church of the Holy Sepulchre.[328] Also, it was suggested recently, the Gnostic sects of the eleventh century in Southern France were seen as successors of the Priscellianitsts in Spain, to have influenced the poems about the Holy Grail.[329] Looking at it closely, this presumption deserves to be considered. But I would like to point out that this influence, *if* it has influenced the *Titurel* and *Parzival*, can only be of poetic nature, since we cannot find actual heretical elements in either poem. It is also pointed, out on a regular basis, that the author's religious and moral way of thinking goes in total accordance with the teachings of the Catholic Church. It is therefore due to either blindness or negligence of the German linguistics if one seeks to find traces of these disgraceful practices and wrong doings in the *Titurel*. Some masters of the Temple should be blamed for this, but certainly not the whole order.[330]

On the other hand one cannot fail to recognise that the poet has taken his clues from this chivalric order in some parts. The same way that the Knights of the Temple got their name from the Temple in Jerusalem, so the Knights of the Grail got their name from the temple of the Grail—and were called Templeisen.[331] They live in a monastery and lived by the rules of Chivalry in the same way as the Knights of the Temple. But unlike them, the master of the

---

327. Tursellinus, Histor. Lauretana; Martorellus Theater. historic S. Dom. Nazar; Benedict XIV. (cardin. Lambertini) de Servor. Dei Benetificat. Lib. IV Pars. 2 cap.7 et 10 p. 34. 53 ff. ; see also Cicognara Storia della Scultura Ed. Fol. I p. 263.

328. Chateaubriand, Itineraisre de Paris à Jerusalem.

329. Leo, Lehrbuch der Geschichte des Mittelalters I (Textbook about mediaeval history I), p. 79.

330. V. Hammer, Mysterium Baphometis in den Fundgruben des Orients VI (The Mystery of the Baphomet in the treasure troves of the Orient VI), p. 24 ff. see further down the comments of verses 15 and 41 of the description of the Temple of the Grail.

331. Derived from the French Templois, like Franzeise from François. Nowadays: Français; Franzeise, Franzeyse and Franzoyse can be found often in the Titurel and Parzival, see also comments about verse 49 and 59.

♦ ♦ ♦

Knights of the Grail can marry.[332] Titurel and nearly all his children and grandchildren are married and in fact there are many women at the court of the cleric Knight-King, all disciplined and respectable. One might remember the monastery Ettal, surrounded by deep forests, which Emperor Ludwig the Bavarian founded for twelve married knights, lead by a likewise married master with his wife leading the wives of the knights. Another similarity between the Knights of the Grail and Knights of the Temple can be found in the actual building. Both temples are round, like the mosque that was built by khalifs between 634 and 714 on the spot where once the Temple of Solomon had been.[333] Not only did the Knights of the Temple own this building, they also modeled every new church or chapel after it. Where [these were] not built in a round shape, they created a polygonal building on a circle instead. This is a shape that was only used for baptisteries or selected churches such as the Church of the Holy Sepulchre[334] and some buildings from pagan times. Most Templar churches are destroyed now. Maybe the slightly different shape was one of the reasons why they were persecuted? However, a few of those buildings are still intact. I will only mention the Templar Church in London[335] and a smaller one in Kobern on Mosel [336], but we do not have any pictures of those.

But enough of this—I need to come back to the temple of the Grail. So, King Titurel wanted to build a temple, worthy of the Grail, which was still hovering high up in the air. He therefore ordered to have the surface of a mountain made from pure onyx polished until it was flat and shiny. One morning he found a ground plan drawn on it, given by the wonderous force of the Grail. The stone was over a hundred fathoms wide and the Temple was round like a rotunda, in such a way that seventy-two chapels would fit around it. The chapels were octagonal and projected outward. Each was unique. The work was arched on iron/bronze pillars [ehern = erz can

332. Titurel, chapter 6, verse 44.

333. An illustration of it can be found in Bernardo Amico, Trattato de Sacri edifizi di Terra sancta Firenze 1620. 4to p. 45 pl. 35; It's also believed that a picture of that mosque can be found in Forbin's *Journey to Jerusalem*.

334. The Church of the Holy Sepulchre, as Constantine the Great had built it, consisted of many churches connected through cloisters/arcades. Amongst them was the actual round Church of the Sepulchre. The Church of the Holy Cross on the other hand, had the shape of a basilica, elongated with a semi-circular finish. Despite many changes over time, the original complex is still recognizable. Eusebius Pamph. Vita Constantini. m. lib. III. Cap 33–39 Edit Hainichen p. 188 and 190 and 501. Valesius, epistol de Anastesi et Martyrio Hierosol. See also Hieronymus in Chronic et Epistol—Cyrillus Hierosol, Cateches. Adamnanus de loc. sanct. Bei Mabillon acta Sancta ord. St. Bened. Saecl. III Pars II p. 450. Bern Amico Loc. cit. p.31–45 pl. 22–33. Chateaubriand Itineraire etc.

335. John Britton, Essay on round churches in Antiquities of Great Britain Vol I.

336. Wiebeking, *Architecture civile* Vol 5, p. 14.

◆ ◆ ◆

be both iron or bronze]. The diaphragm arches were decorated richly with beautiful artwork, all kinds of illustrations and ingenious decorations of gold and mother of pearl. The vaults were blue from sapphires with an emerald disc in the middle. The disc shows a lamb with a banner of the cross made from enamel. The windows were not made from ordinary glass but filled with beryl, crystals and many other coloured gemstones. To calm the burning radiance they also had paintings created on them.

The king ordered a tower to be built at two corners of each chapel, as they stuck out, making thirty-six towers. They surrounded the Temple, each the same, each made from eight walls and the many corners resulting from the chapel they rested upon. Each tower had six levels with three windows each and a spiral staircase inside that was also visible from the outside. In the middle rose a tower twice the size and height of the others. All the towers were made from precious jewels and gold, and the roofs were made from red-gold decorated with blue enamel. Inside the building, in the centre beneath the big tower, there was a far more splendid work, which represented the Temple in miniature and which served to hold the Grail.

I limit myself to those main outlines and have added the drawings for better understanding, following the exact description. It seems most important to me to give a general and as far as possible a clear picture of the building in order to indicate the main points that led me to the claim that the author must have seen German architectural work in its golden age.

These points are: first and foremost the projecting, octagonal chapels, which can be found a lot in old German churches, but nowhere else. Secondly the cross-ribbed vaults, decorated with a disc or capstone in the middle. Thirdly the painted windows. Fourthly the towers with the walls pierced by many windows and inner spiral staircases. Fifthly the repetition of the whole Temple in miniature, which is obviously the same as in our old German churches with their ornate, tower-like tabernacles. Some more evidence results from looking at the decorations of the chapels, altars, pews, stalls, etc., which are described in detail in the following verses.

Görres thought to have found the model church for the Temple of the Holy Grail in the Church of Sophia (Sophienkirche) in Constantinople.[337] It is built in a square shape with a dome, with pillars made from the most beautiful stones. All walls and vaults show mosaic pictures and decorations on golden ground and it has a splendid inlaid floor. But firstly, the shape of this building only partly corresponds with the Temple described [by Albrecht] since the latter is round like the Church of the Holy Sepulchre and the Arabic temple building in Jerusalem, and not a rotunda on a square. Secondly, the Church of Sophia as well as the similarly

337. Lohengrin, introduction XVI ff.

◆ ◆ ◆

decorated Church of St. Marcus in Venice are both missing the projecting, octagonal chapels, the ribbed vaults with capstones, the painted windows, the towers and the tabernacle-like building in the middle—whereas all these things can be found in our cathedral churches with their pointed arches from the thirteenth and fourteenth centuries. So, there is no doubt that the poet Albrecht had those as an example when he described his temple. But because the description of the temple features very early in the *Titurel*, it is very likely that it featured already in Wolfram von Eschenbach's part of the work. In this case the author will have modeled his description mainly after the two churches in Jerusalem, as well as the Church of Sophia in Constantinople; as mentioned previously, in his day there were no significant buildings in the old German style. Therefore, it might be that those parts that remind one of an oriental church in the *[Later] Titurel* are parts that have been retained from the older version. The significant change in description however can be totally explained by the author's sheer admiration for the amazing old German architecture in its golden age, a time in which Albrecht lived. Be that as it may, and let us assume that the description that lies before us has been written by the later author, it becomes then evident, that the author was mindful of the three famous churches of the Orient when he wrote his description of his building—the three churches of the Orient were well known in his time due to the crusades and pilgrimages to the holy land.

The fantastic pomposity of the material and the embellishment of the story appears to have been taken from Oriental fairy tales and poems, the description of priest Johann's palace,[338] and initially the apocalyptic description of the heavenly Jerusalem, which was stated as the perfect example whenever a new church was inaugurated.[339] The heavenly Jerusalem is also clearly stated as the example of the temple in the *Titurel*.[340]

It is worth mentioning that this fairy-tale splendour of the temple of the Grail was manifested on a smaller scale in the chapel of the Holy Cross (heilige Kreuzkapelle) in the castle of Karlstein in Prague, built not long after the poem was finished. Emperor Karl IV ordered its creation within his castle to contain the Bohemian imperial insignia. It still exits, and its walls and vaults are indeed richly decorated with gold, paintings, cut agate, amethyst, chrysoprase and other colorful gemstones. And, oh the windows—of which I saw only fragments in 1811—were made from beryl and amethyst leaded with golden lead. The vaults with their ribs

338. See the following verses, verse 3 and the description of the palace in the Titurel chapter 40, verse 381–409 and chapter 41.

339. See also my "History and description of the Cologne Cathedral" (Geschichte und Beschreibung des Doms von Koeln), page 11 and 12.

340. Chapter 5, verse 20.

and capstones richly decorated with gemstones and mother of pearl show the firmament. A dainty gold-plated lattice with little bows and hooks from which pear-shaped chrysoprase and other gemstones hang freely, separates the chapel in two halves. On it and on the walls, there are more than six hundred gold-plated candelabrums, in which you can light waxen lights; these are mirrored in the big cut gemstones and richly decorated golden floors.[341] Even nowadays the whole thing appears like splendour created by magic. It is even more surprising that this chapel is not recognized in our time, as it contains a rare treasure, the fourteenth-century work of two German artists: Theoderich of Prague and Nicolas Wurmser of Strassburg; and furthermore by an Italian artist Thomas de Mulina and probably also by the lesser known Johann de Marignola of Florence. The latter was a Franciscan monk who travelled to East India in service of Karl IV where, according to his own account, he decorated a church of the Saint Thomas Christians.[342]

Before I get to the poet's own description of the Temple, I need to mention one or two things regarding my adaptation of it: The six handwritten manuscripts and the old print that I have used are named as followed:

The older handwritten Heidelberg manuscript	H I
The newer handwritten Heidelberg manuscript	H II
The Vienna manuscript of his Majesty's library	W
The Berlin manuscript	B
The Regensburg manuscript	R
The Carlsruhe manuscript	C
The old print (Druck)	D

The handwritten manuscripts of the [Later] Titurel are too fragmented to be considered a consistent literary piece of work. I have therefore used the new spelling rules throughout the document to enable not only the adepts of our old German language but also the friends of German literature and art in general to read the description of the temple of the Grail; only with those words not in use anymore have I used the older spelling.

341. A description of this chapel can be found in F. Schlegel's *German Museum* (Deutschem Museum) 1812 II, Volume, page 357 and in the monthly journal of the Bohemiam Museum (Monatsschrift des böhmischen Museums), 1828, a special print of the latter in 1831 by I. M. Schottky.

342. Johann Marignola, Chronic bei Dobner, Monumenta hist. Boem T. II 89.

◆ ◆ ◆

Within the verses I followed the older handwritten Heidelberg manuscript, using four lines in each verse, as this manuscript formed the basis of my research.

So, I close with grateful thoughts and appreciation to J. Grimm, registrar Dümge and Dr. E Braun for transcribing the handwritten manuscripts and to Professor Schmeller for helping me with explanations of the language.

◆ ◆ ◆

BIBLIOGRAPHY

Texts

Allen, Paul M. *A Christian Rosecreutz Anthology*. New York: Rudolf Steiner Publications, 1981.

Barber, Richard, and Cyril Edwards. "The Grail Temple in Der Jüngere Titurel." In *Arthurian Literature XX*, edited by Roger Dalrymple and Keith Busby, 85–102. D. S. Brewer, 2003. [The only previous modern translation of parts of the poem describing the Grail Temple.]

Brewer, Keagan. *Prester John: The Legend and Its Sources*. Routledge, 2012.

Bryant, Nigel, trans. *The Complete Story of the Grail: Chrétien de Troyes Perceval and Its Continuations*. D. S. Brewer, 2015.

———. *Merlin and the Grail: The Trilogy of Arthurian Romances Attributed to Robert de Boron*. D. S. Brewer, 1970.

Bryant, Nigel. *The High Book of the Grail: A Translation of the Thirteenth-Century Romance of Perlesvaus*. D. S. Brewer, 2007.

Budge, E. A. Wallis. *The Kebra Negast: The Book of the Glory of Kings*. Aziloth Books, 2013.

Davies, Sioned, trans. *The Mabinogion*. Oxford World Classics, 1998.

Day, Mildred Leake, ed. and trans. *The Story of Meriadoc, King of Cambria (Historia Meriadoci, Regis Cambrie)*. Garland Publishing, 1988.

de Boron, Robert. *Joseph d'Arimathie*. Translated by H. Lovelich. Early English Text Society, 1874.

de Troyes, Chrétien. *Arthurian Romances*. Translated by William W. Kibler. Penguin Books, 1991.

———. *Conte du Graal (Percevale)*. Translated by Pierre Kunstman. Université d'Ottawa/Laboratoire de français ancien, ATILF, 2009.

———. *Percival: The Story of the Grail*. Translated by Nigel Bryant. D. S. Brewer, 1982.

Durand, William. *Rationale Divinorum Officiorum*. Edited by Joseph Dura. Naples, 1859.

Edgington, Susan B., and Carol Sweetenham, trans. *The Chanson d'Antioche: An Old French Account of the First Crusade*. Ashgate, 2011.

Gilleland, Brady B., and Johannes de Alta Silva. *Dolopathos, or The King and the Seven Wise Men*. Centre for Medieval and Early Renaissance Studies, 1981.

Goldschmidt, Moritz von, ed. *Sone von Nausay*. Bibliothek des Literischen Vereins in Stuttgart, CCXVI, 1899.

Gower, John. *Confessio Amantis: Tales of the Seven Deadly Sins*. Edited by Taylor Anderson. Create Space, 2018.

Hahn, Karl August. *Albrecht: Der Jüngere Titurel*. Druck & Verlag von Gottfried Base, 1842. [The first edition of highlights from the poem.]

Hibbard, Laura A. *Medieval Romance in England*. Burt Franklin, 1963.

Hopf, Charles. *Chroniques Greco-Romaines Inedites ou Peo Connues: Robert de Clari, la Conquête de Constantinople*. Weidmann, 1873.

Ibn Khaldun. *The Muqaddimah*. Routledge & Kegan Paul, 1958.

Jameson, Anna. *Sacred and Legendary Art*. 1911.

Lachet, Claude, ed. *Sone de Nansay*. Honore Champion Editeur, 2014. [The only complete modern edition of the work.]

The Lancelot-Grail: The Old French Arthurian Vulgate and Post-Vulgate in Translation. Edited by Norris J. Lacy, translated by Carol J. Chase. D. S. Brewer, 2010.

Loomis, R. S. *Arthurian Legends in Medieval Art*. Modern Language Association of America, 1938.

✦ ✦ ✦

Malory, Sir Thomas. *Le Morte d'Arthur*. Edited by John Matthews. Cassell, 2000.

Martyr, Justin. *The First and Second Apologies*. Edited by Leslie William Barnard. Paulist Press, 1968.

Matarasso, P. M., trans. *The Quest of the Holy Grail*. Penguin, 1969.

Matthews, C., J. Matthews, and G. Knight. *The Lost Book of the Grail: Restoring the Courts of Joy*. Inner Traditions, 2018. [Includes a new translation of *L'Elucidation*.]

Mickel, Emanuel J. Jr., and Jan A. Nelson, eds. *The Old French Crusade Cycle*. University of Alabama Press.

Mingana, A. *Woodbrook Studies: Christian Documents in Syriac, Arabic, and Gsarshūni*. Heffer & Sons, 1928.

Neale, J. M., and R. F. Littledale, trans. "The Divine Liturgy of St. Mark." In *The Liturgies of SS Mark, James, Clement, Chrysostom, and Basil and the Church of Malabar*. Leopold Classics Library, 2016.

Passage, Charles E. *Titurel: Wolfram of Eschenbach, Translation and Studies*. Frederick Ungar, 1984.

Penninc and Pieter Vostaert. *Roman Van Walewein*. Edited and translated by David P. Johnson. Garland Publishing, 1992.

Signer, Michael A., Marcus Nathan Adler, and A. Asher. *The Itinerary of Benjamin of Tudela: Travels in the Middle Ages*. NightinGale Resources, 2010.

Slessarev, V. *Prester John: The Letter and the Legend*. University of Minnesota Press, 1959.

St. Germanus of Constantinople. *On the Divine Liturgy: The Greek Text, with Translation, Introduction and Commentary*. Edited by Paul Meyendorff. St. Vladimir's Seminary Press, 1984.

St. Paul's Apocalypse. Translated by M. R. James in *Visions of Heaven and Hell Before Dante*, edited by Eileen Gardiner. 1989.

Weston, Jessie L. *Sir Gawain at the Grail Castle*. David Nutt, 1903.

Whiston, William, trans. *New Complete Works of Flavius Josephus*. Revised and expanded. Kregel Academic, 1999.

◆ ◆ ◆

William of Tyre. *The Conquest of Jerusalem and the Third Crusade: Crusade Texts in Translation*. Edited by Peter W. Edbury. Ashgate, 1998.

Wolf, Werner, and Kurt Nyholm, eds. *Albrecht von Scharfenberg Jüngerer Titurel, Deutsche Texte des Mittelalters, XLV, LV, LXI LXXIII.* 1955–95. [The only complete edition of the text in German.]

Wolfram von Eschenbach. *Parzival.* Translated by A. T. Hatto. Penguin, 1980.

Further Studies

Adolf, Helen. "Oriental Sources for Grail Romances." *Publications of the Modern Language Association* LXII (1947): 306–23.

———. *Visio Pacis, Holy City and Grail.* The Pennsylvania State University Press, 1960.

Ashe, Geoffrey. *King Arthur's Avalon.* London: William Collins, 1958.

Barber, Richard. *The Holy Grail, Imagination and Belief.* Alan Lane, 2004.

Barto, Philip S. *Tannhauser and the Mountain of Venus.* Oxford University Press, 1916.

Bogdanow, F. "Robert de Borron's Vision of Arthurian History." *Arthurian Literature XIV* (1996): 19–52.

Boisserée, Sulpiz. *Ueber die Beschreibung des Tempels des heiligen Grales in dem Heldengedicht: Titurel Kap III.* Druck von G. Jaquet, 1834.

Brewer, Elizabeth. *Sir Gawain and the Green Knight: Sources and Analogues.* D. S. Brewer, 1992.

Brooks, Michael E. "Prester John: A Reexamination and Compendium of the Mythical Figure Who Helped Spark European Expansion." PhD thesis, University of Toledo, 2009.

Bruce, J. D. *The Evolution of Arthurian Romance From the Beginnings Down to the Year 1300.* Second edition. Peter Smith, 1958.

Cabaniss, Alan. "Joseph of Arimathea and a Chalice." *Mississippi Studies in English* 4 (1963).

Carey, John. "Henry Corbin and the Secret of the Grail." *Temenos Academy Review* 14 (2011): 159–178.

Carman, J. Neal. "The Symbolism of the Perlesvaus." *PMLA LXI* (1946).

♦ ♦ ♦

Clifton-Everest, J. M. *The Tragedy of Knighthood: Origins of the Tannhauser Legend.* Medium Aevum Monographs, New Series, X, Society for the Study of Medieval Languages and Literature, 1978.

Coyajee, J. C. "The Legend of the Holy Grail: Its Iranian and Indian Analogues." *Studies in Shahnameh.* D. B. Taraporevala Sons and Co., 1940.

Crichlow, K. *Soul as Sphere and Androgine.* Golgonooza Press, 1980.

Dobschütz, Ernst von. "Joseph von Arimathea." *Zeitschrift fur Kirchengeschicht* XXIII (1902).

Duggan, Joseph. "Performance and Transmission, Aural and Ocular Reception in the Twelfth- and Thirteenth-Century Vernacular Literature of France." *Romance Philology* XLIII (1989/90), 49–58.

Elkington, D. *The Quest for the Face of God.* (forthcoming)

Gaster, Moses. *Studies & Texts.* London, 1925–28.

Gerritson, Willem P. ,and Anthony G. van Melle, eds. *A Dictionary of Medieval Heroes.* Boydell Press, 1998.

Greer, John Michael. *The Secret of the Temple.* Llewellyn, 2017.

Hamblin, William J. and David Rolph Seely, *Solomon's Temple, Myth and History.* Thames and Hudson, 2007.

Holmes, Urban Tigner. "The Arthurian Tradition in Lambert d'Ardres." *Speculum* 25, no. 1 (1950): 100–103.

———. *Chrétien de Troyes.* Twayne Publishers, 1970.

———. *A History of Old French Literature.* Crofts and Co., 1938.

———. "A New Interpretation of Chrétien's Conte del Graal." *Studies in Philology* XLIV (1947): 453–476.

Holmes, Urban Tigner, and Sr. Amelia Klenke. *Chrétien, Troyes and the Grail.* University of North Carolina, 1959.

Huff, Dietrich. "The Ilkhanid Palace at Takht-I Sulayman: Excavation Results." *Beyond the Legacy of Genghis Khan.* Edited by L. Komaroff. Brill, 2013.

◆ ◆ ◆

Izquerdo, Josep. "The Gospel of Nicodemus in Medieval Catalan and Occitan Literature." In *The Medieval Gospel of Nicodemus: Texts, Intertexts and Contexts in Western Europe*, edited by Z. Izydorcyk. Medieval and Renaissance Texts and Studies 158, Arizona State University, 1997.

Jackson, W. H., and S. A. Ranawake, eds. *The Arthur of the Germans*. University of Wales Press, 2000.

Jaffray, Robert. *The Two Knights of the Swan, Lohengrin & Helyas*. G. P. Putnam's Sons, 1910.

Kahane, Henry, and Renee Kahane. "On the Sources of Chrétien's Grail Story." *Festschrift Walther von Wartburg*. Tubingen, 1968.

———. "Robert de Boron's Joseph of Arimathea Byzantine Echoes in the Grail Myth." *Jahrbuch der Osterreichischen Bayzantianstik* 38 (1988).

———. "The Secrets of the Grail, apropos of Francesco Zambon's Robert de Boron." *Zeitschrift für Romanische Philologie* 103 (1987): 108–14.

Knight, Gareth. *Melusine of Lusignan and the Cult of the Faery Woman*. R. J. Stewart Books, 2010.

Knight, Gareth, ed. *The Book of Melusine of Lusignan: In History, Legend and Romance*. Skylight Press, 2013.

Lachet, Claude, ed. *Les Metamorphoses du Graal*. GF Flammarion, 2012.

Lacy, Norris J., ed. *The Grail, the Quest, and the World of Arthur*. D. S. Brewer, 2008.

Langlois, Pierre. *La Societe Francais au XIII Siecle*. Hachette, 1904.

Lecouteux, Claude. *Mélusine et le Chevalier au Cygne*. Payot, 1982.

Le Gentil, Pierre. "The Work of Robert de Boron and the *Didot Perceval*." Chapter 19 in *Arthurian Literature in the Middle Ages, A Collaborative History*, edited by R. S. Loomis. Clarendon Press, 1959.

Logorio, Valerie. "Joseph of Arimathea: The Vita of a Grail Saint." *Zeitschrift fur romanische Philologie* 91 (1989).

Loomis, R. S., ed. *Arthurian Literature in the Middle Ages, A Collaborative History*. Clarendon Press, 1959.

———. *Celtic Myth and Arthurian Romance*. Columbia University Press, 1926.

◆ ◆ ◆

————. *The Grail: From Celtic Myth to Christian Symbol*. Princeton University Press, 1963.

Lyons, William John. *Joseph of Arimathea: A Study in Reception History*. Oxford University Press, 2014.

Malcor, Linda. "The Chalice and the Cross: A Study of the Grail Motif in Medieval Europe." PhD diss., University of California, 1991.

Matthews, John. *The Grail: Quest for Eternal Life*. Thames and Hudson, 1980.

Matthews, John, and Caitlín Matthews. *The Complete King Arthur*. Inner Traditions, 2016.

Meeks, Doris, and John Meeks. "The Temple of the Grail." *The Golden Blade* 33 (1981): 52–61.

Michell, John. *The Temple at Jerusalem: A Revelation*. Gothic Image, 2000.

Needleman, Jacob, ed. *The Sword of Gnosis: Metaphysics, Cosmology, Tradition, Symbolism*. Penguin Books, 1974.

Neitze, W. A. *Perceval and the Holy Grail*. University of California Press, 1949.

Nicholson, Helen J. *Love, War and the Grail*. Brill, 2004.

Normand, Kruger. "A Study of the Old French Romance of Sone de Nansay." PhD diss., University of Pennsylvania, 1975.

O'Gorman, R. "Ecclesiastical Tradition and the Holy Grail." *Australian Journal of French Studies* 6 (1969): 3–8.

————. "Robert de Boron's Angelology and Elements of Heretical Doctrine." *Zeitschrift für Romanische Philologie* 109 (1970): 539–40.

Olschki, Leonardo. *The Grail castle and Its Mysteries*. Manchester University Press, 1966.

Owen, D. D. R. "From Grail to Holy Grail." *Romania* 89 (1968): 31–53.

Parshall, Linda B. *The Art of Narration in Wolfram's Parzifal and Albrecht's Jüngerer Titurel*. Cambridge University Press, 1891.

Polarno, H. *The Talmud: Selections from the Contents of that Ancient Book, Its Commentaries, Teachings, Poetry and Legends*. Frederick Ungar, 1876.

Pope, A. U. "A Great Parthian Fortress that Defied Mark Antony." *Illustrated London News* (26 February 1938): 348–349.

✦ ✦ ✦

———. "Persia and the Grail." *The Literary Review* 1 (1957).

Pope, A. U., M. Crane, and D. N. Wilber. "The Institute's Survey of Persian Architecture, Preliminary Report on Takht-e Suleiman, the Significance of the Site, and Summary Description of the Extant Structures." *Bulletin of the American Institute for Iranian Art and Archaeology* 5 (1937): 71–105.

Putter, Ad. "Walewein in the Otherworld and the Land of Prester John." In *Originality & Tradition in the Middle Dutch Roman van Walewein*, edited by B. Besamusca and E. Kooper, 79–99. Cambridge, 1999.

Quinn, Esther Casier. *The Quest of Seth for the Oil of Life*. University of Chicago Press, 1962.

Ringbom, Lars-Ivar. *Graltempel und Paradies: Beziehungen Zwischen Iran und Europa im Mittelalter*. Wahlstrom and Widstrand, 1951.

Scavone, Daniel. "Gospel of Gamaliel: Early Evidence for the Survival of Jesus' Shroud." https://www.shroud.com/pdfs/n60part6.pdf.

———. "Joseph of Arimathea, the Holy Grail and the Edessa Icon." *Arthuriana* 9, no. 4 (Winter 1999): 3–31.

Schayer, Leo. "The Meaning of the Temple." In *The Sword of Gnosis*, edited by Jacob Needleman, 360. Penguin Books, 1974.

Uebel, M. *Ecstatic Transformation: On the Uses of Alterity in the Middle Ages*. New York, 2005.

van Esbroeck, M. "L'Histoire de L'eglise de Lydia dans deux Textes Georgiens." *Bedi Karthlisa: Revue de Karthvaelogie* 35 (1977): 109–31.

von Dobschütz, Ernst. "Joseph von Arimathea." *Zeitschrift fur Kirchengeschicht* XXIII (1902): 4–17.

von Schroeder, Leopold, and Alexander Jacob. *The Grail: Two Studies*. Numen Press, 2014.

Vukovic, Kresimir. "Initiation in the Mysteries of Augustus: The Liberalia and *Forum Augustum*." [forthcoming]

Weinraub, Eugene J. *Chrétien's Jewish Grail*. North Carolina Studies in the Romance Languages and Literatures, 1976.

◆ ◆ ◆

Wesselofsky, A. N. "Zur Frage uber die Heimath der Legende von heilegen Gral." *Archiv fur slavische Philologie* 232 (1901): 321–385.

Wilber, Donald N. "The Parthian Structures at Takht-i-Sulayman." *Antiquity* XII, no. 4 (1938): 389–410.

Wilson, S. R. "The Grail Utopia in Southern Germany." *Temenos Academy Review* 14 (2011): 138–158.

———. "Rene Guénon and the Heart of the Grail." *Temenos Academy Review* 18 (2015): 146–167.

Wood, J. *Eternal Chalice: The Enduring Legend of the Holy Grail.* I.B. Tauris, 2016.

✦ ✦ ✦

INDEX

✦ ✦ ✦

✦ ✦ ✦

❖ ❖ ❖

INDEX

Letter of Prester John, 4, 135–137, 144, 146, 150, 152–155, 201

Libre de Gamaliel, 166

Life of St. Gildas, 99

Logres, 42, 91, 92, 105

Lohengrin, 162, 203–205, 213, 214, 226, 230, 240

Loomis, R. S., 17, 26, 101, 236, 240

Ludwig II, King of Bavaria, 191, 193, 194

Ludwig IV, Emperor of Bavaria, 192–194

Lydda, 176–178, 180, 191

Mabinogion, 79, 80, 183, 214, 235

Mabonagrain, 79

Madoc, King, 67, 68

Malory, Thomas, 2, 95, 99, 158, 188, 195, 237

Manna of Heaven, 18

Margon, 66, 67, 69–71, 76, 106

Marie de France, 186

Marriage of Sir Gawain and Dame Ragnall, 96

Matabrune, 29, 70, 76, 210–212

Matter of Britain, 73

Meleagant, 63, 98–100

Melusine, 75, 213, 240

Menelik, 15, 16

Merlin, 20, 107, 160–161

Merlin, 93, 171, 175, 235

Milon, 67, 70, 76, 106

Le Morte D'Arthur, 2, 95, 104, 158, 195, 201, 237

Muntsalvasche, 21, 111, 114, 122, 123, 126, 128, 152, 198, 204, 214

Nanteos Cup, 1

Nebuchadnezzar, King, 10

Nestorian Church, 150

Normand, Kruger, 26

Norway, 29, 30, 33, 35, 36, 41–44, 46, 48, 49, 53, 57, 58, 67, 70, 78, 80–82, 84, 90–93, 95–98, 212

Odée, 33, 34, 44–46, 48, 49, 53, 54, 57–60, 62–64, 66–71, 76, 81, 93, 95, 96, 98, 102, 106, 213

Oil of Mercy, 136, 187

On the Krater, 169

Oriant, King, 29, 76, 212, 213

Orvale, 49, 53, 54, 57, 96–98

Papagay, 53, 55, 57, 96–98

Parzifal, 7, 16, 74, 75, 108, 109, 112, 113, 121, 122, 125, 129, 130, 135, 151, 152, 155, 157, 191, 193, 195, 214, 226, 241

Pasqual of Jaen, 166

Perlesvaus, 73, 88, 89, 93, 97, 103, 104, 136, 164, 200, 201, 235, 239

Philip, Count d'Alsace, 18

Pitimont, 128

Plotinus, 24

Pope, Arthur Upham, 182, 190

Prieddeu Annwn, 100

Prester John, 4, 22, 84, 115, 128–130, 132, 133, 135–137, 144–155, 162, 178, 181, 183, 184, 194, 195, 200, 201, 205, 235, 237, 238, 242

Pythagoras, 114

Quest del Saint Graal, 73, 91, 136, 195

Quasidus, 142, 151, 154

Rerum Ecclesiarcarum Contemplatio, 173

Rationale Divinorum Officiorum, 175, 236

Repanse de Schoye, 130

Ringbom, Lars-Ivar, 184, 193, 200, 242

Robert de Boron, 8, 13, 16, 20, 24, 73, 87, 90, 106, 125, 132, 133, 146, 157, 158, 161, 164–171, 173, 195, 200, 224, 235, 236, 240, 241

❖ ❖ ❖

248

❖ ❖ ❖

✦ ✦ ✦